latino literacy

the complete guide to
our hispanic history
and culture

latino literacy

◆

FRANK DE VARONA

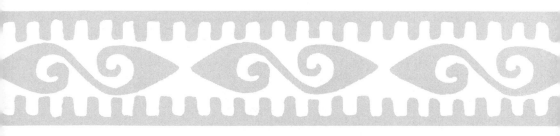

An Owl Book
A Round Stone Press Book
HENRY HOLT AND COMPANY
New York

Henry Holt and Company
Publishers since 1866
115 West 18th Street
New York, New York 10011

Henry Holt® is a registered trademark of
Henry Holt and Company, Inc.

Published in Canada by Fitzhenry & Whiteside Ltd.,
195 Allstate Parkway, Markham, Ontario L3R 4T8.

LIBRARY OF CONGRESS CATALOGING-IN-PUBLICATION DATA
De Varona, Frank.
Latino literacy: the complete guide to our Hispanic history and culture / by Frank de Varona.
— 1st ed.
p.   cm.
Includes bibliographical references and index.
1. Hispanic Americans.   2. Hispanic Americans—History.   3. United States—
Civilization—Hispanic influences.   I. Title.
E184.S75D38   1996
973′ .0468—dc20   96-9162
                              CIP

ISBN 0-8050-3859-0

Henry Holt books are available for special
promotions and premiums.
For details contact: Director, Special Markets.

First Owl Book Edition—1996

A Round Stone Press Book

Directors: Marsha Melnick, Susan E. Meyer, Paul Fargis
Development Editor: Nick Viorst
Contributing Editors: Ronald D. Coleman, Sue Heinemann

Designed by Kathryn Parise

Cartography by Jeffrey L. Ward

Printed in the United States of America
All first editions are printed on acid-free paper. ∞

1   3   5   7   9   10   8   6   4   2

To my wife,
Haydée Prado de Varona

CONTENTS

◆

MAPS

◆

ACKNOWLEDGMENTS

◆

Two people were indispensable for the preparation of this book. One was my wife, Dr. Haydée Prado de Varona, who was of immense help to me during the writing process. She typed all the drafts, helped me with the editing, and even did some research. For that reason, I have dedicated the book to her.

The second person was Nick Viorst, editor at Round Stone Press. Nick read an article that appeared in the *Washington Post* about my work in regard to the Hispanic heritage and called to ask me if I wanted to write a book on this subject. I agreed and worked closely with him for more than two years. He assisted me throughout the entire period with suggestions and by sending me clippings from newspapers and magazines. Of course, any errors or omissions in the book are my own.

Frank de Varona
MIAMI, FLORIDA
April 1996

FOREWORD

by Congresswoman Ileana Ros-Lehtinen

◆

When we left Cuba in 1959, neither my parents nor I ever dreamed that 37 years later, I, a foreign-born woman, would be a U.S. citizen and would have been granted the honor to serve in the United States Congress. As the first Hispanic woman ever elected to Congress, I have had the privilege of not only performing my civic duty by representing the interests of the constituents of the 18th District in South Florida, but also bringing forth issues in Congress that affect us as Hispanics.

My Hispanic colleagues and I have done our best to show our Congressional peers that, as Hispanics, we are indeed a group to be reckoned with. According to a recent U.S. Census Bureau report, Hispanic children, totaling 12 million, are the second largest group of children in the United States. We are the fastest growing minority in the nation and, therefore, will soon be the largest minority in the country. Consequently, we have to work together to make ourselves heard on the issues that are of great importance to us—issues such as welfare reform, bilingual education, and immigration.

One Hispanic in particular has made significant efforts to ensure that our importance in U.S. history is not overlooked or overshadowed. He is Frank de Varona, a Cuban-American, and the writer of the book you are about to read. He has dedicated himself to bringing attention to the many accomplishments of Hispanics in the United States, as well as highlighting the predominant role that Hispanic heritage has played in the Western Hemisphere. Through his work as a teacher, school administrator, writer, editor, and lecturer around the country, he has helped America recognize the tremendous contributions of Hispanics to its history and culture. In many ways, this book is the culmination of his many years of dedicated service, and for this, we shall always be grateful to him.

Hispanic contributions in many different fields—from the creative arts to the gritty reality of the business world—reflect our achievements as a group both here in the United States and throughout the world. Two prime examples of Hispanics who have gained worldwide recognition are singer Gloria Estefan and dancer Fernando Bujones. Ms. Estefan, a resident of South Florida, is known for her beautiful voice and compositions, and Mr. Bujones has captured audiences globally with the grace and ease of his ballet performances. Then there are those Hispanics whose names may not be familiar, but who have played significant roles in American society. Roberto Goizueta, for example, CEO of Coca-Cola, has managed in his tenure to diversify the company's holdings and boost the value of its stock by nearly 60 percent. Dr. Antonia Novello, a Puerto Rican who, thanks to her tireless dedication to public health, was named the first woman and first Hispanic Surgeon General and thus has helped place Hispanic women on the national agenda.

The list of Hispanics who have played significant roles in American society both in the past and in the present is obviously quite long. What we must remember, therefore, is that regardless of color, nationality, ethnic background, or occupation, we share a common heritage and culture and must remain united in order to maintain a strong and cohesive voice.

INTRODUCTION

who are the latinos?

♦

Who are the Latinos? A given Latino may trace his or her ancestry to virtually any spot on the globe. But in the American mosaic, the Latinos have coalesced into a distinct, identifiable—and very special—group of Americans. This book is an attempt to present the outlines of their story, or more properly, their stories. It is a story that is central to understanding America's past and present, and critical to anticipating America's future.

Five hundred years ago half the ancestors of the Latinos—the soldiers and sailors of the great Spanish empire—arrived on the shores of the New World. There they were met (sometimes with open arms, sometimes with whizzing arrows) by the other half, the Native Americans, or Indians, who had been comfortably settled in for millennia. The descendants of these two groups would be the first to explore the vast majority of the New World, name its geography, and people its vast expanses. From the Straits of Magellan at the southern tip of Chile to the Pacific Northwest, these people would change the face of two continents.

Technically, Latinos are people of various racial backgrounds whose ancestors lived in Spain or Latin America. They may speak Spanish at home, or may have learned it in school, or may not know it at all. They come in every color—or better, in the words of a Puerto Rican poet, "all the colors tied." This should be no surprise, since the majority of Latinos are *mestizos*, or people of mixed Spanish and Indian descent.

The Spaniards themselves, after centuries of intermingling with the many peoples who settled and sojourned in Spain, carried the blood of Iberians, Celts, Phoenicians, Greeks, Carthaginians, Romans, Jews, Arabs, and various German tribes in their veins. They mixed with Native American nations such as the Taíno, Aztec, Maya, Inca, and other pre-Columbian civilizations. Soon, enslaved and sometimes free Africans would add to this mix; later still, Asians would contribute to the collection of ethnic backgrounds. Whether in Mexico, Cuba, Puerto Rico, the Dominican Republic, Guatemala, or Nicaragua, or in the lands that would become the southwestern United States, millions of their children would, in the ensuing centuries, find themselves on soil that was, or would become, the United States of America. These people are the Latinos.

No ethnic group's story is more bound up with the American experience than the Latinos', especially if we include their Spanish and Indian forebears. With the exception of the Indians, no other group (*Mayflower* or otherwise) has lived here longer. The Spaniards were the first Europeans to touch ground in most of the New World around the dawn of the sixteenth century. Juan Ponce de León's 1513 expedition to Florida was the first to the future mainland United States. Pedro Menéndez de Avilés founded Saint Augustine, Florida, the first permanent European settlement in North America, in 1565, more than half a century before the Pilgrims landed on Plymouth Rock.

Spain brought the first explorers, missionaries, and settlers to America; the first cattle and horses; the first European grains and produce. Cities and shipyards, industries and businesses were established by the Spaniards, who, while bringing Western law and religion, language and literature, music and dance, art and architecture, found time to build the first hospitals and schools, establish European-style governments, and even invent the cowboy.

In the succeeding centuries Spain explored and came to rule approximately 80 percent of what is now the United States. And as these territories did, gloriously or otherwise, become the United States, Latinos became Latino Americans. Immediately the Latino presence—continually augmented by successive waves of immigration from places such as Puerto Rico, Cuba, Mexico, Central America, and more recently the Dominican Republic made itself felt throughout American life.

Thus the English language is laced with at least 400 words of Spanish origin: words such as "bodega," "rodeo," "rancho," "hacienda," "corral," "sombrero," "adobe," "patio," "plaza," "tornado," "hurricane," "cigar," and "alligator" come directly from Spanish or from Indian languages by way of Spanish. Americans can lift a glass of sangria and enjoy dinners of tacos, burritos, paella, black beans, *picadillo*, and *arroz con pollo*, or perhaps just some chips and salsa, before an evening of theater, film, music, dance, or just a good book either produced or significantly influenced by Latinos. Whether dancing the conga or laughing with Desi Arnaz, cheering the ballpark feats of Bobby Bonilla or enjoying the sounds of Gloria Estefan, Americans have welcomed many Latino contributions to their culture.

Latinos are well represented in more serious areas of endeavor as well. Thirty-eight Hispanics have been awarded the Congressional Medal of Honor, the highest decoration bestowed by the nation for bravery in combat above and beyond the call of duty. These heroes represent only a fraction of the thousands of Latinos who have served in every war America has fought, from the American Revolution to the Persian Gulf. From cabinet members Federico Peña and Henry Cisneros, to members of Congress such as Ileana Ros-Lehtinen and Henry González, through every level of government, Latinos have distinguished themselves in peaceful public service as well. And three U.S. Latinos have been awarded the Nobel Prize—one each in medicine, physics, and chemistry.

Today there are some 25 million Latinos in America, according to the U.S. Census Bureau—nearly 10 percent of the population. Immigrants from the Caribbean, Central America, and Mexico have swelled the numbers of Hispanics in the United States, and will continue to do so. It is predicted that by the year 2050 the Hispanic population will increase to 81 million and make up more than a fifth of this country's population. A group this large, soon expected to pass African Americans as America's largest minority group, has to be considered a serious player in American society. As voters, consumers, citizens, and leaders, what matters to Latinos will matter, in some way or another, to the greater society.

If they do share a common Spanish ancestry, Latinos are and always have been a diverse group. If they share cultural and linguistic similarities and certain economic, social, and political concerns, Latinos nonetheless spring from scores of cultures and have been shaped differently by centuries of different experiences. Their perspectives are informed respectively by their "racial" or ethnic roots, their nations of ancestral or personal origin, and the length of time they or their families have resided in this country.

The differences among Latinos show themselves acutely in how they choose to describe their Spanish heritage. The U.S. Census Bureau first used the term "Hispanic," from *España*, or Spain, in 1980; prior to that, the official term and common usage was "Spanish" or "United States Latin." Some Latinos deride the use of "Hispanic" as an anglicized cheapening of their Spanish roots, and insist on "Latino." "Hispanic" is more common on the East Coast and in Texas and New Mexico, though many Puerto Ricans in New York prefer "Latino" or even "Spanish." The preferred term in California is "Latino."

Certain subgroups of Latinos have their own terms for themselves. Generally Latinos prefer to refer to themselves in terms of their specific nationalities or those of their ancestors. Many Mexican Americans like the term "Chicano," derived from *mexicano* and having radical or activist overtones. Though originally a pejorative term used by Anglos and better-off Mexican Americans, the "Chicano" label was taken up as a badge of honor in the 1960s. New York–born Puerto Ricans sometimes call themselves "Nuyoricans."

Many Latinos also identify with the states or territories where they live; thus the terms *"tejano," "nuevomexicano," "puertorriqueño,"* and *"boricua"* (for Borinquén, the original Taíno name of Puerto Rico). And many descendants of those New Mexico Hispanics who woke up in 1850 to find themselves suddenly U.S. residents call themselves "Hispanos." *Latino Literacy,* aware of the impossibility of pleasing all the people all the time, uses the two most widely accepted terms—"Latino" and "Hispanic"—interchangeably for general purposes.

Innumerable geographical and architectural landmarks stand as silent reminders of America's Spanish heritage. The steps of the conquistadores, missionaries, and settlers echo in plazas, haciendas, missions, churches, and fortifications; in the names of such cities as San Francisco, San Antonio, and Saint Augustine and such states as Florida, Texas, New Mexico, Nevada, Arizona, California, Colorado, Montana, and Oregon.

But it is hardly novel to observe that the official history of our country has, as always, been written by the "victors"—the dominant Anglo-Saxon, Protestant culture. Most Americans consider their history an English march from east to west. Spain, for centuries a prosperous and powerful Catholic monarchy, aroused significant envy in Protestant northen Europe, culminating in the promotion of the anti-Spanish Black Legend by these powers. By this distorted account, the Spanish experience in the Americas was an unmitigated record of rape and plunder that decimated the native populations and left nothing of value behind when it was over. Needless to say, this book hopes to correct whatever remnants of this impression remain today.

At any rate, anti-Catholicism held on as one of the United States' most powerful prejudices until well into the current century. Indeed, until the election of John F. Kennedy to the presidency, Catholics generally were outside the American cultural mainstream. Anti-Catholic prejudice was just one more hurdle for Latinos, who were and are overwhelmingly Catholic, to jump as they sought their rightful place in American society.

These biases made it easy for the majority to join in almost casual war making and territory grabbing by the United States against Spain and Mexico throughout the nineteenth century, wars and actions denounced by the likes of Henry David Thoreau and Abraham Lincoln. In turn, Spaniards and Mexicans became for generations — especially in the Southwest — "enemies." No nation glorifies its enemies or celebrates their culture or heritage.

Latino Literacy does not pretend to describe the complete Hispanic experience in the United States but rather to acquaint Latinos and non-Latinos alike with a world and a culture that rightfully is part of every American's heritage. *¡Adelante!*

I

history

THE NOTION that U.S. history can be told merely as a succession of political and military deeds performed by white men was debunked a long time ago. Its place has been taken by a widespread appreciation of U.S. history as a multiplicity of stories, players, and perspectives. More and more, the unique experiences of women, African Americans, and Native Americans, among others, have been recognized as essential components of the nation's history. The result has been a fresh picture of the past that is complex and somewhat less flattering to the powers that be (and were) but also increasingly rich, more complete, and more honest.

It is in the spirit of helping set the record straight on Hispanics that this section is written. As much as any group, Hispanics have been regarded as extras in the larger, Anglo male drama of U.S. history. The principal aim of this section, then, is simply to breathe life into events and individuals that, in standard tellings, have been at best minimized and oversimplified and at worst distorted or even ignored altogether. It is an opportunity to see American history, as it were, through Latino eyes.

Broadly speaking, the story of the United States' Latino community has two distinct chapters (and this section is broken up accordingly). The first is that of the conquest and settlement of vast portions of the country, from Florida to Texas to California, by the Spanish (and later Mexicans) in the sixteenth to the nineteenth centuries. During this period, Spain vied with other European powers (especially Britain) for control over the continent, control that it held over most of the rest of the hemisphere. This was a struggle the Spaniards eventually lost.

The second, only slightly overlapping, chapter is that of a distinctly minority Hispanic population—ever swelling its ranks with new immigrants—making its way in a predominantly Anglo United States. That chapter began in the mid–nineteenth century and continues to this day.

Although these two phenomena are intimately bound up with the history of the rest of the Spanish-speaking Americas, they nevertheless can be looked at separately from that history. The experience of Latinos in the United States (from even before it *was* the United States) has made them a unique group—different from if still connected with the Hispanics of Latin America. Both the early settlers and the later immigrants faced challenges and rewards in the United States distinct from those they encountered in other parts of the Americas. It is a recognition of this distinctiveness that underlies the discussion of Latino history presented in this section. This also explains why only a limited amount of Latin American (and Spanish) history is related here to illuminate the Hispanic experience in the United States.

the spanish were here

◆

Welcome to the New World

"¡Tierra! ¡Tierra!"

On the cry from the *Pinta*'s lookout, her captain fired the ship's cannon into the dark of the early morning that October 12, 1492. The volley's report meant good news—marvelous news—to Cristóbal Colón, aka Christopher Columbus (see also pages 277–278), aboard the nearby *Santa María:* The two ships, along with the *Niña,* had finally reached land.

At daybreak, Colón and a small party rowed ashore. The flag of his royal patron Isabel (Isabella) de Castilla in hand, Colón claimed for Castile (in modern-day Spain) what he dubbed the island of San Salvador in today's Bahamas. After a short prayer of thanksgiving, Colón was welcomed by the Taíno Indians to the place they called Guanahaní. Thus met two ancient civilizations, in a clash of worlds that would drastically change the course of history.

Though Spain's Colón was not the first European to set foot on the land that would come to be called the Americas, he was the first with a grand mission. Northern European fishermen had plied the waters off Newfoundland, Nova Scotia, and New England, and Leif Eriksson and other Vikings had tried to establish settlements in these areas. But Colón was the first European to sail west on behalf of empire and God. His was the first word of the Western Hemisphere to be publicized widely in Europe. In that sense, for Europe, Colón's was very much a "discovery," which unleashed a centuries-long campaign to incorporate the New World into the Old.

Colón's royal mission was followed by other forays on behalf of Spain—journeys by explorers, soldiers, priests, and settlers. In the decades to come, Spanish ships sailed up and down the Americas' coasts and many of their rivers and bays, penetrating deep into the continents. They established towns and endowed them with homes and hospitals, plazas and fortifications, schools and universities. Great agricultural developments sprung up as Spain put the natives, as well as African slaves, to cultivating the vast lands she ruled. And though fabled for the futility of their search for gold and silver, the Spaniards in fact found and extracted great mineral fortunes in the New World.

Perhaps even more impressive was the quick military conquest of an empire larger than Rome's by only a few hundred Spanish troops, led by Spain's fabled conquistadores (from the Spanish word for "conquerors"). Within two decades of Colón's arrival, the conquests of Hispaniola (1493), Puerto Rico (1508), Jamaica (1509), and Cuba (1511) had made the Caribbean a Spanish lake— and a base for further exploration and settlement of both the South and North American mainlands. In 1521, Hernán Cortés (or Hernando Cortez) captured Tenochtitlán and brought an end to the ancient Aztec empire in Mexico. Twelve years later, Francisco Pizarro conquered the large Inca empire that extended through many modern Latin American countries. It was in these early years, too, that large swaths of the current United States would be claimed by the Spanish. And after subduing these and other ancient American societies, Spain ruled successfully for three centuries, implanting its religion, language, laws, institutions, and culture in the Americas.

The discovery of the Indies, as the Spanish called the Americas, was no less than "the greatest event since the creation of the world excluding the incarnation and death of Him who created it," as a contemporary of Colón's wrote in 1522. This was hardly an exaggeration, for Colón had inaugurated a new epoch, radically altering global culture. For Europe, the New World promised, and delivered, unprecedented opportunity for expansion — of the borders and treasuries of Europe's powers, and of their institutions and ideas. Europe's conquest of the Americas made the eventual Westernization of much of humanity, given those institutions and ideas, virtually inevitable.

"Inevitable," of course, is not the same thing as "desirable" — at least from the perspective of the conquered. Up to 90 percent of some Native American nations were destroyed by Old World diseases. Those who survived were largely traumatized by their intense, un-asked-for contact with European institutions, culture, and species. The first to greet the Europeans were the first to succumb; within a few years of Colón's landing, the Taínos, gentle custodians of the Caribbean, were virtually annihilated by European and, later, African diseases.

Ironically, however, since the early Spanish settlers were mostly men, they perpetuated the seed of the conquered races through the *mestizos*, the mixed-blood children of Indian mothers and Spanish fathers. Even as ancient Indian civilizations were upended, the foundations were being laid — economically, culturally, and even genetically — for the future nations of the Americas.

Spain's Indian Policy and the Black Legend

From the beginning of its conquest of the Americas, Spain insisted it had no higher goal with regard to the Indians than to save their souls. Indeed, Queen Isabel is said to have declared, when Cristóbal Colón presented her with Indian slaves from the New World, "Admiral, how dare you enslave my free subjects!" The Laws of Burgos (1512) and the New Laws (1542) soon enshrined the principle that any Indian who accepted Christianity was to be regarded as a free subject.

Over the centuries, these were principles the Spanish made a serious effort to live by. With Jesuit and Franciscan missionaries often serving at the front lines, Spain devoted tremendous resources to converting, educating, and understanding the Indians. With the missionaries' help, the Indians could at least make a stab at integrating into the colonial society of the Spaniards, and in fact Spaniards could and did marry converted Indians. Today's vast mestizo population of Latinos is itself a testament to the degree of Spanish and Indian intermingling.

By contrast, the English, French, and Dutch colonizers never extended half the presumption of humanity to the natives of the New World that the Spanish did. To the former, Indians were no more than soulless savages, and they undertook methodically to destroy the natives. This difference in attitude did not, however, stop Spain's rivals from spreading the notion that the Catholic Spanish were responsible for endless atrocities against the defenseless natives—the heart of the so-called Black Legend that today still colors the prevailing image of Spain's colonial rule.

To be sure, the Spanish were not always as benevolent in practice as they were in theory. Many Indians died in battle with the conquistadores—some cruelly—and many as well from overwork in the mines and fields. (Ironically, it was to a large degree the freedom Spain offered to critics of the conquest, such as priests Bartolomé de las Casas and Antonio de Montesinos, that provided Spain's enemies with much of their ammunition.) However, this is, in the end, but a part of the story.

La Florida

First Impressions

Although in his second voyage in 1493 Colón did make landfall on territory that would later become part of the United States — specifically, an island he called Santa Cruz (Holy Cross), today the U.S. Virgin Island known as Saint Croix, and at Puerto Rico, or Borinquén as the Taínos called it (and as some modern *puertorrique-ños* still do)—it was not until 20 years later that the celebrated conquistador Juan Ponce de León (see page 278) became the first representative of the Spanish presence on the mainland when he stepped onto the land he called La Florida. (Maps and other evidence suggest that earlier Spanish explorers may have sighted, or even visited, the continent, but Ponce still gets credit for the first landing.)

Legend holds that Ponce de León was in search of the mythical Fountain of Youth when he set out to explore whatever lands might be north of Puerto Rico. More likely, this former crewman of Columbus's second voyage was simply seeking new honors and wealth. He had, after all, not long before been removed from his office as governor of Puerto Rico, which Ponce himself had earlier conquered. On April 2, 1513, after a 36-day voyage, Ponce set foot on the Atlantic shoreline of Florida between modern Daytona

Beach and Melbourne, convinced he was on another island, albeit a big one. Since the date was Easter Sunday *(Pascua Florida)* and the location was awash in blooming flowers *(flor* is the Spanish word for flower), he named the place La Florida. His party then headed farther south and discovered both the Gulf Stream—a warm ocean current that flows along the U.S. east coast—and the Florida Keys. The party also came across the Calusa Indians along Florida's west coast, which they followed as far north as today's Sanibel Island. After six months, filled with many clashes with the natives, Ponce returned to Puerto Rico, eager to put together a colonization mission and secure for himself the governorship of this new island.

Ponce, of course, had vastly underestimated what he had "found." In 1519, the governor of Jamaica charged his friend Alonso Álvarez de Pineda with the mission of exploring the waters to the west of La Florida, what would come to be called the Gulf of Mexico. Pineda determined that La Florida was in fact part of the continental mainland. He also discovered the Texas coast and the mouth of the Mississippi River. La Florida became the Spanish designation for all the land from north of the Florida Keys, west to Texas, and north to the distinctly un-Floridian region of Newfoundland. It would remain so until British, Dutch, and French colonization began chipping away at Spanish claims in the coming centuries.

As for Ponce, his return engagement—seven years later—was not so successful. His expedition landed in the Charlotte Harbor area (near Fort Myers) on La Florida's west coast and was immediately set upon by the Calusas, whom he had fought in the same place on his first trip. This time, however, he promptly suffered a mortal wound by a Calusa arrow. His discouraged party turned without delay and headed back to Cuba, where Ponce de León expired. His honorable but failed settlement effort became the first in a string of such misfires that the Spanish would suffer over the next 40 years.

Exploring the Eastern Seaboard

Fascinating as the New World was turning out to be for the Spanish, in some respects it still remained a big obstacle between Europe and the riches of the East Indies (aka Asia), for which Columbus had initially headed west across the ocean. And for some time Spain continued to send ships in search of a way through to the Pacific Ocean. After Ferdinand Magellan's 1520 discovery that the only southern passage was all the way down below today's South America, Spain in 1525 sent Portuguese sailor Esteban Gómez (see page 280) to try his luck north.

Gómez spent six months sailing up the eastern coast north of Florida. Along the way, he encountered a large bay that he named Bahía de San Cristóbal (later to be called New York Bay) and flowing into it a river he named San Antonio (later to be called the Hudson). Gómez's travels then took him along the coast of the future New England and Cape Cod, all the way up to Nova Scotia. What he did not find was the hoped-for "Northwest Passage." And so while his explorations did reinforce Spain's claims to the region, they did not inspire further Spanish excursions to the chilly lands north.

Spain's interest in La Florida did not abate, notwithstanding Ponce's bad fortune. The territory was seen as a critical strategic point for protecting treasure ships that plied the Atlantic coast or followed the Gulf Stream up from the south before heading east to return to Spain. In 1520, explorer Francisco Gordillo sailed up the Atlantic coast at least as far as the Carolinas and perhaps even to Virginia. Four years later, in an effort to secure the territory,

Gordillo's patron, the appointed governor of unsettled La Florida, Lucas Vázquez de Ayllón (see also page 279), set out from Hispaniola (the island that is now called Santo Domingo and is split between Haiti and the Dominican Republic) on what was to be the "definitive" Florida expedition. It went awry from the start, however, landing too far north, near the Savannah River in modern-day Georgia. The several-hundred-member party set up the first Spanish mission on the mainland at the new settlement of San Miguel de Gualdape—indeed, the first European settlement (Vikings respectfully excluded) ever founded on the mainland—but barely a third survived the winter. Ayllón wasn't one of them. The survivors sailed back to Hispaniola.

Undaunted, Pánfilo de Narváez (see also page 279), veteran of military expeditions to both Cuba and Mexico, decided to try his luck in La Florida. With his aide Álvar Núñez Cabeza de Vaca (see also page 280) and a crew of 600, he set out from Spain in June 1527. During a stop in Santo Domingo, one-quarter of his crew promptly deserted, a misfortune only heightened when sailing on to Cuba for additional supplies he lost two of his ships in a hurricane. Undeterred, however, he sailed to the site of Tampa Bay, where he took formal possession of the territory in 1528. Narváez sent his ships ahead to a site farther west along the Gulf coast, then headed inland. The army of 400 trudged through swamps, prairies, and forest before settling at a spot near present-day Tallahassee. Along the way they lost several of their party to the Indians, including one Juan Ortiz, who would be held captive for more than a decade. In all, Narváez's party spent 25 days looking for gold, but finding none, they finally headed for the coast to meet up with the ships. The ships, however, had sailed home, the sailors having concluded that the landing party was dead. Now Narváez's 200 remaining men were cut off from supplies and under siege by Indians. It looked as if the sailors might end up being right.

After considerable fretting, the party came up with a plan to save themselves. They would kill their horses and use the hides to fashion boats, on which the expedition would sail down to Mexico, now

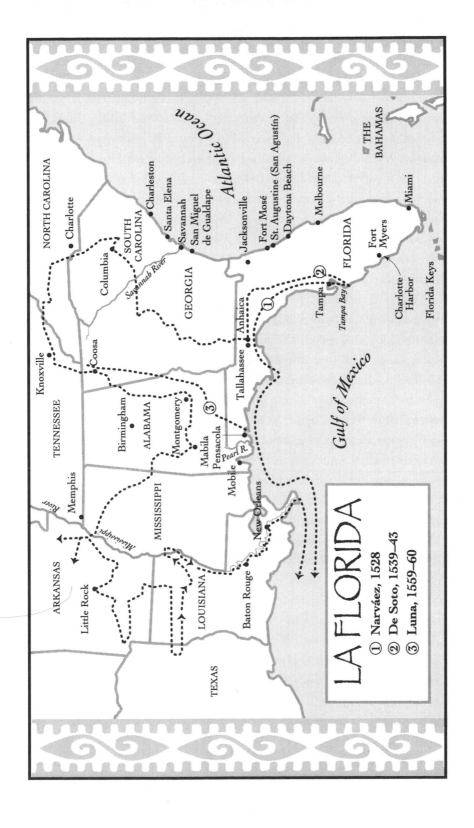

LA FLORIDA

① Narváez, 1528
② De Soto, 1539–43
③ Luna, 1559–60

Atlantic Ocean

Gulf of Mexico

THE BAHAMAS

NORTH CAROLINA

Charlotte

SOUTH CAROLINA

Columbia

Charleston

Santa Elena

Savannah

San Miguel de Gualdape

GEORGIA

Savannah River

Jacksonville

Fort Mosé

St. Augustine (San Agustín)

Daytona Beach

Melbourne

FLORIDA

Miami

Fort Myers

Charlotte Harbor

Florida Keys

Tampa

① ②

Tampa Bay

Anhaica

Tallahassee

Knoxville

TENNESSEE

Coosa

Birmingham

Montgomery

ALABAMA

Mabila

Pensacola

Pearl R.

Mobile

New Orleans

③

Memphis

Mississippi River

MISSISSIPPI

ARKANSAS

Little Rock

LOUISIANA

Baton Rouge

TEXAS

solidly in Spanish hands. The idea might have worked if Mexico had been as close as the Spaniards thought. But not long after the boats (the first built by Europeans on U.S. soil) set out, all but two of them sank at sea, taking their crews down with them—including Narváez himself. The remaining boats continued along the Gulf coast for a month and a half before they wrecked on Texas's Galveston Island in November. It would be almost eight more years before the final four survivors of this expedition found their way back to Spanish civilization.

Certainly if it had taken place 450 years later, the amazing adventure of the survivors of Narváez's ill-fated expedition would have merited no less than a Movie of the Week. The 80 or so castaways on Galveston Island were reduced, by hunger and disease, to 15 by the spring of 1529. They in turn became slaves to the natives, a travail that further winnowed their number to four—including Cabeza de Vaca and Esteban (or Estebanico) (see page 281), an African slave. The four eventually escaped from the Texas Indians, only to face a 6,000-mile journey through mosquito-laden swamplands and scorching deserts, often posing as medicine men to the natives they encountered. After an incredible transcontinental journey—through Texas and possibly New Mexico and Arizona—the survivors were finally found by a group of Spanish slave hunters in northern Mexico in March 1536.

The story of this expedition and the saga of the survivors became the basis for the sixteenth-century version of a best-seller, Cabeza de Vaca's *La relación*, published in Spain in 1542. The full title was *La relación que dio Álvar Núñez Cabaza de Vaca de lo acaecido en las Indias en la armada que iba por gobernador Pánfilo de Narváez desde el año 27 hasta el año 36 que volvió a Sevilla con tres de su compañía*. That is: *The Story Told by Álvar Núñez Cabaza de Vaca of What Occurred in the Indies in the Fleet Led by Governor Pánfilo de Narváez from the Year '27 until the Year '36, which Returned to Seville with Three of Its Company.* Luckily, the book had a nickname—*Los naufragios*, or *The Shipwrecks.*

"They Cure Sickness by Blowing to the Sick"

"[The Indians of Texas] wanted to make us physicians . . . without examining us or asking for degrees because they cure sickness by blowing to the sick and with that blow and moving their hands the sickness is gone. And they asked us to do the same. We laughed and said we don't know how to cure people, then they took our food until we did what they asked. . . .

"The cure was by making the sign of the cross and blowing the sick, we prayed a Paternoster and an Ave Maria asking our God to cure the sick. God in His mercy made well those we were trying to cure. After our prayers the sick told others that they were cured and they treated us well and gave us food, hides, and other things . . ."

—1542 ÁLVAR NUÑEZ CABEZA DE VACA *La relación*

DE SOTO'S TOUR

Hernando de Soto (see also page 282) looked upon Cabeza de Vaca's story not as a cautionary tale but as a dare. He had fought the Incas together with Pizarro in the 1520s and 1530s, along the way appropriating much of their imperial wealth before returning to Spain, and he saw La Florida as another golden opportunity. His plans for a conquest of La Florida won him the backing of Holy Roman Emperor (and king of Spain) Carlos V, who at once appointed De Soto governor of both Cuba—by now the most actively colonized island in the Caribbean—and La Florida. Once in Cuba, De Soto also got Vasco Porcallo de Figueroa, a wealthy veteran of the Cuban conquest and longtime resident of the island, to enlist much of his household and strength in the quest. He had no such luck convincing Cabeza de Vaca to make a triumphant return trip; the former castaway instead accepted the governorship of distant Paraguay.

The Florida expedition (or *entrada*) consisted of nine ships carrying 600 people—including two women—and more than 200 horses, plus other livestock. Leaving behind his wife Isabel de Bobadilla as Cuba's governor (the first woman governor in the New World), De Soto and his fleet departed Havana in May 1539. A week later they arrived near Tampa Bay and set up camp. Shortly thereafter the Spaniards came across Juan Ortiz, lost to the local Indians years before. Ortiz was a great asset to the newcomers, not least in his capacity as an Indian-Spanish interpreter.

Indians were captured and put to severe Spanish servitude, often acting as load-bearers. They were bound in chains even as the expedition marched north across swamps and forded rivers. The group set up winter camp at the Apalachee Indian village of Anhaica, in present-day Tallahassee, where they celebrated the first Christmas on U.S. soil.

The next spring the expedition moved farther north through Georgia and the Carolinas, then west over the Appalachian Mountains into Tennessee. Returning southwest, the Spaniards fought a major battle with the Indians. While licking their wounds, they were attacked again at Mabila (in central Alabama) by natives led by Chief Tascaloosa, with many Spanish casualties.

De Soto, now near the Gulf of Mexico, could easily have returned to his ships. But to do so empty-handed was unthinkable. Instead he moved north and set up camp near Tupelo, in northeastern Mississippi. There the local natives launched a surprise attack and burned down the Spanish winter camp, costing the expedition more casualties than the Mabila battle and nearly all its supplies.

In the spring the army moved on to the west and met the mighty Mississippi, naming it *Río Grande* (Big River). They crossed the river into Arkansas and continued on, passing the future sites of Pine Bluff and Little Rock, where they captured an unfortunate Plains Indian woman who was fleeing Francisco Vázquez de

Coronado's band 300 miles away in Kansas. After another winter near Little Rock, the Spaniards returned to the Mississippi, where de Soto became ill and soon died. De Soto was buried in the river, and the party headed west again in an attempt to reach Mexico. Somewhere near modern-day Austin, Texas, their new commander, Luis de Moscoso, decided to return to the river, build boats, and sail down into the Gulf. In September 1543, after 53 days sailing along the Gulf coast, the 311 survivors (including one of the two women) reached a Spanish settlement in Mexico.

The expedition was regarded as a failure: no riches, no new settlements, and the captain buried in the wild. But the De Soto *entrada* and exploration of 10 present-day southern states provided Spain with valuable information about the interior of North America and again whetted the Spanish appetite for conquest of La Florida.

■ ■ ■

Juan Ortiz and the First Pocahontas

The four survivors of the Narváez expedition who walked across the Southwest to Mexico City were lionized in *La relación*. But at least as amazing is the story of another survivor, Juan Ortiz, who greeted the de Soto party after eleven years of living with the Indians of La Florida. Without taking anything away from Pocahontas, it was an Indian princess in La Florida who first distinguished herself by repeatedly saving the life of a captured European named John (or, more accurately, Juan).

The story runs like this: Ortiz was one of four young sailors captured near Tampa Bay by warriors loyal to Cacique Ucita, who had fought bitterly with Narváez and hated the Spaniards. Although three of them were killed during a religious ceremony shortly thereafter, the chief's daughter (whose name has been lost to the ages) pleaded for Ortiz's life, and he was spared. When the Indians decided to burn him alive over hot coals at another religious ceremony, the princess interceded again.

Kept as a slave and treated miserably, Ortiz found his life again on the line when he was given the thankless assignment of guarding the body of the chief's recently deceased infant son—and fell asleep. Startled by the sound of an animal, he threw his spear into the darkness. At daybreak, when the baby's body was found to be missing, Ortiz was at once sentenced to death—until the body was discovered only a few yards away beside a dead panther with a spear in its side.

The chief's daughter saved Ortiz's life once again when he was designated as an appeasement sacrifice during intertribal warfare. This time she spirited him away to the enemy chief Mococco, who in turn fell in love with the princess. Her "pet" Ortiz was subsequently treated as a member of Mococco's tribe, where he remained for eight years until rejoining the Spaniards on de Soto's arrival.

After eventually regaining his Spanish, Ortiz became invaluable as an interpreter to the Spanish expedition. Ortiz served de Soto for three years, until his death in 1542. De Soto wrote that Ortiz "gave us life. . . . Without him I do not know what would have befallen us."

SETTLING IN

Spain's next attempt to settle La Florida was massive: 500 soldiers, 1,000 colonists, and 240 horses under the command of Tristán de Luna y Arellano. Unlike those before it, however, this *entrada* had its origins in Mexico, also known as New Spain, whose territory throughout the Spanish period ranged from Central America in the south to Kansas in the east to at least the Canadian border in the north. With the sponsorship of Luis de Velasco, the powerful viceroy of New Spain, de Luna left Veracruz on the Gulf coast in June 1559 with 13 ships. He landed in Pensacola Bay on August 14, establishing a settlement called Santa María de Ochuse. A hurricane five days later destroyed all but three of his ships, costing the expedition most of its food and supplies.

Moving into the Indian territory of Coosa in modern-day Alabama, de Luna met a poor welcome. The Indians burned the Spaniards' encampment, forcing a return to the Pensacola area. There, de Luna was relieved by Ángel de Villafañe, another sailor sent by the viceroy of New Spain. Villafañe brought more troops and supplies, then took the colonists and sailed to what is now South Carolina, attempting to set up a colony at Santa Elena, on present-day Parris Island in the Port Royal Sound. Another big storm hit the colonists, however, and they abandoned the enterprise.

It was ultimately a bit of old-fashioned competition that got Spain where it wanted to be in La Florida. French Huguenots (Protestants) had established an outpost called Fort Caroline around present-day Jacksonville. Another party was en route to reinforce the settlement when word of this violation of Spanish territory came to King Felipe II. The furious sovereign called on the realm's finest admiral, Pedro Menéndez de Avilés (see page 284), and instructed him to oust the interlopers.

Menéndez had earned the king's trust. He was a veteran of numerous campaigns in the Old World and the New, and had even shuttled the king when still a prince to London so Felipe could marry his cousin, Mary Tudor, the queen of England. Menéndez was in fact captain general of the Fleet of the Indies for 12 years, with responsibility for all Spanish sea traffic to and from the Americas. Now he was granted the title of governor of La Florida and told to settle the territory once and for all.

Menéndez landed in the Indian village of Seloy on La Florida's Atlantic coast on September 8, 1565; there he founded the settlement of San Agustín (or Saint Augustine), named for the saint whose feast day it was when the party first entered the harbor. In a show of tribute to his creator, Menéndez then invited the local natives to sit down to what was in effect the first Thanksgiving ever celebrated in the land, shortly after which he set out to take the French fort to the north. The French could offer little resistance. Menéndez massacred the inhabitants, then renamed the fort San Mateo.

Over the next decade Menéndez established six more small, fortified settlements, and set up Santa Elena as the territory's capital. The missions he established, the first enduring missions in the land, stretched as far north as Virginia (this one lasted a year before being destroyed by local Indians) and as far south as Miami, where in 1567 a mission named Tequesta (after the local Indian tribe) was constructed. Between 1566 and 1568, one Juan Pardo traveled through South Carolina, North Carolina, and Tennessee, subduing Indians and building forts. After his recall to Spain, Menéndez looked back fondly on the colony he had created: "After the salvation of my soul, there is nothing in the world I want more than to be in Florida."

But even notwithstanding Menéndez's considerable energy, the nascent colony did have considerable growing pains. In 1568, a revenge-minded French force burned down the San Mateo fort. Eight years later, Indians forced the temporary evacuation of Santa Elena. And in 1586, England's Sir Francis Drake—foreshadowing the intense British-Spanish New World rivalry of the coming centuries—sacked Saint Augustine while most of its residents took cover in the woods. This bit of intimidation convinced the residents of the smaller La Florida towns to consolidate in Saint Augustine, which for a time became the sole Spanish city in the colony and the colony's permanent capital. Saint Augustine would survive many more assaults in its future, and today it stands as the first and oldest continuously occupied European settlement in the United States.

Africans in Florida

The first Africans in the New World came not as slaves but as explorers. Juan las Canaries was the first, a black sailor on Columbus's *Santa María* in 1492. Juan Garrido (see also page 279) was known as "El Conquistador Negro," the "Black Conquistador," and was part of Ponce de León's Puerto Rican force as well as a soldier with Cortés in Mexico. And Esteban (see also pages 281–282), a Moroccan African, was one of the four heroes of *La relación* and the first free black to explore the Southwest. Later, free black soldiers fought bravely for Spain, repelling Britain's attack on Saint Augustine. Many blacks fought the British in the American Revolution, notably in the Mississippi Valley campaign and the battles of Mobile and Pensacola under Spanish general Bernardo de Gálvez.

Yet in truth the story of black men and women in the Western Hemisphere in these early centuries is a story of slavery. The first African slaves were imported by Spain to replace Taíno Indians in the Caribbean who were working Spanish mines and farms but were dying of European diseases. Slaves helped populate Lucas Vázquez de Ayllón's colony at San Miguel de Gualdape in 1526 as well as Saint Augustine, which also was home to free blacks who worked at a variety of trades.

The main slave owner in the New World was the Spanish government. Its Africans worked in the royal barracks and hospitals, in construction projects and stone quarries. Black and Indian forced labor built the magnificent Castillo de San Marcos in Saint Augustine. Spanish crown policy on the status of slaves was based on the *Siete Partidas del Rey Don Alfonso el Sabio*, the Seven Laws of King Alfonso the Wise. These principles, derived from the Justinian Code of sixth-century Rome, were adopted by King Alfonso in the thirteenth century. They differed from the British and later American legal conceptions of slavery, which held that slaves were merely "chattel," or personal property. Spanish slaves were themselves entitled to own property, to initiate lawsuits for wrongful abuse by their masters, and to redeem themselves from bondage. And Spanish slaves could not be separated from their families, unlike in America's British colonies.

On the other hand, principles are one thing and application another. Most Spanish-owned slaves lived miserable lives, and despite their legal and religious status, were at best treated only slightly better than slaves were the world over.

COLONIAL LIFE

Now that Spain had a real foothold in La Florida, it began actively to colonize it. The settlements it founded were far from self-sufficient. Each year a financial subsidy, called the *situado,* was sent from Mexico's busy capital at Mexico City to settlers in the region around Saint Augustine. The money was used to purchase food and consumer goods from Havana or other more established Spanish colonial cities, or from the nearby British colonies (although technically it was illegal to trade with the rival British). When the *situado* was late—as it frequently was in those days—the population of La Florida came close to starvation.

Nonetheless, there was a spark of self-sufficiency, typified by the successful cattle ranches in present-day Alachua County, Florida. "Alachua" is likely a corruption of *Rancho La Chúa*—La Chúa Ranch—the largest and most successful seventeenth-century ranch in La Florida. Owned by the Menéndez Márquez family (descendants of Governor Menéndez), La Chúa was huge. Largely because of the demand for meat in the growing Spanish missions and especially in Saint Augustine following the construction of the massive

Castillo de San Marcos (1672–96), the ranch persevered through Indian attacks and reversals and at one point owned a third of all the horses and cattle in La Florida. La Chúa also exported hides to Spain and Cuba and employed scores of black, Indian, and Hispanic *vaqueros* (cowboys). But even this thriving ranch would not ultimately survive the subsequent British assaults on the colony that were to come.

As with much of Spain's success in settling North America, the key was the use of Catholic missions, or chains of missions, staffed by dedicated churchmen who were motivated by the desire to bring salvation's reach to a new and non-Christian world. The story of the Florida missions, in turn, is a Franciscan success story. The first mission actually was founded by secular priests (not affiliated with any particular order) from Menéndez's expedition at Saint Augustine in 1565. Menéndez subsequently brought Jesuits, who set up missions in Georgia, South Carolina, and as far north as Virginia, but they were decimated by Indians and left Florida. The Franciscans fared better, establishing a successful mission system throughout the territory. Thousands of Indians learned Spanish, European-style farming, cattle raising, new arts and crafts, carpentry, weaving—and reading and writing—along with the catechism, from the Franciscans.

The scholarly Franciscans also studied the Indians' native languages and compiled dictionary and grammar books in those tongues. Among the most notable were Father Francisco Pareja's Timucuan-Spanish dictionary, published in 1614, and his Timucuan-language religious books. Some of the priests mastered the Indian languages and initiated bilingual education in the future United States in the seventeenth century. Indian advances in literacy—using a Franciscan-invented spelling system based on the Roman alphabet—impressed observers such as Father Luis Jerónimo de Oré, Franciscan commissary-general of the Indies, who gushed that "with ease many Indian men and women have learned to read in less than two months, and they write letters to one another in their own language."

By 1655 the Franciscans had converted 26,000 Indians living in 38 missions attended by 70 friars. The missions extended from the Carolinas to the Gulf of Mexico. They were ultimately destroyed by British raiders fighting alongside the Yamasee Indians in the first decade of the eighteenth century. Many Franciscans were burned with their missions. Though a few hundred surviving Catholic Indians gained refuge near the guns of the Castillo de San Marcos in Saint Augustine, thousands more were sold as British slaves in the Carolinas.

Besides Saint Augustine, the other notable Spanish city in La Florida was Pensacola on La Florida's Gulf coast, which was reestablished (an earlier incarnation had been abandoned decades earlier) in 1698. Both cities were essentially garrison towns in the far reaches of the Spanish empire. Saint Augustine's population was never more than 3,000; Pensacola was even smaller. Pensacola had much easier access to Havana (by sea) than it did to Saint Augustine, however, and both cities looked to Cuba and not each other for support. In any event, it was needed, for the British had come to Florida, and not as tourists.

■ ■ ■

Fort Mosé

About two miles north of Saint Augustine, Gracia Real de Santa Teresa de Mosé—later known simply as Fort Mosé— was the first free black settlement in North America. It was established in 1738 by escaped British slaves. Spain's king Carlos II had issued an edict in 1687 granting sanctuary to all slaves who escaped from English colonies. (The edict stood until 1790, when U.S. secretary of state Thomas Jefferson pressured Spain to revoke it.) In 1738, the governor of La Florida declared all such fugitives freemen. A group of 38 black families then founded the settlement, named after the "royal grace" *(gracia real)* that won them their freedom, plus the Spanish saint Teresa and the Indian name Mosé.

The leader of Fort Mosé was an escaped slave, a West African Mandingo who had fought the British and their Yamasee Indian allies. At Saint Augustine he had become a Catholic and taken an oath of loyalty to Spain as well as the name of Francisco Menéndez. He was appointed commander of the Spanish Black Militia, with the rank of captain, in 1726—a position he held for nearly four decades. When the British under James Oglethorpe attacked La Florida in 1740, Menéndez's men fought bravely but futilely. Oglethorpe destroyed the settlement. Mosé was rebuilt in 1752, but its inhabitants were evacuated with much of the Spanish settlement of La Florida to Cuba when Spain handed the territory over to England in 1763.

■ ■ ■

JOINING THE BRITISH

Spain and England, Europe's two premier rival empires, were constantly at war. Their colonies were both proxies and prizes in the competition. This became especially true in North America as, throughout the seventeenth century, the British began to establish colonies along the entire Atlantic coast—technically in disregard of Spain's tenuous claim to the region. The circumstances made La Florida, and especially its capital at Saint Augustine (a mere two-day sail from British Charleston), a regular target. As early as 1668, Captain Robert Searles, like Drake 80 years earlier, sacked the city and ransomed a number of hostages.

Two later assaults originated in the British colonies themselves. The first was led by Governor James Moore of South Carolina in 1702. The second was commanded by Georgia's governor, James Oglethorpe, in 1740, and followed a Spanish raid the previous year on British-held Amelia Island off the Florida coast. The campaigns were devastating: Moore's destroyed the missions as well as Rancho La Chúa and others; Oglethorpe's seized several forts and leveled the free black settlement of Fort Mosé. And both hit Saint Augustine with full force. On both occasions, the city took refuge behind the eight-foot-thick walls of the Castillo de San Marcos, built of coquina stone, a shell-like rock that seemed to "swallow" cannonballs. Despite weeks of intense British bombardment, the city's residents emerged safely from the fortress both times—only to find Saint Augustine in ashes. (The Spanish themselves struck back again three years after Oglethorpe's visit with a massive attack on Saint Simons Island off Georgia, only to be soundly beaten.)

In 1756, the Seven Years' War—known in America, where hostilities had actually begun two years earlier, as the French and Indian War—broke out. In many respects this was the true first "world" war; it was fought in Europe, North America, and India. On one side were France, Austria, Russia, Sweden, and the independent German state of Saxony; on the other were England and the German states of Prussia and Hanover. The fight arose over dynastic struggles in Europe and competition between Britain and France in the New World (and India).

Spain entered the war on the side of France in 1762. France essentially capitulated the following year, but not before Spain had opened itself up to intensified British aggression, resulting in Britain's capture of Havana. In 1763, Spain "traded" La Florida to the British to get back Havana, as well as Manila (in the Philippines), which had also been taken the previous year. The entire Spanish population of La Florida (including the Indians and blacks remaining at Fort Mosé), numbering over three thousand, sailed for Cuba.

England now ruled La Florida and divided it into two colonies: East Florida (approximately the area of most of the present-day state) and West Florida (a sliver running from central Florida east of Pensacola to the Mississippi River). Thus from 1763 to 1783— including the years during which the American Revolution raged— the land making up today's United States contained not 13 but 15

British colonies on the Atlantic seaboard. Unlike the rebellious 13 colonies, however, the southernmost (the Florida colonies) joined the northernmost (the Canadian colonies) in remaining loyal to the British crown.

As elsewhere in the New World, Britain considered the settlement of its foreign possessions a private-enterprise affair. It made land grants and left it to loyal grantees to develop the new country. One notable grantee was the Scotsman Andrew Turnbull, who brought 1,400 Minorcan, Greek, and Italian peasants as indentured servants to work his indigo plantation at New Smyrna, 80 miles south of Saint Augustine. These southern European workers eventually added to an increasingly rich ethnic mix in Saint Augustine. (Their descendants, in fact, would include Florida's first territorial delegate to the United States Congress, José Mariano Hernández; the state's first West Point graduate and youngest brigadier general of the age, Stephen Vincent Benét; and Benét's similarly named literary grandson.)

During the American Revolution, Spain—hoping to recover Gilbraltar, Minorca, and Jamaica, as well as Florida—again threw in its lot with France against England, and this time was more fortunate. Spanish victories over England in the Mississippi Valley and the Gulf of Mexico, including the capture of Pensacola by General Bernardo de Gálvez in 1781, resulted in the return of La Florida to Spain in 1783. But notwithstanding its fortuitous choice of allies, Spain returned to La Florida basking only in the sunset of its empire. Now this weaker power faced not merely a rival empire and a rival church. It shared a border with the United States of America, an expansionist young republic imbued with its own near-religious belief that its destiny was to rule the continent.

Nor did that new neighbor waste much time expressing its ambitions: Recognizing Spain's desire to maintain friendly relations with the United States in the face of enduring British-Spanish hostility, the United States cajoled Spain into signing the Treaty of San Lorenzo in 1795. In this treaty, not only did the United States secure navigation of the Mississippi River and access to the port of New

Orleans, but it acquired the northern swath of West Florida consisting of most of present-day central Alabama and central Mississippi.

La Florida's Integrated School

Several years after the reestablishment of Spanish authority in Saint Augustine, the community sought to reopen Saint Augustine's school, which had operated since 1606 but closed at the end of the first Spanish period. That school had been for white children only, but the second time around it was decided to open a single Spanish-language school in 1787 to accommodate all. Attendance was mandatory for whites and optional for all others, but financing came from the royal treasury and no one was charged a fee.

The school may not have been as integrated as modern sensibilities would prefer, but for its time it was quite progressive. Thus the rules required that "If any negroes or mulattos should attend the schools, they shall be placed near the doors in seats apart; but in matters of instruction, spiritual or temporal, the teachers shall do them the same justice as to all the rest." Even as the Continental Congress was drafting the Constitution far to the north, it would be generations before any U.S. school would countenance seating African Americans under the same roof as Europeans—even by the door.

La Florida's Final Chapter

Spain's return to what were now the two Floridas demonstrated that you can, indeed, go home again, but it also begged the question of why you would want to. Saint Augustine reverted to the status of an isolated military outpost dependent on subsidies for its survival. And government of the territory had become more complicated, with local governors having increasing difficulty controlling the local Seminole Indians in the interior.

In fact, goings-on in the Floridas soon became the least of Spain's problems. In 1808, Napoleon—then master of Europe—had thrown aside an earlier alliance with the Spanish, sent French troops into Spain, and placed his brother Joseph Bonaparte on the throne in Madrid. The Spaniards revolted against Napoleon, precipitating the Peninsular War and Napoleon's eventual defeat by the combined forces of Britain and Spain. Napoleon's "Spanish ulcer" kept a large part of his army busy just when he undertook an ultimately disastrous invasion of Russia in 1812. But it kept Spain's forces pinned down as well, leaving them in no position to reoccupy the Floridas aggressively or develop, much less implement, policies that would discourage U.S. ambitions.

Spain, anxious to bring in more white settlers to offset the threatening Seminole population advantage, made the mistake of welcoming U.S. immigration, even providing land grants, into the Floridas. (Spain, and then an independent Mexico, would later make the same mistake in Texas.) As Anglos streamed into West Florida, Spain's hold on the colony weakened. The flow of runaway slaves from Georgia, plus the use of the Spanish border by Florida Indians attacking Georgia plantations, heightened U.S. interest in getting rid of its own "Spanish ulcer" in Florida.

In 1810, Anglo American settlers, with U.S. moral and financial support—and not a little provocation—revolted against Spanish rule and captured the Spanish fort at Baton Rouge, now in the state of Louisiana but then in Spain's West Florida. The rebels replaced the Spanish flag with the standard of the newly proclaimed Republic of West Florida.

After proclaiming its independence, the new republic promptly applied for admission to the U.S. (establishing a model for the Texas Republic years later). Spain, which had provided material and financial assistance to the United States in its war for indepen-

dence against Britain, might well have been confident that its gener-
osity would not so quickly be forgotten. But American ambition
could not be denied: On October 27, 1810, President James Madison issued a proclamation annexing West Florida up to the Perdido
River, at the western edge of the present-day Florida panhandle.
Not just the ingratitude but the boundaries claimed by the United
States were a surprise, since Spain's claim up to the Pearl River,
some 100 miles farther west, had until then been undisputed.
Brushing aside Spanish protests, Congress formalized the annexation of the land between the rivers, which had never even been
claimed by the Republic of West Florida, in 1812. Spain was in no
position to stop the move; it had enough trouble putting down a
small-scale Anglo rebellion in East Florida that same year.

To the eagerly expanding United States, the now reduced Spanish outpost on La Florida's Atlantic shore was a fly in the ointment.
This time, the pretext for action was the recurrent Seminole aggression along the La Florida–Georgia border. In 1817, General (later
President) Andrew Jackson, an avowed Indian- and Spaniard-
hater, was authorized by President James Monroe to pursue Seminoles into Spanish La Florida. He wasted no time in doing so,
exceeding his brief by capturing the Spanish military post of San
Marcos De Apalachee and promptly raising the Stars and Stripes.
Two unfortunate British soldiers found at the fort were tried on
grounds of having encouraged Indian attacks, convicted, and shot.
Jackson went on to Pensacola and removed the Spanish governor,
later expressing regret that he hadn't finished him off, too. Although
Jackson's excessive enthusiasm brought a congressional inquiry
back home and a protest from Spain's ambassador Luis de Onís,
President Monroe refused to condemn the general. Indeed, he may
well have given his prior approval to the actions. And Secretary
of State (later President) John Quincy Adams suggested to Onís
that if Spain could not handle the Indians, it should simply vacate
Florida.

Repeating the sad pattern, and occupied with rebellion in its
other American colonies, Spain ultimately bowed to the inevitable.

In the Adams-Onís Treaty, signed on February 22, 1819, Spain officially ceded both East and West Florida to the United States, which in turn agreed to assume the claims of its own citizens against Spain, an amount estimated at $5 million. (The treaty also settled the United States' western border with Mexico.) Though generally known as the Spanish Cession, the United States' acquisition of Florida is mistakenly thought to have been a $5 million "purchase" of the territory. In fact, Spain received not a single dollar, only the privilege of avoiding military humiliation. In 1821, the Spanish flag was lowered for the last time over the Castillo de San Marcos in East Florida and over its fort in Pensacola in West Florida. And in a bitter irony, Andrew Jackson was appointed the territory's first American governor.

■ ■ ■

"[W]e Shall Certainly Obtain the Floridas"

"We have some claims . . . to go eastwardly [into West Florida] . . . These claims will be a subject of negotiation with Spain, and if, as soon is she is at war, we push them strongly with one hand, holding out a price in the other, we shall certainly obtain the Floridas, all in good time."
—LETTER OF PRESIDENT THOMAS JEFFERSON, 1803

"[Florida] will just as naturally come into our possession as the waters of the Mississippi seek the sea; and anything done to obstruct the operation will be as useless, in the end, as an attempt to arrest and turn back the course of that mighty stream."
—*Niles Weekly Register*, MAY 29, 1819

■ ■ ■

LUISIANA

The territory of what the Spanish called Luisiana extended from the Gulf of Mexico to Canada and north of Texas from the Mississippi River to the Rocky Mountains, encompassing at least part or all of 13 current states. It originally had been claimed for France by René-Robert Cavelier, Sieur de La Salle, who in 1682 had sailed down the Mississippi and named the delta area Louisiana (or, rather, La Louisiane) for King Louis XIV. Eighty years later, France, which had scarcely settled the region, saw Louisiana as a way to compensate Spain, its ally during the Seven Years' War, for its loss of Florida to Britain. As it was, France lacked confidence in its ability to govern and subsidize Louisiana after losing Canada and the land east of the Mississippi River to Britain in the Seven Years' War. It gave control of the territory to Spain under the secret 1762 Treaty of Fontainebleau between King Carlos III and France's King Louis XV.

The Spanish period in Luisiana (without the "o") did not open encouragingly. French colonists petitioned France to reverse its decision to cede the territory to Spain. When appointed governor Antonio de Ulloa, a naval officer and respected scientist, arrived in New Orleans with 80 soldiers in March 1766, the locals refused to acknowledge his authority. In November 1768, a new law requiring that all wine be imported from Spain touched off a rebellion led by the city's French Creole–controlled Superior Council and joined by many German and French settlers. It was the first North American revolt against a European power, and Ulloa was forced to flee.

Spain reacted by dispatching Irish-born Marshal Alejandro (Alexander) O'Reilly (see page 291), along with 24 ships and 3,000 troops, as the new governor. O'Reilly captured 11 leaders of the revolt, tried them, and had six of them executed. He shut down the council and replaced it with a Spanish-dominated body called the Cabildo. As governor, O'Reilly promoted trade, gave land grants, and established good relations with the Indians. He left a peaceful and prosperous Luisiana in 1770. His successor was Luis de Unzaga, who introduced tobacco cultivation and supported the American colonists in their revolt against England, shipping supplies to, among others, General George Washington.

Unzaga was succeeded in 1777 by Colonel Bernardo de Gálvez (see pages 291–292), 29-year-old nephew of Spain's viceroy in the Indies. Gálvez stepped up aid to the colonists, opening the port of New Orleans to rebel shipping, confiscating British vessels, and expelling Britons from the territory. He also increased the flow of supplies and matériel to the rebels. And when Spain entered the war against Britain in June 1779, he led the Spanish forces in the conflict.

Back in Luisiana, Gálvez encouraged immigration, promoted trade and agriculture, and expanded settlement before going on to become governor of Cuba, and later viceroy of New Spain. His successor, Esteban Rodríguez de Miró, was the longest-serving Spanish governor (10 years). Largely with the financial backing of wealthy merchant Andrés Almonester y Rojas (see also pages 288–289), Miró rebuilt central New Orleans after a 1788 fire that destroyed 856 buildings. The extensive Spanish construction, featuring distinctive brickwork and wrought-iron trim and balconies, is the hallmark of the part of the city known, ironically, as the French Quarter.

Subsequent Spanish governors continued to promote trade, undertake public works, and maintain good relations with the natives. By the turn of the nineteenth century, Luisiana had grown from 14,000 to 90,000 inhabitants, and its capital, New Orleans, had more than tripled in population from its original 3,000.

When Napoleon came to dominate the continent of Europe, Spain was forced—in the secret 1800 Treaty of San Ildefonso—to return Luisiana to France, which it did officially in 1803. Only a few years later, in the famous Louisiana Purchase, France sold the million-square-mile parcel to the United States for $15 million. Clearly, Napoleon needed the money; he had arranged the deal with President Jefferson even before Spain had formally returned the territory.

Hispanics and the American Revolution

The Spanish empire's decision to join the upstart colonies in their fight for independence from Britain proved a windfall for the American revolutionaries. Spain itself made vast financial contributions that the Americans used to purchase military supplies. Cuba's governor supplemented this with funds to underwrite General Washington's Yorktown campaign. Meanwhile, British forces were harassed throughout Central America by the viceroy of New Spain Matías de Gálvez, Cuban general Juan Manuel de Cagigal's forces captured the Bahamas, and other Spanish troops attacked British Gibraltar.

Hispanics on the American mainland were especially critical in the struggle. Aid in the form of war matériel came from the Luisiana governor Luis de Unzaga, who shipped supplies to generals Washington and Lee in Virginia and Clark in the Ohio Valley. Father Junípero Serra, founder of the chain of Spanish missions in Alta California, sent money to support French troops on U.S. soil. Spanish forces battled and defeated the British at Saint Louis and in Michigan (where they captured the fort of Saint Joseph). But the most significant contribution was made by Matiás de Gálvez's son, Luisiana governor (after Unzaga) Colonel Bernardo de Gálvez, who not only sent supplies to the rebels but almost single-handedly removed the British from the Mississippi Valley and the Gulf of Mexico.

Even before Spain declared war on Britain, Gálvez had opened the port of New Orleans to colonial shipping and confiscated British ships and cargo in the port, expelling British subjects as well. In June 1779, after the war had begun, Gálvez headed a small detachment of fewer than 1,500 troops and captured the British forts at Baton Rouge and Natchez, among others, along with eight British ships and more than a thousand prisoners, ousting the British from the lower Mississippi Valley. Gálvez, promoted to general, next turned his sights on Mobile—which, with reinforcements (including all-black battalions) from Cuba, he took after a 21-day siege. He was promptly promoted to field marshal.

Gálvez's next target was Pensacola, the capital of Britain's West Florida colony and a crucial stronghold on the Gulf of Mexico. Although unable to secure the assistance of Cuba's captain general and delayed by a hurricane that in 1780 blew many of his ships as far as Mexico, in early 1781, he launched his attack with some 7,700 soldiers of every race and from throughout Spanish America and Spain.

Reinforced by a Spanish fleet and additional soldiers under General Cagigal, Gálvez took Pensacola on May 8 after two months of heavy fighting, during which his forces suffered only 300 casualties. With this victory—detailed in Gálvez's *Diario* ("Diary"), the only contemporary report of a Revolutionary War commander of a major battle—Gálvez prevented the British troops in Florida from reinforcing General Cornwallis at Yorktown, leading to the decisive American victory and the end of the American Revolution.

TEJAS

OPENING THE TERRITORY

In the late seventeenth century the Spanish borderlands in North America were being pressed by both England and France. To the east, Spanish La Florida was at risk as the British moved south into the Carolinas. To the west, France was preparing a challenge to Spain in the Gulf of Mexico and unsettled Texas, which

Madrid had long claimed for its own along with the rest of the future U.S. Southwest and California. Thus it was imperative to establish a stronger presence in what were then the far northern reaches of Mexico if Spain was to deter its rivals.

The earliest settlements in today's Texas were actually along the eastern edge of Spain's Nuevo México territory, an edge that would later be incorporated into the province of Tejas. There, in 1598, explorer Juan de Oñate gave the name *el Paso del Norte* (the Pass of the North) to a pass he discovered in the Sierra Madre mountains. Located on the route between Mexico City and the Nuevo México settlements that were springing up in the early seventeenth century, the site saw its first mission in 1659. By 1682, the missions of Corpus Christi de la Ysleta and Nuestra Señora de la Concepción had been founded nearby to serve refugees from the 1680 Pueblo Revolt. To this day the former mission serves Native Americans; it is the oldest European settlement in today's Texas. And el Paso del Norte is the site of present-day El Paso.

The main body of settlement in Tejas—a word meaning "friends" or "allies" that the Hasinai Indians used to greet the Spaniards— took place, however, on the other side of the territory. And just as the first settlements in Florida a century earlier had come in direct response to a French threat, so, too, did the first settlements in east Tejas. Two years after La Salle's trip down the Mississippi in 1682, he returned to Louisiana with the intention of colonizing the area. As it turned out, though, he ended up making camp and building a small fort on the Tejas coast near Matagorda Bay, which Spain considered its own. Spain reacted quickly to the news, sending military officer Alonso de León (see page 285) to launch a campaign of mission building in east Tejas and to find and root out the French. In 1689, De León found the remnants of the French outpost, who explained that the rest had succumbed to sickness, hunger, Indian attacks, and internal fighting. Indeed, La Salle himself had been killed by his own men.

The following year de León and Father Damián Mazanet founded two missions in the new province, which then included

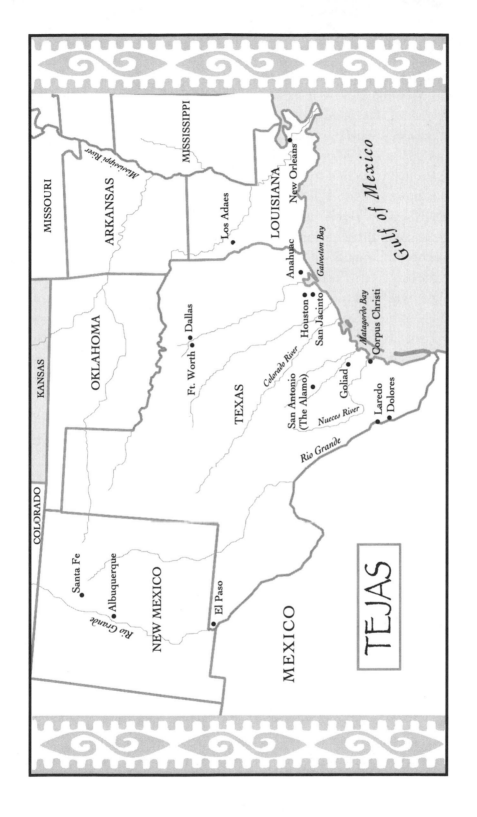

TEJAS

small parts of today's Colorado, Kansas, New Mexico, Oklahoma, and Wyoming, as well as the whole state of Texas. The formerly welcoming Hasinais began to suspect Spain's intentions, and their relationship with the Spaniards deteriorated so seriously that Spain abandoned east Tejas in 1693.

Probably no one was more disappointed with the decision to decamp than Father Francisco Hidalgo, who had served with Father Mazanet, and it was ultimately he who saw to Spain's return to the region—through a little chicanery. Realizing that a bit of foreign provocation was Spain's best incentive, Hidalgo not-so-innocently wrote to French officials in Louisiana suggesting that east Tejas might well deserve some attention. And in the early years of the eighteenth century, French traders began to trickle into the region.

Hidalgo's ploy worked magnificently. In 1716, the anxious Spanish launched a fresh effort in east Tejas. Captain Domingo Ramón led a small expedition (including women, children, and one Francisco Hidalgo) across the Rio Grande and into Tejas. They settled along the banks of the Nueces River, upstream from today's Corpus Christi, establishing the *presidio* (fort) of San Francisco de los Dolores and two missions.

Two years later, Martín de Alarcón, Tejas's governor, founded the city of Béjar (or Béxar), later to be known as San Antonio. There, along with Father Antonio de San Buenaventura de Olivares, the governor saw to the construction of the missions of San Antonio de Béjar and San Antonio de Valero, the latter to gain notoriety more than a century later under the name given to its chapel, El Alamo.

In 1720, a small French force crossed over from Louisiana and occupied the mission of San Miguel de los Adaes, just west of the Red River in what is now the state of Louisiana but was then, in Spain's eyes, part of Tejas. They quickly backed off when challenged by the privately financed army of the marqués de San Miguel de Aguayo, Joseph Azlor Vitro de Vera (see also pages 286–287). Aguayo, who had been named Tejas's governor upon his offer to raise the force, built the presidio at Los Adaes as a lookout over the Louisiana border a dozen miles away. Los Adaes became Tejas's capital and was one of four forts—plus ten missions and the growing settlement at San Antonio—that Aguayo left behind in 1722.

In that same decade the next threat to Spain's Tejas territory arose, now from the Indians. The Apaches were being pushed south onto the Tejas plains by the Comanches. Meeting up with the European enclaves, the Apaches helped themselves to horses, cattle, and sheep, though while they raided missions and ranchos they never broke a presidio stronghold. The Apaches' aggressiveness was a boon to the missions, which sheltered the more peaceable Native Americans who feared the Apaches. The Comanches also raided Spanish settlements. Realizing that Tejas needed more settlers to discourage the Indians, Spain opened the plains to the *rancheros* (cattle ranchers) and the *vaqueros* (cowboys).

The Spanish population of Tejas grew slowly. San Antonio's population reached 500 only when a group of Canary Islanders, led by María Betancour (see also page 287), arrived in 1731. Two small settlements, at Laredo and Dolores along the Rio Grande, were established in 1749 and 1755 respectively. Their founder, José de Escandón, also made many acres available to rancheros in the river valley, helping to establish ranching in the territory. By 1760, there were about 2,500 Hispanics in Tejas, including some 600 in San Antonio. Their life was rough and rude; a visiting Frenchman, Pierre Marie François de Pages, writing in 1767 told of the subsistence existence of the residents of Los Adaes. Though he blamed both lack of water and "the natural indolence of the people" (whom he otherwise admired) for the scarcity of food, de Pages did enjoy the corn victual called *tortillas*, which he called "far from being unpleasant."

The Vaqueros

Although Florida was the site of the first large cattle ranches in the future United States, the Tejas plains proved to be an excellent area to raise cattle and horses, as would the rest of the Southwest. The Spanish, and later the Mexicans, built large cattle ranches and the ranch hands, or *vaqueros* (cowboys), became skilled in the arts of handling cows and horses.

The vaqueros in turn not only passed on their skills to the later Anglo cowboys but provided much of their lore and language as well. Thus the guitar-strumming cowboy, entertaining his pardners and calming those lonesome dogies with doleful ballads, took his cues from the *guitarra*-strumming vaquero, who sang doleful *corridos* around the fire after a long day of *lazo* swinging and *bronco* busting.

Many of the vaqueros, especially in the missions, were Native Americans who, as hard as it is to picture it, were taught their cowboy skills by the *padres*. The tricks of the Spanish bullfighting tradition were put to good use on the great plains.

It is estimated that a fifth of the American cowboys during their late nineteenth-century golden age themselves weren't Roy Rogers look-alikes but were in fact Mexican mestizos, a reality never reflected in John Wayne's "Old West." A number of women were successful vaqueras and rancheras, including Texas's first "cattle queen," María Hinojosa de Ballí (see also page 290), who controlled a third of the lower Rio Grande Valley. The Texas city of Victoria was cofounded by another successful ranchera, Patricia de la Garza de León (see also pages 290–291), one of the richest women in Texas.

MEXICAN INDEPENDENCE AND TEXAS

On September 16, 1810, Father Miguel Hidalgo y Costilla rang the bell in his church in the little town of Dolores, about 120 miles north of Mexico City. The priest asked his congregation the fateful question, "My children, will you be free?" It was a question that would have dramatic repercussions for Mexico, and by extension Tejas as well as other parts of the Southwest that were part of Mexico.

Father Hidalgo's sentiments, and those of his charges, fed on centuries of resentment toward the corrupt Spanish viceroys and the rigid class structure—a pyramid based on ethnic identity and birthplace—that dominated Mexico. Father Hidalgo himself was a *criollo*—a "pure" Spaniard born in the New World. Criollos were excluded from the best opportunities by *peninsulares*, or men born on the Iberian Peninsula (where Spain is located). Further down the chain, Native Americans were particularly dissatisfied with their lot. Under the *encomienda* system, by which native villagers were forced into work details, they were virtual slaves of the landed aristocracy. And since the late eighteenth century, liberal ideology, by way of the 1789 French Revolution, had been filtering into Mexico and changing the terms of the debate.

Father Hidalgo implored his parish, "Long live Our Lady of Guadalupe! Down with bad government! Down with the Spaniards! Long live Mexico!" His cry became known as the Cry of Dolores, or *el Grito de Dolores*, the beginning of Mexico's war of independence, and the date of his impassioned speech is celebrated in Mexico as Independence Day.

After his famous *grito*, Father Hidalgo raised a peasant army of 80,000, as well as substantial criollo support. Despite initial successes, his rebellion was crushed by Spain and the cleric was executed in 1811. The liberation mantle passed to Father José María Morelos y Pavón, a mestizo who declared a Mexican republic in 1814 but who was in turn captured and shot as well. Vicente Guerrero continued the revolution.

By 1820, Spain was racked with political conflict at home and had lost much of its taste for the fight to hold Mexico and the rest of its American empire. On one side were monarchists, who supported the prerogatives of King Ferdinand VII, recently restored to power following the defeat of Napoleon. On the other side were liberals, who had led the Cortes (parliament) in drafting a democratic constitution in 1812 during the Peninsular War, only to have it repealed by Ferdinand. The instability in Spain had brought both conservatives and rebels in Mexico to believe that it would be worth trying their luck as an independent state.

The next year General Agustín de Iturbide, who had defeated Father Hidalgo, joined forces with Guerrero and other revolutionaries and signed the *Plan de Iguala,* which established a separate Mexican monarchy and guaranteed equality for criollos. Although the plan would prove too unstable to endure in the coming years, it did for the moment satisfy the principal competing forces in the land. In 1821, Spain was forced to concede Mexico's independence.

But if independence meant an end to the meddling of Spanish administrators, it also meant the loss of Spanish might. When Spain left, it took along the soldiers who had manned its frontier garrisons, loosening the hold on its distant territories (Tejas, as well as Nuevo México and Alta California) and making them vulnerable to Indian attack. This was not the only cost of independence. After years of turmoil, Mexico now emerged into the world with hardly a peso to its name.

The moment, then, seemed favorable for the United States to make its first attempt at acquiring Tejas—although with few Anglos living there and little else to recommend it, the territory hardly seemed so desirable. (Indeed, only a few years earlier, in the 1819 Adams-Onís Treaty, the United States had conceded a sizable disputed piece of northern Tejas to its then-Spanish claimants.) Still, the United States was in the business of expansion, and in 1825 President John Quincy Adams approached Mexico and offered a fire-sale price for the territory. His successor, Andrew Jackson, did the same four years later. Mexico was not interested, and when U.S. diplomat Anthony Butler offered Mexican officials bribe money to "convince" them of the merit of a sale, he was expelled from the country.

Yet despite the obvious American appetite for Tejas, Mexico welcomed Anglo Americans to settle there and develop it—notwithstanding the Spanish experience with such immigrants in its former West Florida colony. Mexico saw the Anglos as its best hope to counterbalance the vast population of Indians. One important early settler was Stephen Austin, whose father, Moses, had arranged with Spain, before Mexican independence, to bring 300 Anglo families into Tejas. His arrangement with Mexico was explicitly conditioned on a promise to become Catholics and respect Mexican law, including a prohibition on the importation of slaves. Though the new Mexican government was not bound by the agreement, and though Moses died before the exodus could get under way, it was allowed to proceed under Stephen in 1822. Stephen Austin eventually brought 8,000 Anglos to Tejas.

Mexico gave many more land grants to Anglos. By 1830, there were 20,000 Anglos, and (in violation of Mexican law) a tenth again as many slaves, in the territory. Some leading Mexican officials warned that Tejas would be lost to the United States if the flood of immigration was not checked. Despite Mexico's efforts beginning in 1830 to gain control over its U.S. border by officially forbidding immigration, however, undocumented Anglos continued to cross from the state of Louisiana into Tejas.

By 1835, the number of Anglos had increased by half again, to 30,000. The Anglos and their slaves easily outnumbered the 5,000 Mexicans in Tejas. Relations grew strained, not least because Mexico insisted that the immigrants become Roman Catholics and, after 1829, that all slaves in the territories be freed. The immigrants also did not trust Mexico's ability to protect them from the Indians. Finally, the Anglos looked down on Mexican culture and language, and considered Tejas effectively a U.S. enclave ruled by a distant power they neither knew nor respected. Their 1833 application to have Tejas recognized as an independent nation by Mexico City was turned down, building frustration among the settlers.

■ ■ ■

"Texas Could Throw the Whole Nation into Revolution"

"As one covers the distance from Béxar [San Antonio] to this town [Natchitoches], he will note that Mexican influence is proportionately diminished until on arriving in this place he will see that it is almost nothing . . . the Mexicans of this town comprising what in all countries is called the lowest class—the very poor and very ignorant. The naturalized North Americans in the town maintain an English school, and send their children far north for further education; the poor Mexicans not only do not have sufficient means to establish schools, but they are not of the type that take any thought for the improvement of its public institutions or betterment of its degraded condition. . . . It would cause you the same cha-grin that it has caused me to see the opinion that is held of our nation by these foreign colonists, since, with the exception of some few who have journeyed to our capital, they know no other Mexicans than the inhabitants here. . . . Thus, I tell myself that it could not be otherwise than that from such a state of affairs should arise an antagonism between the Mexi-cans and foreigners, which is not the least of the smoldering fires which I have discovered. Therefore, I am warning you to take timely measures. Texas could throw the whole nation into revolution. . . ."

—LETTER FROM GENERAL MANUEL MIER Y TERÁN TO MEXICAN PRESIDENT GUADALUPE VICTORIA, JUNE 30, 1828

■ ■ ■

The Tex-Mex Clash

The monarchy that had been established in Mexico in 1821 lasted only two years. It was replaced with a nominal democracy, characterized by frequent leadership turnover. In 1832, one of the original proponents of republican government, General Antonio López de Santa Anna, rose to the presidency. Three years later, he threw aside Mexico's democratic constitution and began a drive to centralize the Mexican government. His policies and dictatorial behavior roused the already anxious Anglo population into rebellion. In September 1835, Austin, the charismatic firebrand of the Texas rebels, declared that "War is our only recourse. There is no other remedy." And war there was. When Santa Anna dispatched General Martín Perfecto de Cos to enforce the new regime, a rebel force engaged him and sent him into retreat. In November, local leaders met to declare their independence and organize a temporary government.

Most Mexicans in Tejas were loyal to Mexico; some, while denouncing Santa Anna's power play, nevertheless rejected Tejas independence. But a number of wealthy *tejanos* (Mexican Texans), and even some less well-off, had no use for Santa Anna and supported independence. Mexicans Francisco Ruiz, José Antonio Navarro (see pages 300–301), and Lorenzo de Zavala (see pages 299–300) signed the Texan Declaration of Independence, and Zavala became the so-called republic-in-arms' vice president. Other *tejanos* such as Colonel Juan Seguín (see pages 293–294) would soon distinguish themselves in campaigns against Mexico.

The rebel army scored early victories toward the end of 1835, seizing garrisons at Anahuac and Goliad, then ousting a Mexican force from the abandoned mission at San Antonio, familiarly known as the Alamo. While General Perfecto de Cos's troops withdrew to Laredo, Austin had the Alamo fortified in anticipation of the return of Mexican troops. When news of the defeat reached Mexico City, Santa Anna at once gathered a force of 6,000 conscripts, including non-Spanish-speaking Maya Indians, and set out across hundreds of miles of desert to settle matters in Tejas.

In February 1836, Santa Anna led a detachment of 1,400 of those troops in the most memorable military action of the war: the siege of the Alamo. Behind the mission walls, under the command of Colonels William Barret Travis and Jim Bowie, were just 187 Anglo fighters (including Davy Crockett) joined by 10 *tejanos*, including Seguín. A number of Mexican women and children took refuge in the Alamo as well; Andrea Castañón Ramírez Candelaria (see also page 293) served as a nurse during the siege and assisted Bowie. For 13 days, the grossly outnumbered force resisted artillery bombardment. On March 6, Santa Anna's soldiers stormed the Alamo from all sides. The Mexican onslaught was irresistible, and the Alamo was captured, though at tremendous cost. Amazingly, while all but a handful of the Alamo's defenders emerged from the repeated assaults unharmed, the Mexicans sustained approximately 600 casualties. The rebels were taken prisoner and executed. (Seguín, who had been sent outside the walls before the final assault in an effort to raise reinforcements, was one of the few survivors.) Santa Anna's troops then moved east, capturing and executing 365 rebels at Goliad.

At San Jacinto (near Galveston Bay), on April 21, 1836, Santa Anna rested his troops in anticipation of an expected attack the following day. It was a major miscalculation. During the Mexicans' respite, a force led by former Tennessee governor General Sam Houston swooped down and, to shouts of "Remember the Alamo!" and "Remember Goliad!" routed the Mexicans and captured Santa Anna.

The Mexican leader was forced to sign two treaties, requiring Mexico to leave Texas (while the Spanish spelled the name with either a *j* or an *x*, the Anglos settled on the latter) and to recognize Texas's independence. Santa Anna himself was kept in prison for six months and then released. He found refuge in Cuba and eventually returned to Mexico, where he would yet again face American troops in battle a decade later. Although the Santa Anna–less government back in Mexico City repudiated the treaty, it was not for the moment in any position to enforce its view. Thus ended the 14 years of Mexican rule over Texas, and thus began the transition to the inevitable U.S. annexation of the vast territory.

Remembering the Alamo

Today all that remains of the Alamo is the chapel that lent the mission its name, standing in a park in downtown San Antonio. The Alamo—Spain's mission of San Antonio de Valero—was founded in 1718. Construction was completed six years later. Franciscans used the mission until 1793, when the Spanish government abolished it. Its respective buildings were subsequently put to use as a fort, hospital, jail, warehouse, and store. But after the famous battle between Anglo settlers and the troops of Santa Anna, it became a Texas shrine.

The Anglo Americans in Texas generally see the Alamo as the place where Anglo Texans fought against foreign aggression to defend freedom and their own families' safety. In fact, rather than local family men, most of the Alamo's defenders were recent arrivals to the territory in search of fortune and adventure, and they were fighting not foreigners but the legitimate rulers of the territory. Among its most famous figures, William Barret Travis was a fugitive killer; the infamous brawler Jim Bowie, whose fortune was built on slave running, had come to Tejas in search of lost mines; and Davy Crockett had been in the area for all of four months before the Alamo fell, seeking a last fight in his declining years.

As for freedom, one of the biggest forces behind the independence movement was Mexico's abolition of slavery, an institution the arrivals from the United States were not prepared to do without.

Latinos tend to regard the Alamo as an enduring symbol as well—of U.S. aggression against a weak, welcoming neighbor and of the second-class citizenship afforded *tejanos*.

■ ■ ■

THE LONE STAR REPUBLIC

Anglo defenders of the Alamo myth are fond of pointing out that the Texan revolution against Mexico was joined by numerous *tejanos*. They don't often mention, however, that following the Anglo victory these same *tejanos* were discriminated against and even driven off the land for which they had fought. Even Alamo veteran Juan Seguín, colonel of the Texas army and later a member of the Texas Senate and mayor of San Antonio, eventually had to flee to Mexico when Anglo sensibilities came to regard all *tejanos* as traitors.

The 1836 Texas Constitution institutionalized this caste system. Citizenship and the right to own property were denied anyone who had not participated in the war against Mexico. For many Anglos, this translated into the freedom to mistreat any and all Mexicans with impunity. Mexicans were pushed out of central and eastern Texas into the south, and Anglo squatters began moving onto the larger *tejano* properties and claiming land. The courts provided no relief, and the Texas Rangers, the new republic's powerful law officers, enforced the anti-*tejano* decisions. Racial and social segregation in education, housing, and public facilities increased as the Anglo population far outstripped the number of *tejanos*.

To the Texans, however, annexation of their republic by the

United States was crucial. Maintaining an army and navy for the seemingly inevitable next war with Mexico was daunting for a nation with only 70,000 people—1 percent of the population of Mexico. Indeed, for much of life of the Lone Star Republic (so-called because of the single star on its flag, adopted in 1839), a nasty guerilla war raged between Texas and Mexico. In 1841, for example, one Texas general led a 300-man military expedition into Nuevo México with the intention of solidifying Texas's claim to its western border; it was quickly defeated by the militia of Governor Manuel Armijo (see also pages 298–299). The next year, Mexican troops attacked San Antonio, leading Texas to move its capital from Austin north to the Brazos River.

But when Texan leaders first proposed annexation of their republic by the United States in 1836, the reception in Washington was cool. Newly installed president Martin Van Buren saw annexation as an invitation to war with Mexico and a splash of gasoline on the smoldering slavery fire; indeed, as a slave state, Texas was not at all welcomed by the free states of the North. Abolitionists, particularly William Lloyd Garrison, were incensed at the prospect of adding Texas to the Union, declaring, "Texas is the rendezvous of absconding villainy, desperate adventure, and lawless ruffianism—the ark of safety to swindlers, gamblers, robbers, and rogues of every size and degree." Along with France and England, however, the United States did recognize the Texas Republic. And the annexation issue was not about to fade.

NUEVO MÉXICO

IN SEARCH OF THE GOLDEN CITIES

One day in March 1536, a group of Spanish slave hunters in northwestern Mexico saw a strange party approaching them: a white man and a black man heading a group of 11 Indians. The white man explained that he was Álvar Núñez Cabeza de Vaca, and that he, together with the African Esteban and two other Spaniards (a day or two behind them), were the sole survivors of the ill-fated 1528 Florida expedition of Pánfilo de Narváez. After living among the Indians for eight years, as Cabeza de Vaca would soon describe in *La relación*, they had finally been found.

Brought to Mexico City, the group told the authorities about Indian accounts of cities of gold and emeralds—the Seven Golden Cities of Cíbola—said to be located somewhere in present-day northern New Mexico. The viceroy of New Spain, Antonio de Mendoza, could not convince Cabeza de Vaca, who would later turn down a similar offer from Hernando de Soto, to go back and find the golden cities. But he could purchase Esteban from one of the Spaniards, which he did, upon which he placed him at the lead of a new *entrada* to the future U.S. Southwest. It wasn't much of a deal for Esteban. Not long after the expedition set out in March 1539, he and several Indians in his party were killed by Zuni Indians. The remainder of the party, led by Father Marcos de Niza (see page 281), returned empty-handed.

Back in Mexico City, however, Father Marcos's embellishments to the Cíbola stories only whetted the viceroy's appetite. Mendoza didn't have to go near those Zunis, after all. This time, with his own money financing the trip, he tapped the young governor of the Mexican province of Nueva Galicia, Francisco Vásquez de Coronado (see pages 283–284), to lead the way, joined by Father Marcos. The group they organized was huge: more than 1,200 people, including 230 cavalry and 62 other soldiers, along with 1,000 Mexican Indians, 6 priests, and 3 Spanish women.

In late February 1540, Coronado's party set out to search for Cíbola. And, finally, it was Cíbola that they reached—dusty, wretched Cíbola, home to a hundred Zuni families living in adobe huts. Coronado sent the good father home with a note to the viceroy: "Fray Marcos has not told the truth in a single thing that he said."

But Coronado decided to make the best of it and explore the

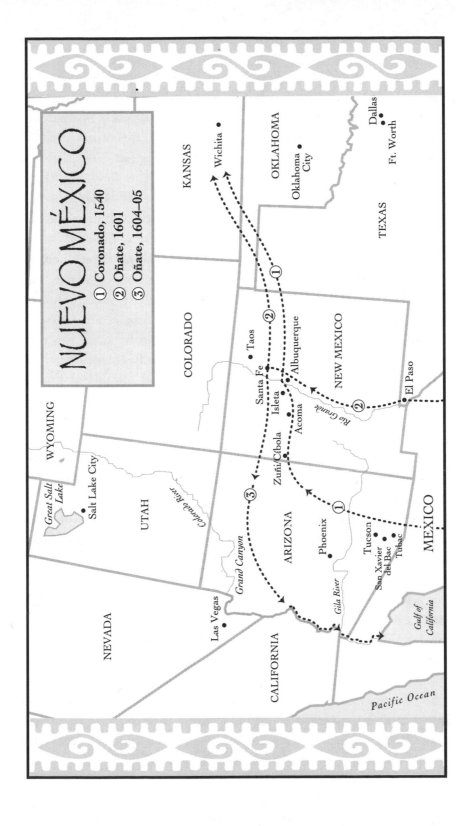

NUEVO MÉXICO

① Coronado, 1540
② Oñate, 1601
③ Oñate, 1604–05

WYOMING

Great Salt Lake

Salt Lake City

UTAH

Colorado River

NEVADA

Las Vegas

CALIFORNIA

Pacific Ocean

Grand Canyon

ARIZONA

Phoenix

Gila River

Tucson

San Xavier del Bac

Tubac

Gulf of California

MÉXICO

COLORADO

Taos

Santa Fe

Isleta

Zuñi/Cíbola

Acoma

Albuquerque

NEW MEXICO

Rio Grande

El Paso

KANSAS

Wichita

OKLAHOMA

Oklahoma City

TEXAS

Dallas

Ft. Worth

region. One of his parties met the Hopi Indians of Arizona. Another, led by García López de Cárdenas, followed up reports of a great river until they reached the roaring *Colorado*—Spanish for "ruddy," since the waters looked red due to the mud—and the majestic Grand Canyon, making López's group in 1540 the first Europeans to see this magnificent site. At the same time, Hernando de Alarcón, who had been instructed to meet up with Coronado and resupply his party, was sailing the mouth of the same river at the Gulf of California. There he encountered the Yuma Indians. But he could not locate the land party. With his ships threatened by worms, he departed—leaving a carved inscription on a tree and letters explaining his whereabouts at its foot, which, incredibly, one of Coronado's officers would discover two months later.

After exploring along the Rio Grande, Coronado set up near present-day Albuquerque for the winter. There his men battled the Pueblo Indians, who, needless to say, resented his use of Pueblo villages to supply the Spaniards with food and women. In the spring, ever hopeful, Coronado pursued an eastward path urged by an Indian nicknamed "the Turk" in search of yet another golden city—Quivira. Coronado's men traversed the Texas panhandle and Oklahoma into Kansas, at which point they found that the land was rich in buffalo but had little that the Spanish wanted. The Turk finally came clean: He had intentionally misled the party out of spite. His belated honesty was rewarded with execution.

Injured in a riding accident at the end of 1541, Coronado led the party home several months later, leaving priests Juan de Padilla and Luis de Ubeda to lead the trek eastward. Both died at the hands of Native Americans, though, becoming the first Catholic martyrs in North America.

For his own part, Coronado died, forgotten, in Mexico City in 1554. Since he hadn't found any gold, his *entrada* was considered a failure. But his explorations of modern-day Arizona, New Mexico, Texas, Oklahoma, and Kansas expanded Spain's knowledge about the interior of the future United States.

"Send Me a Great Cross"

"I sent Esteban Dorantes, the Negro, whom I instructed to take the route towards the north for fifty or sixty leagues to see if by that way he might obtain an account of any important thing such as we were seeking. I agreed with him that if he had any news of a populous, rich, and important country he should not continue further but should return in person or send me Indians with a certain signal which we arranged, namely, that if it were something of medium importance, he should send me a white cross of a hand's breadth, if it were something of great importance, he should send me one of two hands' breadth, while if it were bigger and better than New Spain [Mexico], he should send me a great cross. . . .

"In four days' time there came messengers from Esteban with a very great cross, as high as a man, and they told me on Esteban's behalf that I should immediately come and follow him, because he had met people who gave him an account of the greatest country in the world. . . . [H]e had Indians who had been there, of which he sent me one. . . . He told me that it was thirty days' journey from where Esteban was staying to the first [of seven] cit[ies] of the country, which was named Cíbola. . . . He told me many other particulars, not only of the seven cities but of other provinces beyond them, each one of which he said was much bigger than that of the seven cities."

— FRAY MARCOS DE NIZA, *relación* (report) TO THE VICEROY OF NEW SPAIN, 1539

BACK AGAIN

For 40 years after Coronado's expedition, Spain, occupied throughout the hemisphere and happy to focus on mining the silver near Mexico City, forgot Coronado's not-so-golden land. Then, in 1581, seven soldiers and three Franciscans led by Captain Francisco Sánchez Chamuscado found their way up the Rio Grande to Pueblo territory. They named the area San Felipe de Nuevo México and returned home. The Franciscans stayed behind to convert the Indians. The Indians, however, had other things in mind, and by the time a second expedition, led by Antonio de Espejo, returned, the padres had been killed. Undaunted, Espejo's party stayed on to explore Nuevo México, which under Spanish rule included parts of present-day New Mexico, Arizona, Wyoming, Colorado, Utah, and Nevada.

An unauthorized 1590 *entrada* in Nuevo México, by one Gaspar Castaño de Sosa, earned the brave explorer six years of exile in the Philippines. It was not until eight years later that the Crown decided to settle Nuevo México. Juan de Oñate (see pages 284–285), a *criollo*, was selected by Viceroy Luis de Velasco to head the expedition.

Oñate certainly had the pedigree for the job. His father Cristóbal had been a conquistador in central Mexico and the discoverer of rich silver mines in the territory. His wealthy wife was the granddaughter of conquistador Hernán Cortés and the great-granddaughter of the Aztec emperor Moctezuma. In January 1598 he set out for Nuevo México with 129 soldiers, several of their families and accompanying Mexican Indian servants, 83 wagons of supplies, and 7,000 head of cattle. Oñate was brimming with optimism, writing to the king that "I shall give Your Majesty a new world, greater than New Spain."

As his predecessors to the region had already learned, however, what lay in wait was mostly hardship. Still, Oñate did succeed at his principal mission: to subdue the resident Pueblo Indians to prepare the region for Spanish settlement. This he did with an iron fist. A revolt at the Indian village of Acoma, leading to 12 Spanish dead (including Oñate's nephew), was answered by Oñate's order to level the place. The adult survivors were sentenced to 20 years of servitude, and the children were handed over to priests for Catholic educations. This, Oñate hoped, would be an example for other Indians.

As Nuevo México's governor, Oñate continued exploring, unable to resist the urge to find golden cities. In 1601 he trekked through Oklahoma and Kansas—Quivira again—and experienced the same disappointment as Coronado. Oñate made his way to the Colorado River's outlet at the Gulf of California in 1604, where Alarcón had waited in vain for Coronado in 1540. On the way back his men stopped at El Morro, a promontory between the Acoma and Zuni pueblos. There the Spaniards wrote one of North America's first pieces of graffiti: "There passed this way the adelantado Don Juan de Oñate, from the discovery of the South Sea, on the 16th of April 1605." It can still be seen.

Though the Mexican viceroy was pleased with Oñate's progress, reports of his treatment of Native Americans, unrest among the soldiers, and general mismanagement tarnished Oñate's governorship. Oñate was recalled in 1607.

Historia de la Nuevo México

One of Oñate's captains, Gaspar Pérez de Villagrá (see page 332), was a poet. In 1610, 12 years after marching with Juan de Oñate into Nuevo México, Villagrá published the first epic poem about the future United States: *Historia de la Nuevo México*. Villagrá's poem recounts the hardships encountered by Spaniards in the arid land. This short excerpt finds

Villagrá separated from his party in hostile Indian territory, near death from starvation; he has killed his dog to survive — only to realize he had no fire to cook the dog's meat. Here, he finally happens upon food and water, and is saved when he is discovered by a group of Spanish soldiers.

In downcast mood I now took up my journey,
Leaving the poor dog dead. Sad fate beset me,
Till I descried a towering cliff uprising,
Beneath which flowed a stream of purest crystal.
Blinded and burnt with thirst, into its waters
I threw myself, and drank. This quenched my burning.
A bit of corn I spied, dropped there by someone;
At this, I knelt, and thanked the God Almighty
For this most timely aid. Then, on earth crawling,
Gathered a handful of the corn and ate it.
By rest and food refreshed, I then proceeded,
Seeking the capital, San Juan. Now fortune favored.
Starting upon my way, I soon encountered
Three of our men, out searching for their horses . . .
They called, demanding who I was; I answered,
And, at my name, their joy was so tremendous
That, in delight, they fired their arquebuses.
Heaven-sent impulses! For it chanced the Indians
Following me, were closing in for capture.
Hearing the guns, they turned and fled, believing
That the whole Spanish army lay before them . . .

■ ■ ■

In 1610, Oñate's successor, Pedro de Peralta, established a site for Nuevo México's capital in an unpopulated valley irrigated by a cold stream. Peralta named the new settlement La Villa Real de la

Santa Fe de San Francisco de Asís (the Royal Village of the Holy Faith of Saint Francis of Assissi), now known simply as Santa Fe. Today it is the United States' third oldest city and the oldest state capital.

Santa Fe was capital, however, of very little, from a Spanish point of view. Its own population was only around a thousand in the 1630s, of which three-quarters were Indians and mestizos. Even the 25 Franciscan missions boasted only 25 missionaries to service 50,000 Indians. Nuevo México was neither conveniently located nor wealthy; its scattered settlements stuck close to the green banks of the Rio Grande.

The Spaniards that did come worked the land and raised stock, primarily sheep. Wagons from the south carried on trade with these distant outposts, traveling the 1,500 hot, dry miles from Mexico City to Chihuahua to El Paso and Santa Fe, stopping along the way at smaller hamlets and returning to Mexico City with the products of Nuevo México.

THE PUEBLO REVOLT AND RECOVERY

The continuous demand for cheap labor at Spanish enterprises, coupled with religious persecution, had driven the Pueblo Indians to revolt five times between 1632 and 1650. But in 1680, the Pueblos launched the most successful Indian uprising ever against Europeans in the New World, known as the Pueblo Revolt.

The trigger was a Spanish crackdown on Pueblo religion. In 1675, the Spaniards had raided a meeting of more than three dozen Pueblo religious leaders. Three were executed and the remainder were whipped for the crime of sorcery. One of the "sorcerers" was Popé, a religious leader from the village *(pueblo)* of San Juan. He headed to the northernmost village in Nuevo México, Taos, to plan his revenge: a massive rebellion against Spain.

On August 10, 1680, Popé led 17,000 Indians from 25 pueblos against the Spaniards. Four hundred Spanish men, women, and children were killed, including 21 of the 33 missionaries in the region. The Spaniards, living on small, isolated farms, were easy prey for Popé's rebels. After the initial raids, terrified settlers fled to Santa Fe for refuge, but at Santa Fe, Governor Antonio de Otermín had only 100 soldiers at his disposal. He quickly found himself surrounded by 2,000 Pueblo warriors, who presently cut off the city's water supply and began burning buildings. Otermín, having little choice, fought a path through the Indians with the refugees behind him, heading 300 miles south to El Paso and picking up Spaniards fleeing the tiny village of Isleta along the way.

In a few weeks, Popé controlled all of Nuevo México north of El Paso. He had driven 2,500 Spaniards out of the territory and had destroyed Spanish homes and buildings. But his special fury was reserved for the churches of his oppressors, on whose frames and contents he exacted an unholy vengeance.

Popé controlled this area for almost a decade. He died in 1688, but by then much of his "empire" had fallen apart. Popé could neither maintain strategic unity nor effectively administrate the far-flung, independently minded villages. Occasional Apache raids on the villages weakened the rebellion as well, making them again vulnerable to Spanish encroachment.

By 1691, when Diego de Vargas (see page 286) arrived in El Paso as Nuevo México's new governor, Spain—still relying on only 100 soldiers—had methodically begun to win back control of the territory, one pueblo at a time, using a combination of diplomacy and intimidation. By October 15 of that year he could write to the king that he had retaken 13 Pueblo villages, bragging that close to a thousand Indian children born since 1680 had been baptized. Although Spain would not completely regain its previous dominion of the Pueblo Indians until 1696, Vargas was the toast of Mexico City. One contemporary wrote, "An entire realm was restored to the Majesty of our Lord and King, Carlos II, without wasting an ounce of power, unsheathing a sword, or costing the Royal Treasury a single *maravedí*."

"A Happy Day, Luck, and Good Fortune"

"A happy day, luck, and good fortune were attained, your Excellency, through the impulse which, fervently, spurred by the faith and as a loyal vassal of his Majesty, led me to undertake the [conquest], considering that it is a region so large as to be a kingdom, all of which was in rebel hands for the past twelve years, and only on the confines of which was it known that they had been visited. For their safety, they were living on the mesas, the approaches to which made it difficult to invade them without their being assured of victory. All of these conditions could have justly embarrassed me, but, realizing that the defense of my faith and my king were of greater importance, I scorned them and put into execution the said enterprise. . . ."

— LETTER FROM GOVERNOR DIEGO DE VARGAS TO THE VICEROY OF NEW SPAIN, JANUARY 12, 1693

Though they retook the territory from the Pueblos, the Spaniards mainly learned their lesson in Nuevo México. In the eighteenth century, the Franciscan missionaries used less harshness in moving their spiritual charges away from their old beliefs and practices. The exploitative *encomienda* system was not reestablished, and the colonists cut back on their demand for labor. Both the Spaniards and the Pueblos also realized the value of presenting a common front to the increasingly bold Apaches, Navajos, and Utes.

The end of the Pueblo Revolt to a great degree coincided with the first colonization of the western part of Nuevo México known as Arizona, which before then often had been visited (by Cabeza de

Vaca, Father Marcos de Niza, Coronado, Oñate, and others) but never settled. One reason for delay can probably be found in the origin of the region's name: It comes from the Indian word *"Arizonac,"* meaning "land of few springs." But in 1687, Father Eusebio Francisco Kino (see page 286), a Jesuit, arrived in the *Pimería Alta,* or Upper Pima, an area encompassing the present Mexican state of Sonora and southern Arizona, and set up his headquarters at the mission of Nuestra Señora de los Dolores. From there, Kino made three dozen exploratory forays around the region, including 15 into what is now Arizona. He founded 25 missions, including Arizona's San Xavier del Bac (which today features one of the most beautiful Spanish churches in the United States) in 1700. And the "Padre on Horseback" established 20 cattle ranches and farmed extensively to provide food for the region's Indians.

In 1706, Tubac, in southern Arizona, was established as the territory's first town; it added a presidio in 1752. In the 1730s, a small silver mining industry brought several hundred Spanish settlers into the region. Two hundred people lived in Tubac by 1767, plus its garrison, and Tubac was the springboard for the California expeditions of Juan Bautista de Anza in the decade that followed. (Until 1860, Tubac was Arizona's largest town.) By 1820, the Hispanic population of Arizona was about a thousand, clustered around Tubac and another town in southern Arizona, Tucson, which had begun in the 1690s as a mission called San Cosme del Tucson. These settlers braved a harsh and dangerous life, threatened by inhospitable elements on one hand and inhospitable Apaches on the other.

Throughout this same period, the rest of Nuevo México was riding a rising commercial tide. The Spaniards there developed trade with the neighboring Indians, such as the Utes and the Comanches, when relations permitted. At regional fairs at Taos or Pecos they bought or exchanged military supplies and agricultural products for furs and buffalo hides. Meanwhile, the traffic continued to grow on the trade route to Mexico City—the so-called *Camino Real* (King's Road)—which on a given day might serve as conduit for half a million sheep at a time or for woolen cloth, blankets, dried meat, and chilies heading south from the territory. Madrid awarded huge land grants to individuals and communities, and wheat, corn, and fruit were grown. El Paso established a thriving business in wines. Great, self-sufficient walled estates *(haciendas)* sprung up. By 1760, there would be 20,000 Hispanics settled across the region—including 2,500 in El Paso, nearly 2,000 in Albuquerque (established in 1706), and more than 1,500 in Santa Fe—for many of whom life in Nuevo México had taken on all the trappings of home.

■ ■ ■

Exploring Ski Country

Colorado and Utah, also part of the lands that Spain considered to be part of its Nuevo México, forever remained too distant from the principal New World cities for Spain to bother settling. Indeed, they scarcely had any visitors at all. Among those that did pass through were Father Silvestre Vélez de Escalante and a party of eight, who in 1776 set out from Santa Fe to search for an overland route to Monterey in California, which the Spanish were just beginning to settle. After traversing the region all the way to today's Great Salt Lake, they gave up on finding the passage and returned home (a total of 2,000 miles on horseback, in five months) with information on the fresh geographical discoveries they had made.

■ ■ ■

ENTER THE ANGLOS

The first U.S. troops to cross into Nuevo México came in peace. Lieutenant Zebulon Pike and his men had come into present-day Colorado, entered northern New Mexico, and began to build a fort in 1807. The soldiers were arrested for trespassing and, after being brought to Santa Fe and then Chihuahua, were released.

Nonetheless, as in Florida and Texas, American settlers saw opportunities in these borderlands, and they took them. Fur-trapping mountain men came to Taos to trade, imbibe "Taos lightning," dance the fandango, and court women. Next came Yankee merchants along the Santa Fe Trail, the transcontinental pathway from Missouri across Kansas and Colorado to Santa Fe. Their merchandise made its way to eager Nuevo México and Alta California consumers. The merchants followed as well, with settlement and commerce booming in Nuevo México following Mexican independence in 1821.

While the region's robust economy did wonders for development, the Mexico City government feared the development of what one historian has called "a fifth column, becoming the vanguard for the invasion of New Mexico." The Mexican government began to make its heavy hand felt throughout the region's commercial affairs, imposing higher taxes, among other measures, and antagonizing even Mexican settlers. Indeed, in 1837, Hispanics in the region staged an abortive antigovernment revolt. The stage was set for a big change in the territory's fortunes, and those of Mexico and the United States as well.

■ ■ ■

Latino "Firsts"

In the early years of European discovery, the Europeans doing all the discovering were the Spanish. It's not surprising, then, that numerous historical milestones—for the Europeans, if not for the natives—were first achieved by Hispanic trail-blazers.

DISCOVERY OF FLORIDA

By Juan Ponce de León, 1513. He and his party touched ground near present-day Daytona Beach, inaugurating a more than three-century-long Spanish presence on today's United States mainland.

DISCOVERY OF THE MISSISSIPPI RIVER

By Alonso Álvarez de Pineda, 1519. He came across the mouth of the Big Muddy while exploring and mapping the Gulf of Mexico coastal region. Hernando de Soto and his party were the first to cross the river during an *entrada* 20 years later.

FIRST SETTLEMENT

San Miguel de Gualdape, 1526. Established by governor of Florida Lucas Vázquez de Ayllón in today's Georgia, it collapsed under the pressure of hunger, disease, and the death of Ayllón after only four months. It also boasted the first Catholic mission on the mainland.

FIRST CHRISTMAS

In Anhaica, Florida, 1539. Hernando de Soto, along with his expedition of 600, plus numerous Indian slaves, celebrated the first American Noel in this Apalachee Indian village near present-day Tallahassee.

DISCOVERY OF THE GRAND CANYON

By García López de Cárdenas, 1541. López came upon the big chasm, and the Colorado River running through it, while leading a band from Coronado's expedition.

FIRST BOOK ABOUT AMERICA

La relación (The Story), 1542. Álvar Núñez Cabeza de Vaca's extraordinary memoir of his lost-in-the-New World adventures was published in Spain and became a big seller and a challenge to would-be explorers for decades to come.

DISCOVERY OF CALIFORNIA

By Juan Rodríguez Cabrillo, 1542. He touched down in San Diego Bay while exploring the Pacific coast of Alta California (today's state of California).

FIRST PERMANENT SETTLEMENT

Saint Augustine, 1565. Founded by Florida governor Pedro Menéndez de Avilés, 42 years before Jamestown and 55 years before the landing of the Pilgrims at Plymouth Rock, it is the oldest city founded by Europeans in the United States.

FIRST THANKSGIVING

In Saint Augustine, 1565. Yes, 55 years before Plymouth rock, Pedro Menéndez de Avilés invited the Indians to dine on food brought ashore upon the founding of the settlement after hearing a Catholic mass.

FIRST EUROPEAN BABY

Martín Argüelles, 1566. He was born in Saint Augustine, Florida, shortly after its founding.

FIRST BOOK IN AN INDIAN LANGUAGE

Several religious volumes in the Timucuan language, 1614. Translated by Father Francisco Pareja, they were meant for the improvement of the Florida Indians.

FIRST FREE BLACK SETTLEMENT

Gracia Real de Santa Teresa de Mosé, 1738. Known simply as Fort Mosé, the town was established near Saint Augustine in the wake of Spain's policy of providing refuge to slaves escaping England's colonies.

FIRST INTEGRATED PUBLIC SCHOOL
In Saint Augustine, 1787. When Spain recovered Florida after two decades of British rule, a formerly all-white institution was opened to all races—without a court order.

▪ ▪ ▪

ALTA CALIFORNIA

CALIFORNIA, HERE WE COME

As with Tejas and Nuevo México, the story of Alta (Upper) California begins in present-day Mexico. After his defeat of the Aztecs in 1521 and his establishment as de facto ruler of the territory, conquistador Hernán Cortés wanted to expand Spanish rule to the north along the Pacific Ocean. Cortés wrote Holy Roman Emperor Carlos V (recently elevated from his less lofty role as King Carlos I of Spain) that he would not only conquer new lands but would also locate the elusive Strait of Anián—the fabled waterway connecting the Atlantic with the Pacific. The emperor liked the idea and approved the expedition.

In 1533, Cortés sent sailor Fortún Jiménez north. The explorer discovered the southern tip of the almost 800-mile-long peninsula of today's Baja (Lower) California, which, like Ponce de León with Florida just a few years earlier, he took to be an island. The name "California"—taken from a fictional island of griffins and gold, featured in the popular 1509 romantic novel *Las sergas de Esplandián* by Count Ordoñes de Montalvo—may have been Jiménez's choice. In any event, "California" became the designation for the entire West Coast. Two years later, Cortés himself visited the Baja area and established a small colony there. But it would take yet another expedition, by Francisco de Ulloa in 1539, to determine that this territory was in fact part of the mainland; this Ulloa did by sailing the entire west coast of Mexico to the head of the Gulf of California (aka the Sea of Cortés), then turning south along the eastern Baja California shore, rounding its tip, and sailing three-quarters of the way up the west side.

When, in 1540, Madrid installed Antonio de Mendoza as viceroy of New Spain, he enlisted a veteran of many explorations in South America and the Caribbean, Juan Rodríguez Cabrillo (see also pages 282–283), to explore Alta California—a designation that the Spanish eventually meant to include territory reaching far into today's Canada until the northern boundary was definitively established with the United States in the 1819 Adams-Onís Treaty. In June 1542, Cabrillo sailed north from Navidad, Mexico, a small Pacific port, reaching today's San Diego Bay that September. He and his three ships' crews were the first Europeans to touch ground on the U.S. West Coast.

The expedition soon moved on to the future sites of Santa Catalina Island and Los Angeles, and continued up the coast to the Channel Islands and then past the Golden Gate (which the expedition missed). But upon returning south for the winter, Cabrillo broke his shoulder at San Miguel Island (off Santa Barbara), an injury that would shortly prove fatal. He designated his pilot, Bartomolé Ferrer (or Ferrelo) as his replacement. Ferrer sailed perhaps as far as today's California-Oregon boundary, returning to Navidad in April 1543.

Some six decades later, New Spain's latest viceroy, Gaspar Zúñiga y Acevedo, commissioned Sebastián Vizcaíno, an experienced Pacific merchant sailor, to revisit the coast of Alta California. Vizcaíno in 1602 explored and mapped the California coastline and definitively named many of its sites, including San Diego Bay and Santa Catalina. Farther up the coast, the expedition came across another magnificent bay that Vizcaíno named in honor of the viceroy, who was also *conde,* or count, of Monterrey (spelled then with two *r*s).

Vizcaíno sailed north to Cape Mendocino and, like Cabrillo, missed San Francisco Bay. He decided to return to Mexico after his crew was struck with scurvy, and he brought with him the recommendation that Spain settle Alta California around its great bays. It would be 166 years before Spain, otherwise occupied in Latin America and unaware that it was literally standing on a gold mine, would act on his recommendation.

■ ■ ■

Points Farther North

In 1774, as Spain was working on establishing the Alta California colony, naval officer Juan Pérez was dispatched by the viceroy of New Spain with a fleet to investigate Russian activities to the north. Although bad weather ultimately prevented an intended visit to Alaska, he did survey the coasts of Oregon and Washington, as well as British Columbia and Vancouver Island in Canada, which Spain claimed for itself as part of Alta California. Pérez's party also discovered the mouth of the Columbia River, below present-day Portland. One year later, explorers Bruno de Heceta and Juan Francisco de la Bodega y Quadra did make it to Alaska, sailing all the way up to Juneau.

There was no further Spanish development of these areas. A 1789 scientific expedition by Alejandro Malaspina (see page 290), starting on the Pacific coasts of Chile and Peru, took him in 1790 to Alaska, where a glacier is now named in his honor. His voyage, and those of Pérez and of Heceta and Bodega y Quadra, however, were the basis for Spain's claim (little respected, despite the presence of a Spanish fort at

Nootka Sound, Vancouver Island, from 1790 to 1793) that California extended all the way to the north.

■ ■ ■

UP FROM BAJA

In 1765, the progressive King Carlos III sent José de Gálvez to New Spain as *visitador general* (inspector general) with far-reaching authority to make economic and administrative reforms. Once in Mexico City, Gálvez became concerned about New Spain's northern frontier. Russian fur trappers were sailing the northern Pacific coast in search of pelts, and Britain had continued to show interest in the area.

While inspecting the missions in Baja California, Gálvez met Father Junípero Serra (see pages 287–288), head of the Franciscan order there and administrator of the 17 previously Jesuit missions in the territory. (The Jesuits themselves had been expelled from Spain and its colonies in 1767 in response to their presumed meddling in Spanish politics.) Gálvez also encountered Gaspar de Portolá (see page 288), who was Baja's governor and a military veteran with 30 years experience. Gálvez enlisted both men to lead the colonization of Alta California. Their first charge was to establish a presidio at Monterey Bay.

On January 9, 1769, a band each of clerics and soldiers, headed respectively by Father Serra and Portolá (now governor of both Baja and Alta California), embarked on a coastal march out of Baja, shadowed by two ships. After a six-month journey, punctuated by repeated hostile encounters with local Indians, the Spaniards arrived in San Diego on July 1. There, little more than two weeks later, Father Serra founded the first mission on the West Coast, called San Diego de Alcalá, and held the first thanksgiving ceremony there as well. For Serra, this would be the first in a string of 21 missions that he and his followers would establish as far north as

Sonoma (above San Francisco), thereby decisively determining the character of the Spanish and Mexican settlement there almost until its end.

Portolá soon proceeded north to search for Monterey Bay by land. When his directions indicated he had arrived, he refused to believe it. While the bay was useful, it did not meet the expectations Portolá had formed by reading the exaggerated praises of Father Antonio de la Ascención, chronicler of the Vizcaíno expedition ("the best port that could be desired"). Continuing north, however, was a bay that was indeed wondrous—San Francisco Bay. Father Juan Crespi, Portolá's chronicler, wrote that "doubtless not only all the navies of our Catholic monarch, but those of Europe might lie within the harbor."

Running out of strength and food, Portolá and his party returned to San Diego the next year but, on the inspector general's instructions, returned to what he now acknowledged to be Monterey Bay. Portolá declared Spanish possession over the area on March 24, 1770, established a presidio on the site, and left Alta California for the last time the following July. Monterey was soon designated as Alta California's capital.

Over the next few years, Juan Bautista de Anza (see page 289), a Mexican-born soldier, solidified the Spanish presence in Alta California with a series of excursions there. He started out in Tubac in 1774 with the intention of carving out a land route between Arizona and California. Along with Arizona missionary and explorer Father Francisco de Garcés (see page 289), Anza led a party of less than two dozen men across 600 miles of deserts and mountains to the recently established San Gabriel Arcángel mission just a few miles east and north of the future Los Angeles. Anza then continued north to Monterey, looping back to Tubac by June—a journey of 2,000 miles in five months. Upon his return to Mexico City (another 1,500 miles), he was promoted by the viceroy to lieutenant colonel and charged with the task of heading a larger expedition and finding a site for a presidio at San Francisco Bay.

The second party, which eventually numbered over 240, started

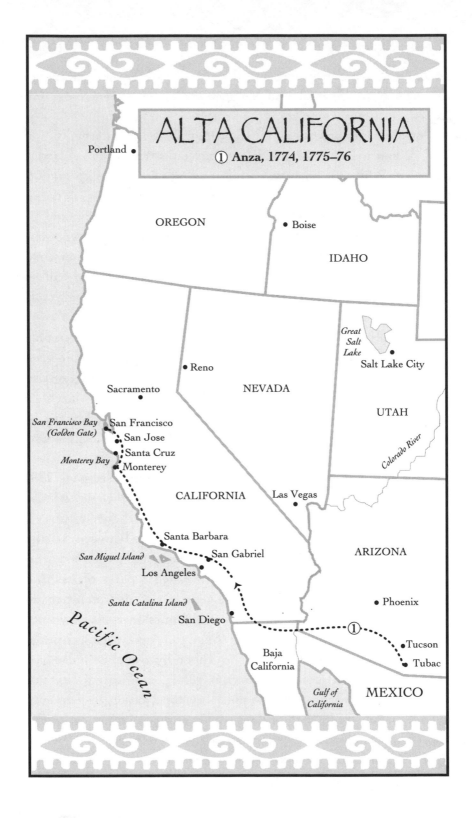

ALTA CALIFORNIA

① Anza, 1774, 1775–76

Portland •

OREGON

• Boise

IDAHO

Great Salt Lake

• Salt Lake City

• Reno

NEVADA

UTAH

Sacramento •

Colorado River

San Francisco Bay (Golden Gate) San Francisco

San Jose

Santa Cruz

Monterey Bay Monterey

CALIFORNIA

Las Vegas •

Santa Barbara

San Miguel Island San Gabriel

Los Angeles

ARIZONA

Santa Catalina Island

San Diego

• Phoenix

Pacific Ocean

①

• Tucson

• Tubac

Baja California

MEXICO

Gulf of California

at Culiacán, Mexico, in the spring of 1775, arrived in Tubac by October, then pushed 1,200 miles to San Francisco Bay. Arriving in March, Anza established a presidio at the Golden Gate.

The Alta California Colony

By 1794, Alta California boasted four presidios—in San Francisco, Monterey, Santa Barbara, and San Diego—with slightly more than 200 soldiers among them, whose job it was to protect what settlers had come to Alta California and serve as the first line of defense against any encroaching foreign powers. In addition to the presidios, three small pueblos were established in this first wave of settlement: San José, along the Guadalupe River, in 1777; the Pueblo de Nuestra Señora la Reina de los Ángeles Porciúncula (Village of Our Lady the Queen of Angels of Porciúncula), modern-day Los Angeles, in 1781; and Branciforte, at modern-day Santa Cruz, in 1797 (though it was later abandoned). For the most part, however, the pueblos were peripheral to the life of the colony.

The cornerstone of Spanish settlement, a population that would grow to 3,200 Hispanics by the year of Mexican independence in 1821, was the missions. Each mission controlled thousands of acres of prime land, which would be worked by Native Americans. (Technically the land belonged to the Indians and was held in trust by the Franciscans.) The natives in return would learn Christianity, Spanish, and various arts and crafts from the priests, as well as ranching skills. Though they at first had trouble with the Indians (the San Diego mission was burned down in 1775) and for some time relied on food shipments from Mexico, the missions eventually became self-sufficient and more. They grew vegetables and grains (up to 120,000 bushels of grain a year among them) and raised hundreds of thousands of cattle, hogs, sheep, and goats—and all this in a region where only a few years before there had been not a single grain of wheat or a domesticated animal. They produced wool blankets and leather. The Franciscans even founded Alta California's wine industry with plantings brought over from Spain. At their height in the early nineteenth century, 60 Franciscans in the 21 missions served 31,000 Indians.

But they also produced friction with the military. The soldiers did not appreciate the priests' criticism of their treatment of native women. The groups frequently had to be kept apart and often had to turn to Mexico City for resolution of their conflicts. Other settlers, especially ranchers and would-be ranchers, resented the missions' possession of the best lands and lobbied Mexico City to abolish the missions and permit them to develop ranchos on their sites.

Ultimately, the missions' detractors won out. When Mexico gained its independence in 1821 the influence of the Church—which had supported and in return been a beneficiary of Spanish rule—could only decline. The Mexican Congress's 1833 Secularization Act, allowing the government to confiscate mission property, was the final nail in the missions' coffin. Application of the law went slowly, but by 1839 the missions were for all practical purposes defunct.

Were the Missions Good for the Indians?

During its centuries of rule, Spain established more than 200 Spanish missions in what is today the United States, from Florida to California. But were the missions slavery with a religious face or a relatively benevolent process of assimilating the Native Americans into Spanish society?

Critics of the system point to the regimented, monotonous life of mission Indians. They were subject to both the ravages of European diseases—such as smallpox, measles, dysentery, typhoid, and tuberculosis—and the stress of adapting to an un-asked-for alien culture. Others argue that, given the on-

slaught of European conquest, the missions provided the Indians with an important buffer.

The friars were undoubtedly sincere in their desire to
peacefully integrate the natives into Spanish society, if in a
subordinate role. They protected the Indians from abusive
soldiers and settlers as well as from more aggressive Indian
nations. The Franciscans also taught the Indians crafts and
trades—something few African slaves or Indians under the
British were permitted.

In fact, comparison to the worldwide treatment of conquered nations and to non-Spanish colonizers shows the missions in a good light. Most Anglo settlements operated on a
strict policy that "the only good Indian is a dead Indian." Few
Protestant churches welcomed Native Americans, and virtually no attempts were made to integrate them into Anglo
society.

The later U.S. policy of placing the Indians on reserva-
tions, while in some respects superficially similar to the mission system, differed in a critical way: Whereas the missions
were situated on the most fertile land, the U.S. reserva-
tions were located on the worst land available. Indeed, the
missions were theoretically supposed to be turned over to the
control of the Indians themselves when they were "ready" to
take them on. The missions were abolished before anyone
could test whether the theory would succeed in practice.

At any rate, the missions did breed a certain unhealthy
dependency among some Indians. After the missions were
abandoned, many who had come to rely on the mission community for their livelihood and on the missionaries for guid-
ance had trouble adapting to the new circumstances. While
some did become vaqueros or turn to trades and farming,
many, without the advice and care of the knowledgeable
priests, simply failed and faded away.

■ ■ ■

In the aftermath of the collapse of the missions, it was only to be expected that the rancheros, who had pushed so hard to undermine the Franciscans, should rise to a dominant position in Alta California. A land-grant system had been introduced in the region in 1784, but only 20 nonmission grants had been made before 1833. Over the next 13 years, however, Mexico City made 700 land grants, many of them portions of the former missions. Ultimately, some 800 rancheros held 8 million acres of land, and several individual ranches had more than 300,000 acres themselves. Self-contained communities typically supporting up to a hundred people or more (including extended family, vaqueros, and dozens of Indian servants), ranchos became the territory's center of economic activity during the final decade of Hispanic rule in Alta California. In 1835, the capital was moved from Monterey to Los Angeles, in the heart of rancho country.

As they had been elsewhere across Mexico's northern regions, however, circumstances were rapidly changing. Anglos began to move to Alta California in the 1830s and 1840s. Some came on ships from New England to trade products of the industrializing Northeast and for cattle hides and tallow. Others came overland, looking to homestead. Although the earliest individual Anglo settlers comfortably integrated themselves into Hispanic society, often marrying Mexican women, later groups behaved otherwise.

Mexican rule over Alta California was vulnerable, as it had been in Texas. The distance to Mexico City was great. Governors came and went with the ebb and flow of local and Mexican politics. Once again the notion of amputating Alta California (and perhaps even Baja) from Mexico and then transplanting it to the United States was not far from Anglo minds—they had seen it work in Florida and Texas, after all. And again, as elsewhere, there was no shortage of Mexicans who thought separation from their home country might serve their interests, too. The independence-minded Alta California residents were only further encouraged when Mexico, tired of trying to balance the various conflicting interests in the region, recalled its governor in 1844 and sent no replacement.

"Never More Happy People"

"It seems to me that there never was a more peaceful or happy people on the face of the earth than the Spanish, Mexican, and Indian population of Alta California before the American conquest. We were the pioneers of the Pacific Coast, building towns and missions while General Washington was carrying on the war of the Revolution. . . ."

—RANCHERO GENERAL MARIANO
GUADALUPE VALLEJO,
MEMOIRS, 1890

MANIFEST DESTINY: THE MEXICAN WAR AND THE GADSDEN PURCHASE

EYES ON THE PRIZE

In 1844, President John Tyler submitted to the Senate a treaty to annex Texas. A firm believer in the ideology soon to be dubbed Manifest Destiny—that the United States had been divinely ordained to spread Anglo American culture (notably democracy and Protestant Christianity) from sea to shining sea—the Southerner Tyler supported adding another slave state to the Union and foresaw quick statehood for the territory. A still-wary Senate rejected his proposal. The presidential campaign later in the year, however, increased national support for Manifest Destiny's promise of a coast-to-coast America. Unfortunately for Mexico, half of its territory (approximately a million square miles) stood between Texas and the Pacific.

James K. Polk campaigned on Manifest Destiny—focusing specifically on a border dispute with Britain in the Pacific Northwest—

and won. Tyler, now a lame duck, at once used the new mood to reintroduce the treaty before Polk's inauguration. This time it passed, but without the two-thirds majority required by the Constitution for treaty approval. Declaring that annexation was different from treaty approval, Tyler introduced a joint resolution approving annexation, which was passed by close majorities in both houses. Notwithstanding the constitutional quibbles, the vote stuck and was gladly acted on by Polk (who took office three days after Tyler signed the bill into law). Texas agreed to the terms of the resolution in July of 1845.

Mexico had warned the United States that annexation of Texas would be considered an act of war. Not the least reason was the novel claim of the Texas Republic that its boundary with Mexico was the Rio Grande, instead of the Nueces River, located at least 100 miles north of the Rio Grande at points. Texas also claimed land as far west as Santa Fe, in Nuevo México. As it was, the Mexican government suspected that the United States had been behind the original 1835–36 Texas rebellion in the first place. When Congress ignored Mexico's threat and approved annexation, even recognizing Texas's boundary claim, Mexico at once broke off diplomatic relations.

But Polk was determined to support Texas's claims. At the end of the year, President Polk ordered General Zachary Taylor and 4,000 troops into the disputed territory between the Nueces River and the Rio Grande. Ignoring the warning of the ranking Mexican commander to withdraw, Taylor in March moved his troops to Point Isabel, at the mouth of the Rio Grande. There he constructed a fort to blockade the river. Mexico regarded Taylor's actions as an invasion. On April 26, 1846, Mexican forces crossed the Rio Grande and attacked a U.S. patrol, killing or wounding 16 and capturing several dozen more.

This was all the excuse Polk needed to get his war with Mexico. Even before he learned of the clash, he and his cabinet had been trying to conjure up a rationale for war. One half-baked pretense was Mexico's unwillingness to negotiate a price for Texas and its rejection (hardly surprising) of an American offer of $25 million for New Mexico and California, made several months earlier. In fact, on May 9, the very day Polk learned of the Mexican attack, his cabinet had agreed to present a declaration of war to Congress, the precise language of which they would determine the following day. Now Polk had a more palatable excuse for war.

The May 11 war message stated in part, "[N]ow, after reiterated menaces, Mexico has passed the boundary of the United States, has invaded our territory and shed American blood upon the American soil." Two days later, on May 13, Congress formally declared war by a vote of 174 to 14 in the House of Representatives and 40 to 2 in the Senate.

There were dissenters, mainly among abolitionists. Whig congressman Abraham Lincoln opposed the war and asked the Polk administration to identify the precise "spot" on American soil where this blood had been shed. Other Whigs accused Polk of cynically manufacturing the war, provoking Mexico by sending troops into disputed territory. One such dissenter was the future Civil War hero and president, General Ulysses S. Grant. "I had a horror of the Mexican war . . . only I had no moral courage to resign," he admitted later.

MAKING WAR

Mexico was no match for the United States. The latter's non-Indian population was 20 million, including 3 million slaves, compared to Mexico's 7 million, including Indians. Mexico, after only 23 years of independence from Spain, was in political, economic, and social disarray. Militarily it fared no better; most of the soldiers were poorly equipped Indian conscripts, while the generals were distracted by political infighting. Some Mexican states and cities even refused to provide assistance to the Mexican army in defending their country against the invading enemy.

The U.S. forces defeated the Mexicans at almost every battle. Both sides left bloody trails of atrocities. Many Americans know of

Santa Anna's mass executions at the Alamo and Goliad in Texas's battle for independence 10 years earlier. But few have learned of the hundreds of civilians, as well as prisoners of war, murdered by U.S. troops in the Mexican War. Yet these events, including the particularly brutal conduct of the volunteer Texas Rangers, are documented in diaries and other works written by the likes of Grant and another future Civil War hero, George Gordon Meade. This war and its aftermath left a legacy of resentment on both sides of the Rio Grande, a resentment that thrives even today.

"I Would Not Pretend to Guess the Number of Murders"

"Since we have been in Matamoros a great many murders have been committed, and what is strange there seems to be a very weak means made use of to prevent frequent repetitions. Some of the volunteers and about all the Texans seem to think it perfectly right to impose on the people of a conquered city to any extent, and even to murder there where the act can be covered by dark. And how much they seem to enjoy acts of violence too! I would not pretend to guess the numbers of murders that have been committed upon the persons of poor Mexicans by our soldiers, since we have been here, but the number would startle you."

—LETTER FROM ULYSSES S. GRANT TO JULIA DENT, JULY 25, 1846

The U.S. attack came on all fronts. Taylor, invading the heart of Mexico across the Rio Grande, captured Matamoros immediately,

Monterrey (due east of Matamoros) in September, and Saltillo (just to Monterrey's south) in November. To the northwest, Nuevo México fell without resistance from its corrupt territorial governor, Manuel Armijo, who withdrew to Chihuahua (in today's northern Mexico), probably with a hefty bribe in his pocket. The victorious U.S. commander, Colonel Stephen Kearny, leading a force of 1,500, entered Santa Fe in August; four months later, one of his officers, Alexander Doniphan, thrust southward, taking El Paso and Chihuahua. Kearny, meanwhile, had moved into Alta California, only to find that technically it had already been taken: Commodore John Sloat had sailed into Monterey and raised the Stars and Stripes with little fighting on July 7.

Sloat had himself received help in the form of the old independence trick: Shortly after the outbreak of war, a group of Anglos (allied with a number of independence-minded Mexicans), encouraged by John C. Frémont—a U.S. Army captain who probably entered Alta California with Polk's complicity—seized Sonoma and declared the territory's independence. Following the West Florida and Texas examples, the rebels raised their own flag, the bear flag (which is still California's state standard), on behalf of the new republic (the "Bear Republic") and named Frémont president. Frémont defeated Mexican troops in a brief skirmish, then led the Bear Flaggers to Monterey, where he met up with Sloat and recognized the American government.

But while *Californios*—Hispanic residents of the territory—in the north largely cooperated with the invading forces, those in the south did not. Pro-Mexican insurgents repeatedly clashed with Kearny's men as they arrived from the east. In December, in the Battle of San Pascual, a force led by Andrés Pico and his cavalry for a time held off Kearny's efforts to enter San Diego, and the general himself was wounded by one of Pico's lancers; only the help of Commodore Robert Stockton (Sloat's replacement) from the sea allowed the American troops to get through. The following month, pro-Mexican forces rallied again and captured Los Angeles, only to be decisively routed by Kearny and Stockton. The subsequent surrender of the Californios put a final end to the fighting in Alta California.

Nuevo México also faced a brief insurgency. There, Mexican peasants and their Pueblo Indian allies revolted and killed the military governor and five others. Colonel Sterling Price rode out of Taos and swiftly crushed the rebellion, killing about 150 Mexicans and executing 25 to 30 more afterward; others were publicly flogged. A subsequent trial resulted in guilty verdicts for 15 accused of high treason—notwithstanding the fact that, as Mexican citizens, they were combatants during a time of war between the United States and Mexico, and entitled to treatment as prisoners of war.

After General Taylor had heroically scattered a large Mexican army led by Santa Anna himself at Buena Vista (near Saltillo) in February 1847, Polk decided to turn his sights on Mexico City and bring the war to a decisive end. He selected General Winfield Scott to command a 200-ship, 10,000-soldier expedition, which captured Veracruz on the Gulf of Mexico in March. Following another fierce clash with 12,000 men under Santa Anna at Cerro Gordo, Scott took the capital in mid-September. On February 2, 1848, Mexico surrendered and signed a treaty at the village of Guadalupe Hidalgo, a suburb of Mexico City.

The peace treaty signed by the combatants did more than secure the Rio Grande border for the United States. Under the Treaty of Guadalupe Hidalgo, Mexico ceded most of the territory that is now New Mexico, Arizona, California, Nevada, Utah, and parts of Colorado and Wyoming—totaling a full third of the area of Mexico. (The acquisition also increased the size of the United States by a third.) The United States would pay Mexico $15 million in return and assume just over $3 million in American claims against Mexico. The treaty also granted that the Mexicans who chose to remain in the territory would become American citizens, with full civil rights and with their religious and cultural freedoms guaranteed. Some opponents of the treaty's ratification by the Senate argued that the United States should annex *all* of Mexico. This clamor was largely quieted by the observation that the United States would then have to incorporate millions of mestizos and Indians into its population.

On March 10, the U.S. Senate ratified all but Article X of the treaty by a vote of 28 to 14. Article X contained comprehensive guarantees concerning the rights of Mexicans in the newly acquired territory to titles in property. A protest by Mexico—which had ratified the treaty in February—resulted in a May 26, 1848, Statement of Protocol restoring those rights. These included the right to retain and bequeath their lands, even if they journeyed or immigrated to Mexico, and to dispose of them as they pleased.

The Treaty of Guadalupe Hidalgo

The Treaty of Guadalupe Hidalgo ended the war between Mexico and the United States, and was ratified by Mexico in February 1848 and by the United States in March. Among the guarantees it made to the new residents of the United States:

Article VII

"Mexicans now established in territories previously belonging to Mexico, and which remain for the future within the limits of the United States, as defined by the present treaty, shall be free to continue where they now reside, or remove any time to the Mexican Republic, retaining the property which they possess in the said territories, or disposing thereof and removing the proceeds wherever they please, without their being subjected on this account to any contribution, tax, or charge whatever. . . .

"In the said territory, property of every kind, now belonging to the Mexicans, not established there, shall be inviolably respected. The present owners, the heirs of these, and all Mexicans who may hereafter acquire said property by con-

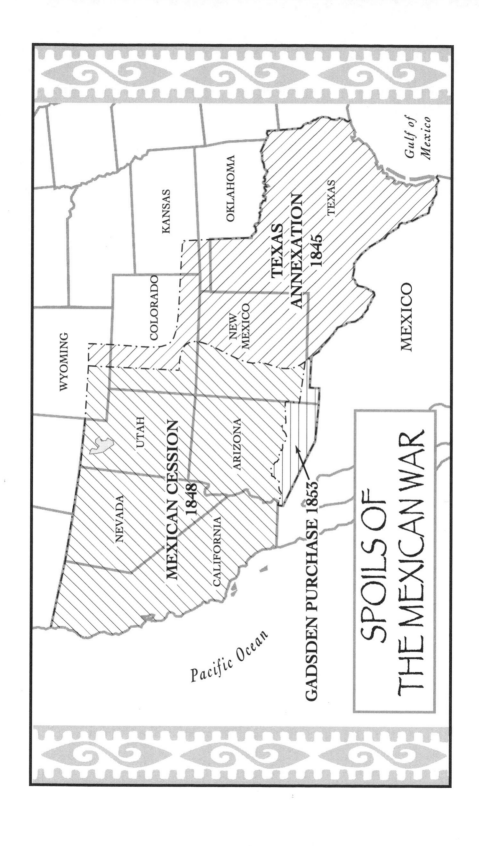

SPOILS OF THE MEXICAN WAR

TEXAS ANNEXATION 1845

TEXAS

MEXICAN CESSION 1848

GADSDEN PURCHASE 1853

WYOMING

UTAH

NEVADA

CALIFORNIA

ARIZONA

COLORADO

NEW MEXICO

KANSAS

OKLAHOMA

MEXICO

Gulf of Mexico

Pacific Ocean

tract shall enjoy with respect to it, guarantees equally ample as if they belonged to citizens of the United States."

Article IX

"The Mexicans who, in the territories aforesaid, shall not preserve the status of citizens of the Mexican Republic . . . shall be incorporated into the Union of the United States and be admitted at the proper time (to be judged of by the Congress of the United States) to the enjoyment of all rights of citizens of the United States according to the principles of the Constitution; and in the meantime shall be maintained and protected in the free enjoyment of the liberty and property, and secured in the free exercise of the religion without restriction."

After the Mexican government protested the U.S. Senate's failure to ratify Article X of the treaty, a particularly explicit guarantee of Mexican property rights, the U.S. government issued a Statement of Protocol in May. It declared:

"The American government by suppressing the Xth article of the Treaty of Guadalupe Hidalgo did not in any way intend to annul the grants of lands made by Mexico in the ceded territories. These grants . . . preserve the legal value which they may possess, and the grantees may cause their legitimate [titles] to be acknowledged before the American tribunals."

The Gadsden Purchase

About 80,000 Mexican citizens living in what was now the U.S. Southwest became nationals of another country overnight. Many of the several thousand Mexicans who crossed the new border into Mexico to avoid just that, however, were in for a surprise.

As Santa Anna would later put it, "With knife in hand the Washington government was attempting to cut another piece from the body which she had just horribly mutilated." Railroad magnate James Gadsden was sent to Mexico City in 1853 to purchase Sonora and other mineral-rich Mexican states, including Baja California. Santa Anna refused to sell off a large amount of his country but, threatened with war again, agreed to let the Americans buy what is today the southernmost slice of New Mexico and Arizona — the most logical avenue for an envisioned transcontinental railroad. The Senate ratified the purchase in 1854. Mexico was given $10 million for the approximately 30,000 square miles of the Mesilla Valley, south of the Gila River. This was the last piece of Mexican land "bought," or otherwise obtained, by the United States.

Adiós to All That

For 335 years Spain, and later Mexico, dominated nearly continuously most of North America. Never before had an entire continent been transformed as radically as this one in so little time. A huge expanse of wilderness populated by largely nomadic tribes came to be settled, dominated by, and, to some extent, assimilated into an alien culture, society, and race. Yet by the end of that period the dominators themselves had been banished from the continent, their empire in a decline from which it would never recover.

Left behind were shadows of a splendid conquering civilization. The splendor lives on in Spanish place-names that still dot the map, from Florida to Texas and up and down the Pacific Coast, in outposts that became great cities, and in the very existence of European civilization made possible only by Spaniards who literally blazed trails for faith and country.

Left behind, too, was a new race of people — of mixed Spanish, Indian, and African blood, fundamentally shaped by the institutions of Spanish colonial civilization but sharing the cultural heritages of all their ancestors. These people, the Latinos, would now have to find their place in the alien land of the United States.

Latino "Oldests"

It was not long after the Spanish opened the door to the discovery of the New World that they also set about the business of building a civilization there as well. Though the cruel hand of time (and to some degree, the Anglos) has done its dirty work, a vast treasury of the products of this civilizing endeavor—cities, missions, houses, ranches, and more—still stand tall in the United States. Among them are some of the oldest of their kind in the country.

OLDEST CITY
Saint Augustine, Florida. Founded in 1565 as San Agustín by Pedro Menéndez de Avilés, governor of the province of La Florida, Saint Augustine is today a city of 12,000. It also boasts the oldest house, the oldest hospital, and the oldest school.

OLDEST MISSION
Nombre de Dios in Saint Augustine. Its founding was among Menéndez's considerable accomplishments in 1565.

OLDEST FORT
Castillo de San Marcos at Saint Augustine. Construction of the only Spanish masonry fort on the mainland began in 1672.

OLDEST DOCUMENT
First page of the parish registers of—once again—Saint Augustine. Dating from June 25, 1594, it records the birth of an infant named María.

OLDEST GRAFFITO
On El Morro, a cliff in New Mexico. A member of an early exploratory mission carved in honor of his leader, "There

passed this way adelantado Don Juan de Oñate, from the discovery of the South Sea, on the 16th of April 1605."

OLDEST STATE CAPITAL

Santa Fe, New Mexico. Pedro de Peralta, Mexico's governor of New Mexico, established this city in 1610. Santa Fe also has the oldest state building in the country—the Palacio de Gobernadores, or Governors' Palace.

Chronology of Events

1492 On October 12, led by Cristóbal Colón (Christopher Columbus), the Spanish first land in the Americas, on an island in the Bahamas. On his return to Europe, Colón publicizes his discovery of a new world.

1493 On his second voyage Colón lands on Santa Cruz (now Saint Croix in the U.S. Virgin Islands) and Puerto Rico. He also starts a colony on Hispaniola.

1496 Santo Domingo (the present-day capital of the Dominican Republic and oldest ongoing European settlement in the Americas) is established.

1508 Juan Ponce de León conquers the native Arawak people and sets up a permanent Spanish settlement in Puerto Rico.

1511 Diego de Velázquez de Cuéllar defeats the Arawak and Taíno Indians to establish a permanent Spanish settlement in Cuba.

1513 Ponce de León is the first known Spaniard to land on what is now the U.S. mainland, in a place he calls La Florida.

Vasco Núñez de Balboa discovers the Pacific Ocean after crossing the Isthmus of Panama.

1519 Alonso Álvarez de Pineda explores the Gulf of Mexico from present-day Florida to the Texas coast and charts the mouth of the Mississippi River.

Hernán Cortés first lands in Mexico.

1520 On the first trip around the world, Ferdinand Magellan discovers the route to the Pacific Ocean at the southern tip of South America (now called the Strait of Magellan).

1521 Cortés captures Tenochtitlán and brings down the Aztec empire in Mexico.

1525 Esteban Gómez sails along the American coast north of Florida, as far as present-day Nova Scotia.

1526 Led by Lucas Vázquez de Ayllón, the Spanish establish their first mission on the mainland, in what is now Georgia.

1528 After exploring inland Florida, Pánfilo de Narváez and most of his men perish at sea, but four members, including Álvar Núñez Cabeza de Vaca and the African-born explorer Esteban, survive and travel eight years across Texas and parts of the Southwest before reaching Mexico in 1536.

1533 Francisco Pizarro conquers the Inca empire.

Fortún Jiménez reaches the southern tip of Baja (Lower) California, believed to be an island.

1539 Following the coastline, Francisco de Ulloa proves Baja California is not an island.

Hernando de Soto lands in Tampa Bay and explores the North American interior, traveling west to present-day Arkansas. He dies during the expedition, in 1542, but others travel to Texas and sail down the Mississippi to the Gulf and reach Mexico in 1543.

1540 For two years an expedition led by Francisco Vásquez de Coronado explores the Southwest, traveling through parts of present-day Arizona, New Mexico, Texas, Oklahoma, and Kansas.

1541 García López de Cárdenas, a member of Coronado's expedition, is the first European to see the Grand Canyon.

1542 Cabeza de Vaca publishes the first memoir on North American exploration, *La relación (The Story)*, recounting his journey of 1528–36.

Sent to explore Alta California, Juan Rodríguez Cabrillo and his crew are the first Europeans to set foot on the West Coast, touching down in San Diego Bay. Cabrillo dies, but his pilot, Bartomolé Ferrer, sails as far north as present-day Oregon.

1559 Tristán de Luna y Arellano and then Ángel de Villafañe try but fail to establish a large-scale Spanish colony in La Florida.

1565 Pedro Menéndez de Avilés founds the settlement of San Agustín (Saint Augustine) in La Florida and holds the first "Thanksgiving" feast with the Indians. Over the next 10 years Menéndez establishes six more fortified settlements in La Florida. Also at this time the first Spanish missions are started in La Florida.

1566 The first known European baby born in the present-day United States is Martín Argüelles, in Saint Augustine.

1585 The British set up a short-lived colony on Roanoke Island, off the coast of North Carolina.

1586 British forces under Sir Francis Drake sack Saint Augustine, but the city survives.

1588 Attempting to invade England, the Spanish Armada is defeated by the British fleet.

1598 The Earl of Cumberland briefly wrests San Juan in Puerto Rico from the Spanish.
Juan de Oñate heads an expedition to settle Nuevo México territory and brutally crushes an uprising by the Pueblo people in Acoma.

1602 Sebastián Vizcaíno maps much of the California coastline and names such features as Monterey Bay.

1607 The English found their first permanent colony in America, Jamestown in Virginia.

1610 Poet Gaspar Pérez de Villagrá, a member of Oñate's expedition, publishes the first epic poem about America, *Historia de la Nuevo México.*
Pedro de Peralta establishes Nuevo México's capital, Santa Fe.

1614 Father Francisco Pareja publishes a Timucuan-Spanish dictionary and religious books in the Indian language.

1620 The Pilgrims arrive on the *Mayflower* and establish a colony in Plymouth, Massachusetts.

1655 The Franciscans have established 38 missions from the Carolinas to the Gulf of Mexico, although most are later burned by the British.

1665 The British burn Saint Augustine, but it is rebuilt.

1672 Construction begins on Castillo de San Marcos, a masonry fort in Saint Augustine, completed in 1695.

1680 After a 1675 Spanish raid on a meeting of Pueblo religious leaders, Popé leads 17,000 other Pueblo Indians in a revolt against the Spanish and takes control of all of Nuevo México north of El Paso.

1682 Led by William Penn, Quakers begin settling Pennsylvania.
Explorer René-Robert Cavelier, Sieur de La Salle, claims the Mississippi Delta area—Louisiana—for France.
In Texas the missions of Corpus Christi de la Ysleta and Nuestra Señora de la Concepción are founded around this time.

1690 Alonso de León and Father Damián Mazanet found two missions in east Texas.

1691 Diego de Vargas arrives in El Paso as governor of Nuevo México and completely regains the territory from the Pueblos by 1696.

1698 The Spanish definitively establish the city of Pensacola on the Gulf coast.

1700 Father Eusebio Kino founds the mission San Xavier del Bac in what is now Tucson, Arizona.

1702 British governor James Moore of South Carolina destroys the missions and Rancho La Chúa in La Florida.

1706 Tubac is the first Spanish town in the territory of Arizona.

1716 Captain Domingo Ramón affirms Spanish control of east Tejas.

1718 Martín de Alarcón, governor of Tejas, founds Béjar, later called San Antonio.

1719 Joseph Azlor Vitro de Vera, the marqués de San Miguel de Aguayo, drives the French from east Tejas and builds a presidio at Los Adaes, which becomes the capital of Tejas.

1738 Fort Mosé, established by escaped British slaves near Saint Augustine, is the first free black settlement in North America.

1740 British governor James Oglethorpe of Georgia seizes several forts in La Florida and destroys Fort Mosé.

1754 The last French and Indian War starts in America; it becomes part of a European "world" war, the Seven Years' War (1756–63), primarily between France and Great Britain.

1762 Spain sides with the French in the Seven Years' War, the British capture Havana in Cuba, and France rewards Spain with control over Louisiana Territory.

1763 To regain Havana and Manila in the Philippines, Spain gives La Florida to the British, who divide it into two colonies: East and West Florida.

1768 French Creoles rebel against the Spanish in New Orleans, but the revolt is soon quelled.

1769 Father Junípero Serra founds the first of many missions on the West Coast, in San Diego de Alcalá.
Traveling overland from San Diego, Gaspar de Portolá reaches San Francisco Bay.

1770 Portolá builds a presidio in Monterey Bay, which becomes the capital of Alta California.

1773 The Boston Tea Party protests British import taxes.

1774 Juan Pérez surveys the coasts of Oregon, Washington, and parts of Canada.

1775 Explorers Bruno de Heceta and Juan Francisco de la Bodega y Quadra sail as far as Juneau, Alaska.

1775 The American Revolution breaks out, lasting to 1783. East and West Florida remain loyal to the British, but Spain later aids the American revolutionaries.

1776 The U.S. Declaration of Independence is signed.
Explorer Juan Bautista de Anza establishes a presidio in San Francisco.
Father Silvestre Vélez de Escalante travels to the Great Salt Lake from Santa Fe in search of an overland route to Alta California.

1779 Spain declares war on England and becomes a cobelligerent of the thirteen colonies.
Bernardo de Gálvez, governor of Luisiana, ousts the British from the lower Mississippi Valley.

1781 Gálvez takes Pensacola, the British capital of West Florida, and thus prevents British troops in Florida from reinforcing General Cornwallis in the decisive Battle of Yorktown.
The Spanish begin settling Los Angeles.

1783 The Treaty of Paris officially recognizes the nation of the United States and returns La Florida to Spain.

1787 The U.S. Constitution is signed.
The first integrated public school opens in Saint Augustine.

1788 Under Governor Esteban Rodríguez de Miró, the Spanish rebuild New Orleans, including the so-called French Quarter, after a major fire.

The U.S. Constitution is ratified, and George Washington becomes the first U.S. president in 1789.

1790 Alejandro Malaspina leads a scientific expedition from Chile to Alaska.

1795 The Treaty of San Lorenzo cedes the northern part of West Florida (today's central Alabama and Mississippi) to the United States.

1800 With Napoleon's victories in Europe, Spain agrees to return Luisiana to France.

1803 With the Louisiana Purchase, the United States buys the territory from France.

1804 The Lewis and Clark expedition leaves Saint Louis, reaching the Pacific Coast in 1805.

1808 Napoleon invades Spain and puts his brother Joseph Bonaparte on the throne in Madrid.

1810 Anglo American settlers revolt against Spanish rule in West Florida, and President James Madison annexes the area, which becomes part of the new state of Louisiana in 1812.

A Mexican revolt against Spain starts when Father Miguel Hidalgo y Costilla issues his *grito* (cry) for independence *(El Grito de Dolores)*. His peasant army is defeated in 1811, but others continue the fight.

1812 The United States fights Great Britain in the War of 1812, lasting to 1815.

1817 General Andrew Jackson attacks the Seminoles in Spanish East Florida and takes over Pensacola.

1819 With the Adams-Onís Treaty, Spain officially cedes Florida to the United States. The treaty also establishes an agreement on the U.S.'s western border with Mexico.

1821 Spain grants independence to Mexico; Mexico's first government is a monarchy, followed by a republic in 1823.

1822 Stephen Austin establishes the first Anglo settlement in Tejas.

1823 The United States issues the Monroe Doctrine, opposing any further European colonization or intervention in the Americas.

1829 Mexico abolishes slavery.

1833 Under Mexico's new Secularization Act, the government can confiscate the property of missions, speeding up their decline.

1835 Stirred up by Stephen Austin, Tejas settlers rebel against Mexican rule and defeat General Martín Perfecto de Cos.

1836 Led by General Antonio López de Santa Anna, Mexican forces retake the Alamo in San Antonio after a 13-day siege. But the Mexicans are soon routed by General Sam Houston and his troops at the Battle of San Jacinto, and Santa Anna signs a treaty granting Texas independence.

The new Texas Constitution denies citizenship and property rights to those who did not fight against Mexico; even *tejanos* who fought for independence face discrimination.

1837 Hispanics in Nuevo México revolt unsuccessfully against higher taxes.

1845 Ignoring Mexico's objections, the United States annexes Texas and supports its claim to a Rio Grande border.

Florida and Texas become states.

1846 After U.S. general Zachary Taylor builds a fort at the mouth of the Rio Grande and Mexico attacks to defend its territory, the United States enters the Mexican War.

Backed by John C. Frémont, Anglos raise the bear flag in Sonoma and proclaim an independent republic in California.

1847 Taylor defeats Santa Anna, and General Winfield Scott leads the takeover of Mexico City.

1848 Mexico surrenders and signs the Treaty of Guadalupe Hidalgo, agreeing to the Rio Grande border and ceding most of what is now New Mexico, Arizona, California, Nevada, and Utah as well as parts of Colorado and Wyoming. The treaty is supposed to grant full civil rights, religious freedom, and property rights to Mexicans residing in these areas.

The gold rush begins.

latino america

◆

INTO THE MELTING POT?

In the centuries before the United States began acquiring pieces of Spain's North American Empire, a smattering of Spaniards as well as Latinos from Mexico, Cuba, Puerto Rico, and the rest of Latin America had made their homes in the British, Dutch, and French colonies that would later become the United States and in the young United States itself. Most curious perhaps was a tiny community of Sephardic Jews who had settled in Dutch New Amsterdam (later New York City) in 1654. But with the exception of the brief period of British rule over Florida, by and large neither the colonies nor the United States had ever had a distinguishable population of Hispanics.

The acquisition of Florida between 1810 and 1821 marked the first real such occasion. But with the departure of the Spanish soldiers, the earlier dissolution of the missions, and the general depopulation that had occurred when the British took over, only small and relatively isolated pockets of Latinos remained in Florida, settled for the most part in the region's two main cities, Saint Augustine and Pensacola. (One of those Latinos, plantation owner José Mariano Hernández [see page 300], quickly took the oath of allegiance to the new nation and was appointed Florida's first territorial delegate to Congress.) And as Anglos from the north began to pour in—a movement that increased after statehood in 1845—the few Hispanics in Florida became almost invisible.

It was another matter when the smoke had cleared from the conflicts with Mexico. Suddenly, the United States had 80,000 Mexicans under its authority, a population that dominated the newly acquired territories. Dating, at least in part, from before the United States even existed and indeed before the first Anglos had settled on the continent, this population had long lived according to its own laws, religion, and traditions, and, of course, spoke its own language. It was an established community that had not willingly come to the United States. (As the saying goes, "We never crossed a border. The border crossed us.") And this community was not particularly eager to be its subject. This was an altogether new challenge for the United States.

It was a challenge the country did not meet very impressively. Notwithstanding the explicit promises of the Treaty of Guadalupe Hidalgo, the Mexican Americans were for the most part treated like anything but equal citizens. Anglos flowed into the new territories and, especially in the states of Texas and California, stripped the Hispanics of their lands, their civil rights, and their social status. Far from offering protection, the laws and leaders of the United States either encouraged this behavior or turned a blind eye. Within a few decades of their admission to the United States, the proud Mexican Americans of the Southwest had largely been relegated to the status of second-class citizens.

As it turned out, however, this mistreatment would often prove far less burdensome than the deprivations suffered by Latinos in their home countries as wars and economic dislocations repeatedly rocked the Spanish-speaking Americas over the next century. The result was wave after wave of Hispanic immigrants seeking better lives: Cubans, Puerto Ricans, more Mexicans, and, later, Central and South Americans. Not only did the Southwest see its Hispanic population expand exponentially and Florida see the return of a large Latino community, but more Hispanics would appear in prevously all-Anglo regions, such as New York, Chicago, and many smaller northeastern and midwestern locales.

The new groups of immigrants, however, were not simple carbon copies of the Mexican Americans who had become attached to the United States in the mid-nineteenth century, nor were they identical to one another. Each of these groups had, over long centuries, developed discrete cultures that reflected the distinct histories of their homelands. Mexicans, Puerto Ricans, Cubans, Dominicans, and the rest each had (and still have) religious, culinary, racial, linguistic, and innumerable other characteristics that distinguish them from the others. These differences deeply influenced each community's development in their new home. As a result, each community's experience here has been in many ways unique; there has been no singular "Latino experience."

For its part, the United States would be little more enthusiastic about these newcomers than it had been about the Mexican American population it had inherited earlier—even if, at various times, it encouraged their entry for economic or political reasons. With the partial exception of the Cubans, the same formal and informal vehicles of discrimination were extended to the range of Latino immigrants even as the population established itself and grew to be a greater and greater part of the American landscape. Indeed, it would not be until the social upheaval of the 1960s civil rights movements that the ground was laid for Hispanics to take the integral place in the country's social, political, economic, and cultural life they have today.

TEXAS

THE LONE STAR STATE OF AFFAIRS

By the time Texas's short-lived experiment with independence had come to an end in 1845 and the territory had been annexed to the United States, the political power of the Mexican population had all but disappeared. The total (non-Indian) population, which less than a decade earlier had stood at 35,000, was now closing in on 140,000—with Mexicans outnumbered at least six to one. And, attracted by cheap land and the prospects for cotton farming and cattle ranching, more Anglos were on their way. Even if the Anglo community had not otherwise used its resources to make Hispanics feel unwelcome in the territory's political life, it is hardly surprising that only one *tejano*, José Antonio Navarro (see pages 300–301), was elected to the state constitutional convention held that same year.

Though the state constitution ultimately granted Mexican Americans the right to vote once the new state was established, it hardly made a difference. *Tejanos* were "discouraged"—by poll taxes, literacy tests, and old-fashioned intimidation—from casting ballots. Nor was their participation in decisive whites-only Democratic primaries welcome. All across the state, even in the *tejano* stronghold of San Antonio, Hispanics lost political control. When the state legislature took office in 1850, not a single Texas- or Mexico-born member was among them. (That same year, in the Compromise of 1850, Texas agreed to cede to federal control parts of the territory now in New Mexico, Oklahoma, Colorado, and Wyoming; this land would, of course, later be allotted to other states.)

Officially and unofficially, the Texas Latinos were subjected to acute discrimination. Schools and public facilities were segregated, jobs were kept off-limits, and Spanish was forbidden. Bit by bit, *tejanos* were stripped of their land as Anglos challenged their titles and Anglo-controlled courts upheld the challenges. *Tejanos* were pushed to the southern part of the state and the bottom rung of the socioeconomic ladder. The emergence in the 1850s of the racist, antiforeigner, and anti-Catholic Know-Nothing Party on the national political scene only led to an increase in anti-Mexican discrimination in Texas and throughout the Southwest.

Purely racial prejudice became more pronounced. In the early settler days, when there were few Anglo women in the region, Anglo men would occasionally marry light-skinned *tejanas*. *Tejanos*, for their part, welcomed the Anglos as sons-in-law, since such marriages offered some protection against discrimination. But as white women came into the territory, intermarriage became a thing of the past. And the wealthy *tejanos*, who at first had allied themselves with the Anglos in controlling the Mexican peasantry, soon found themselves the victims of mistreatment as well—often by those same sons-in-law.

Mexican Americans, along with African Americans, were frequent victims of the casual violence that was a way of life in Texas, where Indian fighting was a constant. They were targeted for their alleged involvement in the traffic of runaway slaves to freedom in Mexico and often even for the meager economic success they did have.

Social *Bandidos*

The constant abuses and violence against *tejanos* and their exclusion from Anglo society did bring resistance by daring individuals—though admittedly the line separating their behavior from standard criminality was sometimes a bit hazy. Their rebellion has been described as social banditry, and their personalities formed the basis of the stereotype of the

Mexican *bandido* or "desperado," the latter term from *desesper-ado*, or "desperate one."

Among these was Juan "Cheno" Nepomuceno Cortina (see also pages 306–307), the son of wealthy landowners and a Brownsville, Texas, resident, who in 1859 shot an Anglo marshal he found brutally pistol-whipping a *tejano* peasant. He then gathered several dozen followers and rode into Brownsville to raise the Mexican flag. He killed three Anglos accused of abusing Mexicans, emptied the jails of prisoners, and published a manifesto condemning the Texan Anglos. In 1860, federal troops commanded by General Robert E. Lee chased Cortina across the border and into Mexico, but he eluded capture and became a hero to Mexican Americans throughout the Southwest. (Cortina, later a Mexican soldier and governor of the Mexican state of Tamaulipas, is rumored to have provoked the riots of the 1877 El Paso Salt War.)

Tejano Gregorio Cortez (see page 310) became a hero when, in 1901, he shot and killed a sheriff attempting to arrest him in a mistaken identity incident. Chased by a sizable posse for 10 days, he was finally captured, tried, and sentenced to jail before ultimately being pardoned in 1913. His story has been immortalized in a string of *corridos* (ballads) and even a movie (see page 223).

Other regions of the Southwest, particularly California, had their own *bandidos*. The legendary Joaquín Murieta (see also pages 307–308) was a California miner, wrongfully turned out of a gold mine by lawless Anglos (who may even have killed his brother)—and who then turned to crime for revenge. Bandit Juan Flores led a gang of about 50 around San Juan Capistrano until captured and hanged in 1857. Californio Tiburcio Vázquez (see also page 308) and his gang, responsible for many robberies and murders, declared before his execution that because of the overbearing domination of Anglos, "a spirit of hatred and revenge took possession of me."

■ ■ ■

UNHAPPY ENCOUNTERS

One notable flare-up of Anglo violence toward *tejanos* was the Cart War of 1857. Mexican and Mexican American porters dominated the teamster ranks, carrying merchandise between the Texas coast and interior cities such as San Antonio for less than their Anglo counterparts. Soon, Anglo teamsters began attacking Mexican freight carts, beating or killing Mexican porters and stealing or destroying the merchandise they were carrying. The violence got so bad that in response to a Mexican government complaint federal troops were sent to quell the fighting. The Mexicans' and Mexican Americans' willingness to work for less than Anglos also caused resentment after the emancipation of slaves in 1863 created a market for cheap labor. Another by-product of the Civil War—in which Texas had joined with the Confederacy—was a deluge of unemployed army veterans on the prowl for easy victims. Latinos were a natural choice.

Conflicts, big and small, came and went. Another conflagration was the El Paso Salt War of 1877. Since the 1860s *tejanos* had been taking salt from the salt lakes at Guadalupe, which were widely regarded as communal property. In 1866, and again in 1877, the salt lakes were claimed by Samuel Maverick and Judge Charles Howard, who posted notices that a fee would be charged to anyone who took salt. The dispute escalated when Howard shot Luis Cardis, a Mexican American leader of the effort to keep the lakes available to everyone. A mob of Hispanics killed Howard and a number of others. Soon the area was ablaze with rioting, looting, and murder, and federal troops had to restore order in 1878. The *tejanos* in the end had to pay for the salt.

Industrial age "progress" at the end of the century did not mean progress for the *tejanos*. Though the post–Civil War period of Reconstruction—during which comparatively liberal Republicans controlled the state—saw some easing of constraints on Latinos, it did not last. Democrats returned to power in 1874 and pushed through a restrictive new constitution two years later. Politically and socially, Latinos remained segregated from the dominant Anglo culture. Economically, they were no better off. The coming of the railroads, the invention of barbed wire, commercial farming, and the great cattle booms made their land more valuable, and hence their ownership rights more vulnerable to Anglo chicanery. Their labor was needed more than ever, but only in the aggregate. Few individuals' labor mattered enough—or was irreplaceable enough—to earn wages suitable to raise a family.

■ ■ ■

"I Am Ready to Offer Myself"

"Mexicans! When the State of Texas began to receive the new organization which its sovereignty required as an integral part of the Union, flocks of vampires, in the guise of men, came and scattered themselves in the settlements, without any capital, except the corrupted heart and the most perverse intentions. . . .

"Many of you have been robbed of your property, incarcerated, chased, murdered, and hunted like wild beasts, because your labor was fruitful, and because your industry excited the vile avarice which led them. . . . It would appear that justice had fled from this world, leaving you to the caprice of your oppressors, who become each day more furious towards you. . . .

"Mexicans! My part is taken; the voice of revelation whispers to me that to me is entrusted the work of breaking the chains of your slavery, and that the Lord will enable me, with powerful arm, to fight against our enemies, in compliance with the requirements of that Sovereign Majesty, who, from this day forward, will hold us under His protection. On my part, I am ready to offer myself as a sacrifice for your happiness. . . ."

— JUAN NEPOMUCENO CORTINA, PROCLAMATION TO THE
MEXICANS OF SOUTH TEXAS, NOVEMBER 23, 1859

NEW MEXICO AND ARIZONA

THE ANGLO AUTHORITY

Though a final fierce Mexican and Pueblo uprising against the U.S. military authority in New Mexico ended in 1847, for years afterward the peace was an uneasy one. It was not until March 1851 that New Mexico's first civilian governor took office. (By this time, the territory was only a shadow of its former Nuevo México self. Though a year earlier it had recovered a large slab of eastern real estate that Texas claimed in 1845, New Mexico's northern border now stopped at today's Colorado and Utah—and in 1863, Arizona would be separated from it as well.) But the transition to statehood was slow, despite the territory's large population.

The main reason was New Mexico's Latino population of about 60,000, by far the largest in the Southwest, and a figure that dwarfed the few thousand Anglos living there. Not wanting a state controlled by or even especially protecting the rights of Hispanics, powerful Anglos both in the territory and in Washington were willing to delay statehood indefinitely, or at least until enough Anglos came into the region to even the odds. The delay also promised Anglos and their rich Mexican (*rico*) allies more time to secure ownership of lands and mines—often at the expense of poor Mexican American owners and in violation of the Treaty of Guadalupe Hidalgo—before tough state laws could get in their way.

And to some degree they were successful. As in Texas, and most notoriously in California, Anglos and *ricos* used a variety of ruses to acquire lands long in the possession of *nuevomexicanos*. They challenged legitimate Mexican American landownership in courts, and as the disputes took years to be resolved, often forced unfair settlements on the owners. They knowingly purchased communal property from individuals who simply had no authority to sell it, and won the ensuing court battles, too. The land rush that followed Washington's 1862 passage of the Homestead Act only accelerated the trend.

After the Civil War, during which New Mexico sided with the North, a small group of Anglo merchants, lawyers, bankers, and politicians, along with a number of *ricos* (including Miguel A. Otero [see page 301]), formed a small clique that conspired to control territorial politics and all major land and business deals. The so-called Santa Fe Ring even controlled the press: Member Max Frost, editor of the *New Mexican*, the territory's largest newspaper, praised the ring's activities regularly and ensured that its enemies were cowed and its illicit dealings were cloaked. As the region saw the beginnings of industrialization, the establishment of vast commercial farms, the opening of the Santa Fe Railroad in 1877, and a major cattle boom, the ring oversaw the transfer of land out of the hands of hundreds of Mexican Americans, especially in the north.

Despite the notoriety it eventually gained, the ring was never punished. Even the U.S. Supreme Court, in 1887, upheld the ring's power: Through the scandalous Maxwell Land Grant, the ring was allowed to maintain control of more than 1.7 million acres of land—in disregard of the valid claims of Native Americans, *nuevomexicanos*, and squatters.

LATINO RESISTANCE

New Mexico's Latino leaders took numerous approaches to fighting the Santa Fe Ring and other manifestations of government corruption. The so-called People's Party succeeded at winning county and assembly seats until it fell apart as a result of internal bickering and disorganization. Elsewhere, the newspaper *La Voz del Pueblo* (the *People's Voice*), founded in 1890, railed against Anglo injustices. But perhaps the most formidable protest group was the *Gorras Blancas* (White Caps). Organized by Juan José Herrera (see also page 309) about 1877, the 1,500 *Gorras Blancas* had a mission: cutting fences. Fencing, whether wooden ties or barbed wire, was the tool by which railroads, land speculators, and others appropriated public lands and cut Mexicans off from water, timber, and grass for their herds.

A leader in the Knights of Labor (an early union), Herrera had been inspired to form his vigilante group after unscrupulous fellow Hispanics started illegally "selling" off pieces of a vast communal land grant to Anglos. The *Gorras Blancas* really hit the *ricos* where they lived. When the Santa Fe Railway appropriated land for its lines, for example, the *Gorras Blancas* cut 9,000 ties. Although Anglos and *ricos* called it a "criminal organization," among poor Mexicans it was an instrument of social justice—even if, ultimately, its victories were little more than symbolic.

Still, the Anglos never completely succeeded in dominating New Mexico as they had Texas. Although more Anglos did move in with the railroads, they never made a notable dent in the overwhelmingly Hispanic population, which was itself increasing due to a rising demand for labor. Latinos—and not just the *ricos* among them— were players in the political life in the territory and completely controlled its legislature until the 1890s. After the disappearance of the Santa Fe Ring in the 1880s, they had access to some of the appointed positions previously reserved for Anglos and their *rico* allies.

And the Anglo foot-dragging could only go on so long; the trans-

parent motives for the delay were becoming something of an embar-
rassment to the nation. When the state constitutional convention
was finally held in 1912, the power of the Latino population was in
full evidence. Led by future New Mexico governor and U.S. Senator Octaviano A. Larrazolo (see pages 303–304), *nuevomexicanos*
were guaranteed the right to vote, run for office, serve on juries,
and use Spanish in public documents. This was in fact the only state
in which Hispanics were granted such extensive protections. (It
was also the only state that would eventually go on to elect Hispanic
U.S. Senators.)

"We Want No 'Land Grabbers' "

"Our purpose is to protect the rights and interests of the
people in general and especially those of the helpless
classes. . . .

"We want no 'land grabbers' or obstructionists of any sort
to interfere. We will watch them.

"We are not down on lawyers as a class, but the usual
knavery and unfair treatment of the people must be stopped.

"Our judiciary hereafter must understand that we will sustain it only when 'justice' is its watchword."

— PLATFORM OF THE *Gorras Blancas*, 1890

ESTABLISHING ARIZONA

Latinos in the Arizona territory, for so long part of Nuevo México and then New Mexico, were not so fortunate. With its comparatively small Latino population (less than 4,000), Arizona separated

from New Mexico in 1863 after an abortive attempt to join the Confederacy. Arizona saw Hispanic influence begin to erode almost at once. The mining potential of the region (especially in copper and silver) and, after the passage of the 1862 Homestead Act, the opportunities for commercial farming had stimulated a dramatic influx of Anglos. The trend only continued in the 1880s as the Santa Fe and Southern Pacific railroads and associated development came in. Between 1880 and 1887, Arizona's population jumped from 40,000 to 90,000, and although as in New Mexico some of these newcomers were Mexicans eager to profit from the expanding economy, enough were Anglos to make them a solid majority in the territory. The Desert Land Act (1877) and the Carey Act (1894), like the Homestead Act before them, further encouraged Anglos to settle and develop the territory.

The sense of cooperation that had existed early on between Latinos and Anglos abruptly ended. Intermarriage was no longer practiced, and Anglo-Latino business partnerships were no longer formed. As elsewhere, those Mexican Americans who did own land quickly found themselves the victim of Anglo land grabbers. The Anglos challenged preexisting Mexican land grants and often either won their cases outright or forced the disheartened owners—who frequently waited years for the resolution of their cases—to sell the land for a fraction of its value. The capital-rich Anglos paid Mexicans and Mexican Americans barely subsistence wages to work the mines and farms, and confined them to segregated housing (known as *Chihuahuitas*). Lawlessness against Latinos was common.

The so-called Federal Ring, an Anglo group, rose to control territorial politics, barring all Hispanics but a handful of *ricos* from important appointed positions. The seat of government was moved from Latino Tucson (the capital since 1867) to Anglo-dominated Prescott in 1877. (It was moved again, to Phoenix, in 1889.) What political power remained to Hispanics was limited entirely to the southern part of the territory. In 1912, when Arizona became a state, Latinos had few of the protections offered in neighboring New Mexico.

The Rest of the West

While the early history of Texas, New Mexico, Arizona, and California under U.S. rule was marked by Anglo-Hispanic clashes of all sorts, the same was not the case in the six other future states whose territory came (in whole or in part) from the lands taken from Mexico in the 1840s: Nevada, Utah, Colorado, Wyoming, Oklahoma, and Kansas. The simple reason is that these were really never Mexican lands more than in name. Distant as they were from the political and commercial centers of Mexico, they had never been actively settled and hardly even visited. As a result, when the United States acquired them, there were scarcely any Hispanics in these regions; the principal non-Anglo population that Anglo settlers encountered there was Native American. Although some of these states, such as Colorado, would later come to have sizable Latino communities, they would not carry with them quite the same legacy of ill will toward Hispanics that some of their neighbors did.

CALIFORNIA

AFTER THE GOLD RUSH

On January 24, 1848, just weeks before the signing of the Treaty of Guadalupe Hidalgo, gold was discovered just northeast of Sacramento, California. What followed was one of the greatest shifts of population in U.S. history. California's population of 15,000 in 1848 swelled to 260,000 only four years later.

The gold rush brought complete disruption to the Californios' way of life. News of the find swept the East like an epidemic, infecting every city, town, and rural area from the Missouri to the Atlantic. People sold their houses, farms, and businesses; government officials left their posts; breadwinners left their jobs; and all headed west with a thirst for gold as bad as any conquistador's. In short order the forty-niners far outnumbered the Mexican Americans, who found themselves strangers in their own land.

By the time the former Bear Republic convened a constitutional convention in 1849 to consider statehood, the population of California numbered about 100,000, of which only 13,000 were Hispanic. But although the more established Californios were able to elect 8 of the total 48 delegates, they constantly broke ranks, beset by differing interests and petty rivalries. They did manage to defeat a measure that would have restricted the vote to white males only. Delegate Pablo de la Guerra, a wealthy ranchero from Santa Barbara, argued successfully that depriving Mexican Americans of the vote would violate the Treaty of Guadalupe Hidalgo—for which Anglo leaders still showed some respect. Latino delegates also secured a requirement that all state laws be printed in Spanish as well as in English. On October 12, 1849, the eight Californios signed their names to the constitution that enabled California to become the 31st state one year later.

As the convention had foreshadowed, though, statehood did not improve the lives of the Latino population. Their treatment by the hordes of gold-seekers was particularly telling. In 1849, there were 80,000 Anglos, 8,000 Mexicans and Californios, 5,000 South Americans, and thousands more from Europe, China, Australia, and even Hawaii seeking their fortune in the gold fields. Only three years later, the number of gold-seekers would nearly triple. Most people, of course, did not find significant amounts of gold, and the disappointed majority began to urge that all the so-called greasers—both native-born Californios and émigré Mexicans and other Latin Americans—be expelled from the mines. (Ironically, it was Latinos who had taught most of the early gold-seekers how to work the mines.)

Although the state government did not go as far as that, it did set its sights on noncitizen Mexicans and other Latin Americans who had come to cash in on the gold rush. In 1850, California's Foreign Miners Tax Law required that non-U.S. nationals pay a then-exorbitant $20-a-month fee just to look for gold. The real target of the law was no secret; its sponsor, state senator Thomas Jefferson Green, had gone on record stating that he could "maintain a better stomach at the killing of a Mexican than at the crushing of a body louse." European and non-Spanish-speaking foreigners were virtually never required to show their permits (which they seldom bought). The Mexicans got the message and flocked out of California. When the sudden drop in customers sent many Anglo businesses to ruin, the law was repealed. But not before the Mexicans had been effectively ousted from the gold mines.

Hostility toward foreign miners and those whom most Anglos wrongly considered foreign miners—the Californios—also took the form of violence. Lynching of Mexicans and Californios became common, so much so that one mining camp became known as Hangtown to Latinos. Miner violence often strayed far from the gold fields, into the countryside and the cities where Californios and other Spanish-speaking arrivals lived. Lynchings, public whippings, and brandings became the order of the day. One vigilante mob, called the Hounds, attacked and looted a Chilean neighborhood in San Francisco in June 1849, killing one woman and raping two more. In July 1850, four Mexicans were lynched without a trial. On July 5, 1851, a kangaroo court in the town of Downieville "convicted" a pregnant woman who had killed a drunken gambler who had attacked her on Independence Day. Two thousand cheered as she was hanged from a nearby bridge. Conditions reached the point where the Mexican government again had to protest the violations of the rights of Mexicans in California. Many Californios saw that the bitter Anglos were uninterested in their status as U.S. citizens and returned home rather than face violence in the mines.

"California Has Fallen into the Hands of the Ambitious"

"California has fallen into the hands of the ambitious sons of North America who will not stop until they have satisfied their passions, by driving the first occupants of the land out of the country, vilifying their religion, and disfiguring their customs."

— Francisco P. Ramírez, editorial, *El Clamor Público,* May 10, 1856

"Oh! Misfortune! Mexicans alone have been the victims of the people's insane fury! Mexicans alone have been sacrificed on the gibbet and launched into eternity . . . ! This is the *liberty* and *equality* of our adopted land! Scan the history of the state since the gold discovery, and one must conclude that 'California is lost to all Spanish-Americans.' "

— Francisco P. Ramírez, editorial, *El Clamor Público,* August 2, 1856

Fall from Grace

But even beyond the mines, Mexican Americans had little protection. Soon, powerful Anglos set out to nullify many of the very rights guaranteed only a few years before at Guadalupe Hidalgo — just as they were doing throughout the rest of the Southwest, only far more systematically. Represented by U.S. Senator Gwin, California Anglos resented that 800 wealthy Californio families controlled 14 million acres of land, just as a rising demand for beef throughout the region was making ranching extremely profitable. (There was less concern that almost 12 million acres were controlled by *one* owner, the Southern Pacific Railroad.) In 1851, Gwin drafted a measure, the California Land Act, that essentially guaranteed Anglo squatters the ability to pick off Californio landholdings. It would set up a three-member board with the power to invalidate all land titles if no proof of their validity was made within two years. California's other senator and one-time Bear Flagger John C. Frémont—himself owner of the 44,000-acre Rancho Mariposa—opposed the bill. His father-in-law, Senator Thomas Hart Benton, called the bill "the most abominable attempt at legislation that has ever appeared in a civilized nation."

But with the support of powerful senators such as Henry Clay, the bill was passed. The system was stacked against Californios. Hearings were set in San Francisco, far from the southern California ranchos in the age before fast and easy travel. They were held in English only, adding the cost of translators to the exorbitant fees charged by unscrupulous lawyers. And, most significant, few rancheros even had written evidence of landownership, since Spain and later Mexico did not follow the title recording practices of the United States.

The disputes took years to be resolved, with some appeals going all the way to the Supreme Court. Needless to say, during the period of the appeal process the rancheros could not sell the land whose title was in dispute. Meanwhile, many had to borrow money at rates as high as 10 percent a month to get by. Many were simply ruined by exorbitant legal fees and property taxes. In the north, Anglo squatters marched onto Californio ranches as law-enforcement officials stood by, ignoring the Californios' rights. Those who in the end did keep their titles often became the victims of Anglo violence.

By 1856, the northern California ranchos were largely gone. The bell tolled for the southern ones as well, which were eventually taxed out of existence or decimated by natural and economic disasters. Some rancheros sought protection in marrying off their daughters and granddaughters to Anglos, but often the sons-in-law turned around and grabbed the ranchos for themselves. A new element was introduced in 1862, when the federal Homestead Act encouraged squatters to claim lands in the West. Many took the easy way to homesteading by jumping on already-developed Mexican American lands. The courts provided little support to the original owners.

One by one, the promises made to Mexican Americans at Guadalupe Hidalgo and at the state constitutional convention were broken. In 1856, the California Assembly resolved to end its former practice and stopped translating legislation into Spanish. One "anti-vagrancy" law was simply an authorization for officials to detain Hispanics at will, and explicitly stated that it was meant to apply to "all persons who are commonly known as 'Greasers.'" Other so-called greaser laws harassed Californios by prohibiting bullfights, cockfights, and other Latino customs.

In April 1857, a judge applied the Civil Practice Act of 1850 — which forbade Native Americans and Chinese from testifying against whites in court—to bar testimony in a case by one Manuel Domínguez. Domínguez was a wealthy man, a former delegate to the California constitutional convention, and a Los Angeles city supervisor, but he was also, like most Californios, a mestizo. Henceforth, whatever their status, mestizos would be systematically excluded from participation in the criminal and civil justice systems.

By 1870, Mexican Americans, who two decades earlier made up 15 percent of the population, had fallen to 4 percent as Anglos continued to stream in. The once influential Los Angeles newspaper, *El Clamor Público*, a champion of Latino rights, had closed in 1859. The arrival in 1876 of the Southern Pacific Railroad in Los Angeles—which soon made it a predominantly Anglo town— spelled the end of the last remnants of influence for the Mexican American population in the south, just as the gold rush had done in the north. Throughout the region, Mexican Americans lost what political power they had and quickly found themselves subject to the same exclusion and discrimination as other Californios. As in Texas and the Southwest, only a tiny handful of wealthy Mexican Americans who allied themselves with rich Anglos managed to remain political players in the state—but only in a limited capacity. In 1875, Lieutenant Governor Romualdo Pacheco (see also pages 301—

302) briefly assumed the governorship in California (becoming the state's first and only Hispanic governor) after the elected governor was appointed to the Senate. Pacheco, however, failed to win the support of his own party for the nomination the next year. (He ended up in Congress instead.)

More than 120,000 Anglos came to the Los Angeles area in the late 1880s, including many grain farmers and merchants. Between 1870 and 1900 a second generation of Californios came of age, all but indistinguishable from recent arrivals from Mexico. And throughout California, stores, restaurants, and businesses began to post a sign in their windows that was being seen all across the Southwest: NO MEXICANS.

■ ■ ■

Latinos in the Civil War

Approximately 10,000 Hispanics fought in the Civil War. Like their Anglo neighbors, some fought for the Confederacy and others for the Union. There were Latino regiments led by Latino officers—such as Salvador Vallejo's all-Californio Union regiment—but others fought side by side with Anglos in regular army or volunteer units.

The most celebrated is no doubt David Glasgow Farragut (see page 293), of "Damn the torpedoes! Full speed ahead!" fame. Commander of the Union ships charged with blockading Confederate ports, he captured New Orleans in 1862 and was launching an assault on heavily protected Mobile two years later when he uttered his bold cry. Farragut did manage to avoid the torpedoes (floating mines), enter the harbor, sink the feared ironclad ship *Tennessee,* and capture the town. For his heroics Farragut in 1866 became the first officer in the nation awarded the rank of four-star admiral.

Another Union hero was Manuel Chaves (see page 294),

known as *El Leoncito* (the Little Lion), who led 490 *nuevomexi-canos* in a spectacular attack—involving a 200-foot rope descent—on a Confederate supply train. Cuban-born Lieutenant Colonel Federico Fernández Cavada (see also pages 295–296) did airborne reconnaissance (from hot-air balloons) for the Union and fought gallantly at Antietam, Fredericksburg, and Gettysburg. Captured at the last of these battles, he was held at Libby Prison in Richmond, Virginia, where he wrote the 1864 book *Libby Life*.

Colonel Santos Benavides (see page 295) was the Confederacy's highest-ranking Hispanic officer. As mayor of Laredo, Texas, he formed a cavalry regiment of Mexican Americans to fight the rebel cause. In November 1863, his unit successfully drove Union troops away from Laredo. But perhaps the most intriguing Confederate hero, or heroine, was Cuban-born Loreta Janeta Velázquez (see page 295), who became a soldier and spy for the Confederacy. Disguised as a man, she fought at Bull Run in 1861, was discovered and discharged, reenlisted again as a man, and fought (and was wounded) at Shiloh in 1862. Velázquez later worked as a spy for the South and described her adventures in the book *The Woman in Battle*.

INTO THE CARIBBEAN: THE SPANISH-CUBAN-AMERICAN WAR

ISLANDS OF DISCONTENT

In the second half of the nineteenth century, Spain had only two colonies left in the Western Hemisphere (having lost all the others to independence by 1825): Cuba and Puerto Rico. Both of them itched for greater autonomy or even independence. Although in the details their concerns differed somewhat, on the larger issues these two islands were in accord. Both felt that their Spanish masters exploited them by denying proper representation in Madrid, maintaining wrongheaded tariffs, discriminating against native-born *criollos*, demanding unfair taxes, limiting free expression, and encouraging slavery. Although Puerto Rico had as early as 1812 begun to see some of these issues addressed, agitation for independence there, as in Cuba, continued throughout the century.

In 1868, both Puerto Rico and Cuba exploded. The spiritual leader of Puerto Rico's uprising was Dr. Ramón Emeterio Betances (see also page 307), who had fled to New York City a year earlier to escape a Spanish crackdown on independence leaders, then to Santo Domingo (the Dominican Republic) to continue organizing rebellion. He managed to establish a considerable network of revolutionaries in Puerto Rico, but when Spanish authorities began to infiltrate it, one group of insurgents decided to act. On September 23, a *criollo*-led band of 400 to 1,000 rebels descended upon and took control of the town of Lares. The next morning, in the famous *Grito de Lares* (*Cry of Lares*), they declared the Republic of Puerto Rico and proclaimed their adherence to a wide range of political and personal liberties—only to be crushed in short order by Spanish forces.

It was a much less simple matter in Cuba. There, on October 10 in Oriente province, sugar mill owner Carlos Manuel de Céspedes issued a *grito* of his own, the *Grito de Yara*. With support from other wealthy landowners as well as small farmers and merchants, he declared Cuba's independence, proclaimed freedom for the island's slaves, and called for a democratic republic and free, open trade.

Although Spain struck back with an iron fist, the rebels proved much more resilient than those in Puerto Rico. The 1868 uprising grew into a ten-year struggle—aptly called the Ten Years' War— between the so-called Cuban Liberation Army and thousands of Spanish troops. The guerilla hit-and-run tactics of the rebels, led by Dominican-born Máximo Gómez and Antonio Maceo, a black Cuban, resulted in burned plantations, slaughtered herds, and general devastation throughout eastern Cuba.

Spain eventually subdued the uprising, signing a treaty with the rebels in 1878 called the Pact of Zanjón. In the pact, Spain promised to improve conditions and allow for more self-determination for Cubans. Those promises were quickly broken, however, and schemes for reform tossed aside (although slavery was abolished, as promised). But Spain's vulnerability had been established.

Cuban revolutionaries, many in U.S. exile, began to plan a new rebellion. Their leader this time was the eloquent poet and journalist José Martí, who himself spent much of the next few decades in exile, recruiting troops, gathering money, and writing of Cuban independence.

On February 24, 1895, Cubans rose in revolt again, commencing with the *Grito de Baire,* an uprising against Spanish forces in Oriente province. Though Martí and Maceo died in early battles, the Cuban Liberation Army—which had disbanded in 1878—was revived, its veterans in Cuba and abroad joined by younger soldiers in this new effort. It had increasing success with its guerilla-style engagements of the huge Spanish army. As had been the case a quarter century earlier, the clashes left the countryside devastated, with mills and farms burned and cattle destroyed.

Its last outposts threatened, Spain sent the largest army ever up to that time to cross the Atlantic to fight the rebels: almost 200,000 troops commanded by 40 top generals, as well as thousands more soldiers from the colony itself. Latin America's famous liberators, such as Simón Bolívar (liberator of Venezuela, Colombia, Panama, Ecuador, Peru, and Bolivia), José de San Martín (liberator of Argentina, Chile, and, with Bolívar, Peru), and Father Miguel Hidalgo y Costilla (who died fighting for Mexico's freedom), never faced Spanish forces numbering more than 30,000. Not even George Washington had had to face such a huge European army.

Part of Spain's strategy was to remove the peasants from the rebel-controlled countryside and concentrate them in centrally located garrison towns. Any who resisted this *reconcentrado* policy were shot. More than 400,000 Cubans died of starvation and disease in history's first known concentration camps.

At the same time, Spain tried diplomatic means to end the conflict. The costs of holding Cuba were fast becoming far greater than its value to the mother country. In 1897, the Spanish offered to both Puerto Rico and Cuba a degree of autonomy neither had ever possessed, including the right to control most of their own affairs in a self-elected legislature. Although the Puerto Ricans were pleased with the offer and agreed to the terms, the Cubans, already betrayed by the Spanish before, saw no reason to concede—and continued their fight for independence.

■ ■ ■

José Martí

No Cuban leader did as much to unite Cubans in Latin America and the United States as the poet and revolutionary José Martí, the "Apostle of Independence," regarded as the greatest Cuban who ever lived by Cubans on both sides of the Straits of Florida. (Indeed, his political writings, stressing both socioeconomic and liberal justice, have been put to good use by both Fidel Castro and anti-Communist Cubans.)

Martí, exiled from Cuba because of his revolutionary activities, spent about 15 years in the United States, chiefly New York City. He wrote his best poems, *Los versos sencillos* (*The Simple Verses*), on U.S. soil in 1891. His journalistic writing on U.S. society and institutions had vast influence on readers in Argentina, Mexico, Venezuela, and elsewhere in Latin America. His straightforward literary style, *modernismo*, was a fresh break from the venerable Spanish tradition of florid, obtuse expression. (Some of his verses would even be incorporated decades later in Pete Seeger's hit song *"Guantanamera."*)

While in the United States he put his masterful oratory to work demanding Cuban independence, raising funds, and organizing the Cuban Revolutionary Party (PRC) in 1892. Martí believed that Cuban independence had not yet occurred because the struggle had been so badly organized. He managed to persuade the leading veterans of the Ten Years' War, including Generals Gómez and Maceo, to work with him. And although he had great affection for the United States, he forcefully argued against its annexation of Cuba, which he considered merely "a change of masters."

Martí died on the front lines on May 19, 1895, in the Battle of Dos Ríos, making his sacrifice for Cuba's independence total.

■ ■ ■

WAR OVER CUBA

For some time, the United States had been eager to see Spain removed from the Caribbean so it could assert itself as the premier colonial power in the region. In fact, the U.S. government had even made several offers to purchase Cuba in the previous decades, dating back to 1848, often backed by implicit threats of military action; America had also offered encouragement to insurgent activity on the island. So it was with enthusiasm that the United States watched Cuba seek to free itself from Spanish control, even granting formal recognition to the rebels in 1896. At the same time, American business interests in Cuba were considerable ($50 million was invested in sugar plantations), and the longer the conflict went on, the more those interests suffered. The question arose, then, as to whether the United States should enter the fray and put an end to the Spanish presence and the war once and for all.

American public opinion certainly leaned toward helping Cuba. Indeed, some U.S. citizens had even volunteered to fight in the earlier clashes with Spain. And word of the atrocities in the concentration camps—publicized by William Randolph Hearst's *New York*

Journal and its rival, Joseph Pulitzer's *New York World*—particularly inflamed public opinion against Spain.

The matter was definitively settled when, on February 15, 1898, the USS *Maine*, sent to Cuba to protect U.S. citizens and property, was sunk by a tremendous explosion. Some 260 sailors were killed, and although responsibility for the blast was not pinpointed, the widespread assumption was that it was an act of Spanish infamy. On April 11, President McKinley sent a war message to Congress, which hesitated for the moment but passed a resolution demanding Spain's withdrawal from Cuba. A call-up of 125,000 volunteers followed a few days later. Spain recognized the American actions as a declaration of war in all but name, and on April 24 made it official by declaring war on the United States. The next day, to cries of "Remember the Maine!" the United States responded in kind, but made its declaration of war retroactive to the 21st.

Hostilities began a few weeks later. In mid-May, the U.S. Navy blockaded the harbor of Santiago de Cuba, where the Spanish fleet was at anchor. Several weeks later, a U.S. force of 17,000 men sailed from Tampa for Cuba, landing at Daiquirí, in Oriente province, where they met up with Cuban general Calixto García Íñiguez's troops. The joint American-Cuban forces attacked the forts at El Caney and the undermanned Spanish defenses on Kettle and San Juan hills, the heights outside of Santiago de Cuba. One celebrated unit that fought bravely in these battles was the Rough Riders, whose second-in-command was (future president but at the time undersecretary of the navy) Lieutenant Colonel Theodore Roosevelt. The Rough Riders included many African Americans, Native Americans, and Hispanics, including Captain Maximiliano Luna (see page 296) of New Mexico. On July 5, when the Spanish fleet tried to leave the harbor to escape, it was destroyed by navy ships. The allies captured Santiago de Cuba on July 17. Although Spain technically continued to hold most of the island's other cities, by now its troops were completely demoralized and decimated both by the fighting and, even more, by disease.

A few days later, a U.S. force led by General Nelson A. Miles, fresh from fighting in Cuba, invaded Puerto Rico. There was little resistance from the 7,000 Spanish soldiers on the island, who had by then heard about the losses in Cuba. In 17 days they were routed, with U.S. troops sustaining only a handful of deaths. With the earlier (May 1) successes of Commodore George Dewey in capturing the Philippines and destroying the Spanish fleet at Manila, Spain's chances for victory had evaporated. The weakened Spanish, with no heart left for the fight, surrendered on August 12.

The Spanish-Cuban-American War was a most popular one in the United States. America fought Spain for only 113 days. Of the 2,400 or so U.S. casualties, fewer than 400 died in battle (the others succumbing to disease or spoiled food). The U.S. ambassador to London said, "It has been a splendid little war, begun with the highest motives, carried on with magnificent intelligence and spirit, favored by that fortune which loves the brave." But one historian who fought in the war later wrote, "Not one American in 10,000 realizes how important the Cuban army was in our Spanish war. . . . Our histories simply state that we did it all. . . . Isn't honor overdue where honor was earned?"

On December 10, 1898, the United States and Spain signed a peace treaty in Paris that effectively put an end to Spain's imperial status. It first and foremost granted full independence to Cuba. For some time, though, Cuban independence would remain no more than nominal: U.S. occupation forces governed the island until May 20, 1902. Before leaving, the United States also ensured that Cuba's 1901 constitution include a provision known as the Platt Amendment, which gave the United States the right to intervene in Cuban affairs practically at will and paved the way for the establishment of the U.S. naval base at Guantánamo Bay. In 1906, amid civil strife on the island, the United States would even briefly replace Cuba's elected president with an appointed American governor. It would not be until President Franklin D. Roosevelt—facing rising Cuban nationalism and widespread criticism at home—abrogated the arrangement in 1934 that Cuba was permitted to remove the yoke of the Platt Amendment. The naval base remains to this day.

For its part, the United States—in return for a payment of $20 million—took possession of the Philippines, the Pacific islands of Guam (captured by the U.S. without a fight in June) and Wake, and, most significantly for the Hispanic presence in the United States, Puerto Rico.

New Faces in the United States

The First Cubans

As early as the 1830s, a small population of Cubans had established itself in the Florida Keys, based around a flourishing cigar-manufacturing industry in Key West, or *Cayo Hueso* (Cape Bone) to the Cubans. But the first significant wave of immigrants did not begin to arrive until the massive unrest and dislocation of the wars of independence sent many in search of more secure pastures. Throughout the last third of the nineteenth century, thousands of Cubans made their way to the United States—some, especially merchants and professionals, as far north as Philadelphia and New York City. Most, however, gathered around the preexisting community in nearby Florida, where many found work in the cigar industry.

By the 1870s, Key West was a predominantly Cuban town, and by 1885 it boasted 100 cigar factories and 3,000 Cubans. Substantial Cuban communities simultaneously arose in the Tampa Bay area, including West Tampa and Ybor City, the latter of which was founded in 1885 and 15 years later had a Cuban population of 3,000. Cubans also settled in Jacksonville and Martí City (now Ocala).

The Cubans who settled in these southern Florida towns for the most part found themselves free of the discrimination that so oppressed the Mexican American population of the Southwest. To some degree this was a function of the history of relations between Cubans and Anglos — or rather the lack thereof. Unlike the Mexicans, the Cubans had never been an enemy of the United States; had never found themselves the subjects of a hostile, permanent U.S. occupation; and had never possessed prized lands that Anglos coveted (and eventually snatched). Anglos, therefore, had not cultivated a legacy of hatred and contempt toward the Cuban community. Nor did the Cuban arrivals inspire such sentiments. They kept to their own communities and developed for themselves a strong economic foundation that could in no way be seen as a challenge to the Anglo population.

There is yet another reason for the Cubans' relative freedom from discrimination, and it is the worst reason of all: their skin color. Unlike the generally mestizo Mexicans, most of the early Cuban immigrants were light-skinned, with more "European" features. In a nation as race-conscious as the United States, this counted for a lot. In fact, those Cubans who were dark-skinned (a full 15 percent of Ybor City), despite their relatively good relations with the rest of the Cuban community, found themselves subject to the same Jim Crow laws as any other blacks in the Deep South.

In a few short decades, the Cubans built up a substantial body of social and political institutions. They founded labor organizations within the cigar industry and led strikes to improve wages and working conditions. They published Spanish-language newspapers. They threw themselves into local politics (another prerogative denied Mexican Americans), even electing Cuban mayors in Key West and West Tampa, the latter of whom, Fernando Figueredo Socarrás (see page 302), had also served as a state legislator. They formed mutual aid societies, which for a small monthly fee would provide free medical services, burial benefits, and financial assistance for their members, and also functioned as social clubs, arranging entertainments for the community.

During and after the Ten Years' War, they set up revolutionary clubs to support the independence movement, raising money on behalf of figures like Carlos Manuel de Céspedes and José Martí. Cigar makers in Key West and Tampa even donated one day's pay a week to the war effort. Indeed, for the efforts of its Cuban community, Tampa was called "the cradle of Cuban independence."

When Cuba became free of the U.S. occupation in 1902, many returned to their native island. But a great number remained in the United States, having grown attached to those communities where they had purchased homes, held jobs, and were busy raising families. With the flourishing Cuban enclave in Florida and active commerce between Cuba and the United States, Cuban immigration remained steady, if limited, into the middle of the twentieth century. Spikes of immigration would occur in times of political turmoil on the island, such as during the struggle against the dictatorship of Geraldo Machado y Morales in the 1930s and, twenty years later, against dictator Fulgencio Batista. A Cuban American population of 20,000 grew to close to 40,000 by the early 1950s. A more substantial wave would come only in the wake of another Cuban revolution—this one led by Fidel Castro.

El Lector (The Reader)

An interesting institution unique to the Cuban cigar manufacturing culture was the use of a *lector*, or reader, in the factories. Cuban and Spanish workers pooled their own money to hire well-educated—and strong-voiced—people to read aloud on the shop floor while the workers rolled cigars. The custom of using *lectores* began in Cuba and was transplanted to Key West, West Tampa, and Tampa. Besides providing intellectual stimulation, the *lectores* were often initiators of class consciousness and social resistance.

An elected workers' committee selected what the *lector* would read. Current events were always an interest, as were classical and popular literature, but the writings of Karl Marx and other political scientists were also well represented. Thus the *lectores* were the true intellectuals at the vanguard of the working classes and became active in union organization. This did not endear them to the factory bosses, however, who sometimes stooped to having particularly nettlesome *lectores* kidnapped and thrown out of town. Eventually, the workers' self-improvement proved to be a threat to the owners, who put a stop to the practice.

■ ■ ■

THE COMMONWEALTH OF PUERTO RICO

When the United States acquired Puerto Rico from Spain in 1898 as a result of the Spanish-Cuban-American War (see pages 120–122), its plan for the island, unlike that of Cuba, did not include independence, nominal or otherwise. Puerto Rico's strategic location at the gateway to the Caribbean simply made it too important for the United States to give up.

After two years of military rule, Congress passed the Foraker Act. Under this scheme, Puerto Rico would be governed by a bicameral legislature, which had jurisdiction over internal matters. Although the lower house would be elected by the people of Puerto Rico, the upper house and, more significantly, the governor were to be appointed by the president of the United States. Puerto Ricans also would be permitted to send a nonvoting delegate to Congress.

The Foraker Act did not particularly please the Puerto Ricans, for it actually gave them much less than they had been granted by Spain only a few years earlier. Under that 1897 agreement, Puerto Rico had been given not only self-rule but the right to send representatives to the Cortes, the Spanish legislature in Madrid. And, indeed, the first Puerto Rican legislature—led by longtime independence agitator Luis Muñoz Rivera (see also pages 302–303)—had been elected in March of 1898, and its members sworn in only eight days before U.S. forces landed and closed the parliament.

After the U.S. takeover, Muñoz Rivera spearheaded the calls for more Puerto Rican autonomy through his Federalist Party and his newspaper *La Democracia*. He became Puerto Rico's delegate to Congress in 1910, and spent the rest of his life working without success for an amendment to the Foraker Act.

It was only in 1917, a year after Muñoz Rivera's death and with the United States eager for recruits for the Great War, that Congress passed the Jones Act granting all Puerto Ricans U.S. citizenship and the right to elect their upper house delegates — but still not the governor. The president continued to appoint the governor and other key officials. Notably, the Jones Act also applied the Selective Service Act to Puerto Ricans, making them eligible for the draft.

Through the 1920s and 1930s, Puerto Ricans clamored for greater self-rule, and some, fearful of the cultural hegemony of the United States over Puerto Rico, advocated independence. The discontent on occasion even led to violence: One abortive uprising in Ponce left almost 20 people dead. But the U.S. government was unmoved. After World War II, however, with the dismantling of the colonial empires of Great Britain, France, and other powers, the United States began to take measures to end its colonial relationship with Puerto Rico. In 1947, a year after President Harry S. Truman had appointed the island's first native-born governor, Jesús T. Piñero, the power to elect a governor was turned over to the Puerto Ricans. Two years later, Luis Muñoz Marín (see page 304), the son of Luis Muñoz Rivera, became the first Puerto Rican native elected governor of the island, a position he would hold for 16 years. And on July 4, 1950, Truman signed into law the Puerto Rico Constitution Act, which proclaimed that "the people of Puerto Rico may organize a government pursuant to a constitution of their own adoption."

The following year, a constitutional convention agreed to establish Puerto Rico as an *estado libre asociado*, or associated free state, also known as a commonwealth. Under this arrangement, which began officially in 1952, the people of Puerto Rico would elect their own governor, legislature, and delegate to Congress, and have their own flag. While remaining U.S. citizens, Puerto Ricans would not pay federal income tax on local income or vote in federal elections unless they emigrated to the mainland. But all social services and federal programs available in the 50 states were made available in the commonwealth. This arrangement continues to the present day. (Since 1992, however, Puerto Rico's delegate has been permitted to vote on the House floor, not merely in committee.)

■ ■ ■

Borinquén

"Borinquén" was the name the Taíno Indians gave to the island now known as Puerto Rico. It means "the land of the brave lord." Today Puerto Ricans, particularly those who live on the mainland, call each other *"boricua."* Colón's original name for the island was San Juan Bautista (Saint John the Baptist), which alluded both to the saint and to the young heir to the Spanish throne, Prince Juan. But it was another Juan, Juan Ponce de León, who subdued the island for Spain, and who exclaimed, upon sailing into one of its magnificent harbors, *"¡Qué puerto rico!"*—"What a rich port!" The city built at the port retained the island's original name, San Juan. San Juan is Puerto Rico's capital today.

■ ■ ■

PUERTO RICANS ON THE MAINLAND

Just as it had under Spain, Puerto Rico under United States control painted a bleak economic picture: a small, overpopulated island with few industries, dominated by a handful of large sugar plantations, farms, and ranches worked by impoverished *jíbaros* (peasants). This condition only grew more acute when, in the early years under U.S. rule, Americans established additional sugar plantations, which dispossessed more small farmers of their land and brought in cheap finished goods, which undermined what few local industries existed. The net effect was a rising tide of jobless peasants. When with the onset of World War I demand for labor began to soar on the U.S. mainland, it was there that the natives streamed in search of opportunity. But unlike the Cubans, whose cigar-making community was a truly unique phenomenon, the Puerto Ricans did not head to Florida. Rather, their destination was the same as that of most of the European immigrants flooding the United States in this period: New York City, the point of entry to the labor-hungry industrial Northeast.

They were not, to be sure, the first Puerto Ricans to settle on the mainland. Merchants, plotters against Spain, members of the *criollo* middle class, skilled artisans and laborers, students, garment workers, and cigar makers had all found their way over to New York in the decades before and the years immediately after the Spanish-Cuban-American War. By 1910, there were about 1,500 Puerto Ricans living on the mainland. But the swelling wartime labor market and the passage of the Jones Act making all Puerto Ricans U.S. citizens opened the floodgates. By 1930, there were 53,000 Puerto Ricans in the United States and more than 45,000 in New York City alone.

Although a full 20 percent of mainland Puerto Ricans returned to the island as mainland jobs disappeared during the Great Depression of the 1930s, during and especially after World War II the migration was renewed with even greater intensity. In 1946 alone, the net migration of Puerto Ricans to the mainland was 40,000. Encouraged by a postwar economic boom and newly affordable air transportation, the Puerto Rican population grew to 675,000 by 1955 (with half a million in New York) and 900,000 by 1960. Although the vast majority continued to settle in the neighborhood known as Spanish Harlem and in nearby Brooklyn, working in the garment and service industries, many Puerto Ricans found jobs in other parts of the industrialized Northeast and Midwest, as well as in Florida and California. Chicago eventually grew to have the second-largest Puerto Rican population on the mainland.

When migration began to level off in the 1960s, it was a function of revolutionary economic developments back on the island—developments whose roots dated back a quarter century. In 1938, future governor Muñoz Marín, influenced by the government programs of the New Deal, had established the *Partido Popular Democrático* (Peoples' Democratic Party, or PDP)—known as the *Populares*—advocating sweeping economic and social changes under the slogan "Bread, land, liberty." The PDP was carried to victory in the 1940 legislative elections and, in the years that followed, instituted a string of incentives to bring mainland businesses to and otherwise improve the island. The centerpiece of this program was Operation Bootstrap, launched in 1948, which encouraged investment and tourism through a system of low-interest loans, tax exemptions, and other incentives; improved health care and education; cleared slums and built new housing; and promoted agricultural production. Though Puerto Ricans were to remain far poorer than their mainland compatriots, within a decade Operation Bootstrap had managed to lift the island to the highest per-capita income in Latin America. Even though unemployment remained high—indeed, some of the very businesses Operation Bootstrap brought in actually put people out of work—ultimately it was enough to convince many natives it was worth staying home.

If life was better for Puerto Ricans on the mainland than on the island, it was nevertheless difficult. The jobs they had come for paid meagerly and left them mired in poverty and, like most immigrants, settled in wretched housing and congregated in urban neighborhoods they called *barrios*. Although the northern cities in which Puerto Ricans mostly lived had few segregated public facilities, the newcomers—especially dark-skinned *puertorriqueños*—were subject to other insidious forms of discrimination: job and housing discrimination, mistreatment in the courts, police brutality. Like African

Americans and Mexican Americans, they were even occasionally the victims of Anglo violence. In 1926, Anglos in New York ransacked the Puerto Rican barrio, beating residents in the so-called Harlem Riots.

Puerto Ricans did have one advantage not available to Latinos in many other parts of the country. After the passage of the Jones Act, they were granted the right to vote. Far from trying to prevent them from acting on this right—as was common for Latinos throughout the Southwest—the big-city political "machines" actively encouraged their participation. Their involvement with the machines did often win them attention from the local governments, which made sure at least some municipal services were provided and doled out patronage jobs to lucky Puerto Ricans. But by and large, Puerto Rican involvement in electoral politics did not measurably improve their lives.

To provide some degree of comfort for themselves in this rather inhospitable environment, the Puerto Ricans as early as 1910 created mutual aid societies, what they called *hermandades* (brotherhoods). These *hermandades*, like their Cuban and Mexican counterparts, would act as both social clubs and insurance companies, providing medical care and offering financial aid when needed. They also made their buildings available for weddings and other celebrations and served as the centers of activity on holidays. In addition to the mutual aid societies, Puerto Ricans formed a range of labor groups, which occasionally, though not especially effectively, agitated for better wages and working conditions.

Later in the century, other organizations would build on the base of these earlier institutions and address a broader range of concerns. In the 1950s, the Puerto Rican Forum was established in New York with the aim of studying and eliminating the problems associated with poverty in the community. ASPIRA was founded early in the 1960s to encourage school-age Puerto Ricans to finish high school and attend college.

Latinos in World War I

Puerto Ricans were quickly given the opportunity to show their loyalty to the United States, which entered World War I shortly after the Jones Act was passed. The San Juan government promptly drafted 17,000 Puerto Rican men, and approximately 20,000 eventually served in the conflict.

Similarly, Mexican Americans, despite being victims of intense discrimination, volunteered for the armed forces in a higher percentage than any other ethnic group in the country. Though many of the volunteers could neither speak nor write English, they distinguished themselves against the Germans. Young private Marcelino Serna attacked a German trench with grenades and his rifle and forced the surrender of 24 German soldiers. He received the Distinguished Service Cross but not the Congressional Medal of Honor—his officers claimed he did not know enough English to fill out the necessary paperwork.

One Mexican American who did win the Medal of Honor was David Barkley. Barkley volunteered to reconnoiter enemy positions. Though killed in action, his maps, passed on to a comrade, enabled his unit to overcome the enemy. Another Mexican American, Nicolás Lucero, received the French *Croix de Guerre* for destroying two German machine-gun positions.

THE GREAT MEXICAN WAVE

REVOLUTIONARY IMPULSES

The discriminatory and often brutal treatment served up to His-panics in the southwestern states in the years immediately following Guadalupe Hidalgo acted, as no doubt expected, as a terrific deter-rent to further Mexican immigration. Although technically there were no limits on immigration, Mexicans kept to their side of the border—despite the perpetually grim economic shape of their own country. But as the railroads looked to extend their reach into the Southwest in the 1880s, the demand for cheap Mexican labor began to soar. This became especially true after the 1882 Chinese Exclu-sion Act (and less explicit actions targeting the Japanese) all but put an end to immigration from that quarter. With new opportuni-ties opening up in mining and agriculture—both rising along with the railroads—the impoverished Mexicans crossed into the United States to take advantage of them. By 1910, there were some 380,000 Mexicans and Mexican Americans in the country.

It was not, however, principally the "pull" factor of better wages but the "push" factor of a devastating, decade-long revolution that brought the first massive influx of Mexican immigrants to the United States. When it started in 1910, the Mexican Revolution had been at least 30 years coming. Since he had taken dictatorial control in 1876, General Porfirio Díaz had overseen the rapid in-dustrialization of the country, fueled largely by foreign money. But the benefits found their way into the hands of very few: Most of Mexico's land was owned by a few thousand families, and a handful of foreigners and privileged Mexicans dominated the industries. The vast mass of Mexicans, and especially the long-disfavored Indi-ans and mestizos, only sank further into poverty.

In 1910, liberal landowner Francisco Madero, for years a vehe-ment opponent of Díaz, initiated a popular revolt when the 85-year-old dictator betrayed his promise of a free and fair presidential election. It was the beginning of a prolonged and deadly crisis of leadership. When the extent of Madero's support became clear, Díaz resigned and in 1911 Madero became president. Madero's vague plans to overhaul the economy, however, never gained the backing of either the left or the right, and in 1913 he was gunned down by right-wing forces and replaced by the autocratic general Victoriano Huerta. Huerta was in turn challenged by Venustiano Carranza, a state governor who had inherited Madero's liberal following. With the backing of U.S. troops who captured the city of Veracruz on his behalf, Carranza took power in 1914. Although in 1917 Carranza put forward a decidedly reformist constitution — including, among other provisions, some land redistribution and the nationalization of profitable mineral resources — he never bothered to implement it. In 1920, he was deposed by General Álvaro Obregón, whose subsequent election to the presidency marked the end of the severe political disruptions of the period.

Throughout these years, Mexico was in a state of almost complete chaos. Violent champions of more radical reform — most famously Francisco "Pancho" Villa and Emiliano Zapata — roamed the land with rebellious bands, fighting federal troops, destroying the railroads, dispossessing landowners of their property, and becoming folk heroes in the process. (Both Villa and Zapata were eventually assassinated, although not before Villa had crossed into New Mexico in 1916 and killed nineteen U.S. citizens, then four more in Texas two months later, as "punishment" for American meddling.) Repression became severe. The bloody conflicts left a million Mexicans dead. The economy fell into tatters.

North of the border, meanwhile, the economy was booming. World War I sparked a fresh demand for laborers, especially for work in war industries and on farms. The 1917 Immigration Act made Mexican laborers welcome, opening the doors to "temporary" workers. It did contain a literacy requirement and charge a head tax, but this was soon revoked for agricultural laborers — which the farm industry desperately needed. The economic expansion continued throughout the 1920s, and even as the United States was closing the door to other foreigners with the Emergency Quota Act of

1921 and the Immigration Act of 1924, pressure from business leaders made sure no quotas were set on Mexican (or other Latino) immigration. (Congress did, however, create the U.S. Border Patrol in 1925 to stop unauthorized immigration from Mexico; it quickly established its reputation, still preserved, of virtual ineffectiveness.)

INTO THE NORTH

Mexicans streamed north in droves to escape the horrors of the revolution and take advantage of the opportunities there. By 1920, the United States' Mexican American and Mexican population was up to 650,000. Between 1910 and 1930, a full 10 percent of the entire population of Mexico relocated to the United States. Their principal destinations were rural and urban areas of California, Texas, New Mexico, and Arizona, but in the 1920s Mexicans and Mexican Americans spread throughout the Midwest—Kansas City, Omaha, Saint Louis, Detroit, Gary, and even as far east as Philadelphia—often trying to keep one step ahead of the newest wave of arrivals into the Southwest. Chicago saw its Mexican population increase fivefold in the decade, and it soon had the largest Mexican American community outside the Southwest.

Some Mexican immigrants, especially those that came in the 1920s, were members of Mexico's upper and middle classes. Well educated, they often had the skills to adjust to life in the United States, sometimes just transferring their professional practices or businesses to their new home. But most were illiterate in both Spanish and English and had to do unskilled work, notably as farm laborers. Indeed, by the late 1920s, a full 80 percent of southern California's farmworkers were of Mexican descent. Others worked the mines, operated the assembly lines, and laid the railroad tracks, and in the Midwest worked in steel mills and other factories and in meatpacking plants. The payment was rarely better than a subsistence wage and the working conditions generally miserable, but compared to the situation in Mexico, the jobs were a godsend.

For the most part, the life of a farm laborer was a migrant one.

Living in communities called *colonias*, the Mexican workers moved from state to state, harvesting cotton, fruit, vegetables, and sugar beets. As the need for pickers moved with the seasons, the Mexican workers moved and formed new *colonias* wherever they stopped. In the cities, Mexicans settled in barrios, the largest of which was in Los Angeles, with a population that reached 30,000. As Puerto Ricans were themselves discovering on the other side of the country, barrio life offered the support of a network of family, friends, and countrymen, but little else. Its chief feature was poverty. The barrio was last and least in receiving basic government services (such as garbage collection). And it was made up of overcrowded, dilapidated tenements, most without gas, electricity, or indoor plumbing.

Like the Cuban and Puerto Rican communities in other parts of the country, Mexican immigrants developed mutual aid societies, which they called *mutualistas*, to look after their own. The *mutualistas* helped the migrant workers and the Mexicans of the barrios adjust to American life, providing them with financial and other support. They also helped Mexicans retain their cultural heritage, sponsoring social and cultural events and with traditional fiestas.

The incoming Mexicans experienced prejudice everywhere they went. Throughout the Southwest, they were subject to the same mistreatment that Mexican Americans had been living with for decades: segregated public facilities, job discrimination, and, especially in Texas, occasional violence and vigilante justice. Pancho Villa's deadly 1916 raid and wartime rumors of a Mexican pact with Germany that would return the Southwest to Mexico—both of which raised questions among Anglos about Mexican loyalty—only further poisoned the atmosphere. The cities of the Midwest and East offered up their own varieties of discrimination, for example, relegating Mexicans, along with African Americans, to separate sections of movie theaters. And, of course, Mexicans never were paid on a level with Anglo workers.

Mexicans particularly incurred the hostility of other urban ethnic immigrants, who felt (sometimes justifiably) their own jobs threatened by the newcomers. Though they shared the Catholic faith, Central and Eastern Europeans in Chicago and elsewhere refused to invite the Mexicans into their churches. Even the more established Mexican Americans often turned up their noses at these struggling immigrants, whom they referred to derisively as *mojados*, the equivalent of the disdainful Anglo term "wetbacks" and a reference to the newcomers' supposed crossing of the Rio Grande.

Anglo prejudice extended to the labor movement as well. Since the beginning of the great Mexican migration, labor leaders, such as Samuel Gompers of the American Federation of Labor (AFL), had resented the effect that cheap Mexican labor was having on the wages of native workers. They had protested, to no avail, Congress's repeated decisions not to curtail Mexican immigration. The labor movement, then, was little inclined to help Mexicans improve their lot, even in areas such as migrant farming, where Anglos played a comparatively minor role. The Mexicans were for the most part forced to create their own unions, and they did have some success: In 1917, three Arizona mine locals had 5,000 Mexican workers, and in 1927 southern California's *Confederación de Uniones Obreras Mexicanas* (the Confederation of Mexican Workers, or CUOM) had 3,000. These, however, were exceptions, and successful strike activity was even rarer. For the most part, in the century's first decades, few Mexican workers—and no migrant farmworkers—were organized.

■ ■ ■

Corridos, or ballads, have a long tradition among Mexican Americans as anthems of social protest (see also page 234). One early-twentieth-century *corrido*, "*Los rinches de Texas*," lamented abuse by the Texas Rangers. It opened:

Es una triste verdad	It's a sad truth
De unos pobres campesinos	about the poor peasants
Que brutalmente golpeados	who were brutally beaten
Esos Rinches asesinos . . .	by those murderous Rangers . . .

Another, *"El deportado"* ("The Deported One"), assaulted the United States for its repatriation campaign against the Mexicans in the 1930s:

Los güeros son muy maloras	The whites are very evil
Se valen de la ocasión	They take advantage of the
Y a todos los mexicanos	situation/And all Mexicans
Los tratan sin compasión	Are treated without pity

■ ■ ■

MEXICANO, *Go Home!*

When the Great Depression hit in the early 1930s, throwing a third of all Americans out of work and dramatically lowering the wages of those who kept their jobs, Mexican Americans in the Southwest and Midwest, as well as Latinos across the country, were hit harder than most. As factories and other businesses closed or shrank, Mexican Americans were the first to lose their jobs, and the ranks of migrant farmers swelled with the unemployed, sending wages tumbling to a fraction of what they had been in previous years. Wages of Mexican farmworkers in California, for one, fell from between 35 and 50 cents per hour in 1931 to 15 or 16 cents in 1933. In 1933, President Franklin D. Roosevelt introduced his New Deal, with a wide range of programs to assist unemployed and struggling workers, including public works projects and expanded minimum wage laws. But they turned out to be of only limited help to the recent Mexican immigrants because they were not available to noncitizens or applicable to farm labor.

As was the case with workers across the country, Mexican Americans turned to their unions to defend them. Union membership soared, often with women workers in the forefront, and strikes flared up throughout the Southwest among both agricultural and industrial workers. But though they had some success—a strawberry pickers union at El Monte (near Los Angeles) won a considerable wage increase in 1933, and Los Angeles dressmakers with the International Ladies Garment Workers Union (ILGWU) in 1936 doubled their salaries after a strike, for example—most met with frustration.

A celebrated case in point: San Antonio's 10,000 or so Mexican pecan shellers were making a meager $2 a week when, in 1938, management cut their wages. Under the leadership of Communist firebrand Emma Tenayuca (see page 311) and labor agitator Luisa Moreno (see pages 310–311), the two unions into which the workers had organized—*El Nogal* (The Walnut Tree) and a company union, the Pecan Shellers Workers Union—struck. But their strategy misfired. The employers "settled" the strike by making workers unnecessary: They bought and installed automated shellers. By 1941, the company needed only 600 workers.

Meanwhile, as is always the case in hard times, the country was looking for scapegoats for its ills. Mexican immigrants, who for so long had been accused of depressing wages and taking Anglo jobs, became an obvious target. To many, then, the solution seemed obvious: Throw them out. Newspaper editorials, politicians, and labor unions began to demand that Mexicans be deported.

And so they were. Systematically in large cities, more haphazardly in smaller towns and rural areas, local authorities throughout the Southwest and Midwest began rounding up Mexicans and returning them south of the border. Civil rights and common decency were simply brushed aside in the effort, which caught up not only recent immigrants and the U.S.-born children of immigrants but thousands of U.S. citizens as well. The complaints of Spanish-language newspapers, among the few institutions to protest this campaign, simply were ignored.

In Los Angeles, by far the hardest hit city, Mexicans were given train fare back to Mexico and a small stipend to tide them over. Between 1931 and 1934, nearly 13,000 were ejected from the city. Texas, which had more Mexicans than any other state, also deported more than any other state: 130,000. Only New Mexico's strong and well-integrated Mexican community escaped any substantial repatriation. In total, close to half a million Mexicans and

Mexican Americans were sent across the Rio Grande during the 1930s—including 200,000 repatriated in 1932 alone. Although the Mexican government by and large cooperated with the program, it had few resources to reintegrate the "new" Mexicans, and many languished in refugee camps.

■ ■ ■

"These People Are Not Aliens"

"Long before the 'grapes of wrath' had ripened in California's vineyards, a people lived on highways, under trees or tents, in shacks or railroad sections, picking crops—cotton, fruits, vegetables, cultivating sugar beets, building railroads and dams, making barren land fertile for new crops and greater riches. . . . These people are not aliens. They have contributed their endurance, sacrifices, youth, and labor to the Southwest."
— LUISA MORENO, IN A 1940 CONGRESSIONAL HEARING

■ ■ ■

REOPENING THE DOORS

The United States had only just finished saying good-bye to hundreds of thousands of repatriated Mexicans when suddenly it needed them back. In 1941, World War II came to America, and just as in the previous conflict, a manpower shortage and a sudden boom in war-related industries created an enormous demand for labor. Although Mexicans once again crossed into the United States, they were not doing so fast enough or in large enough numbers to meet the existing need.

The U.S. government quickly realized that circumstances required a more formal arrangement and turned to the Mexican government for help in guaranteeing a steady supply of workers — or, as the Mexicans called them, *braceros*. Mexico, for once in the driver's seat, insisted on a minimum wage of 30 cents an hour for the *braceros* and on adequate transportation, housing, and work conditions. It also refused to send *braceros* to Texas, where discrimination and violence against Mexicans was considered unacceptable. The U.S. government agreed to the conditions, and in 1942 a provisional arrangement to bring 250,000 migrant farmers was put in place. By 1945, another 68,000 were in the railroads' employ. During the same period, many more Mexicans not associated with the *bracero* program continued to enter the United States as well.

Although the *bracero* program proved immensely valuable to the U.S. economy during the war, the *braceros* themselves did not profit as much as the Mexican government had anticipated. The agreed-upon standards, opposed from the beginning by agricultural interests, were for the most part simpy ignored — and Mexico was in no position to enforce them. (The *bracero* program would nonetheless continue until the end of 1964, involving 4.5 million Mexican workers, until felled by mutual dissatisfaction with the program, labor opposition to it, and, most of all, automation.)

The renewed influx of Mexicans throughout the 1940s was met, as was by now the custom, with widespread Anglo animosity. Police brutality against Mexican Americans increased sharply across the country. More alarming still was a rise in violence toward young Mexicans and Mexican Americans in the Southwest — a rise that would culminate in the notorious zoot suit riots.

Many Mexican American youths during the period adopted a flashy clothing style called a zoot suit: an oversize jacket with padded shoulders coupled with oversize pants that rose halfway to the chest and were severely tapered at the cuffs. This was topped off by a broad-brimmed fedora. The young zoot-suited Mexican Americans became known as "pachucos." The style was a big hit with gang members, and though few pachucos were actually in gangs, a zoot suit was often assumed by Anglos to signal gang affiliation.

Many Anglos took it as their right to assault anyone wearing the flashy clothing.

The zoot suit became an issue in the 1942 Sleepy Lagoon case in Los Angeles. When a young Mexican American man was found dead, authorities indicted 22 pachucos who were members of the 38th Street Club gang. The accused were not permitted to cut their hair and were required to stand trial dressed in their zoot suits. To no one's surprise, the threatening-looking pachucos were convicted. (A state appeals court eventually overturned the conviction, finding, in a unanimous opinion, that the defendants had been denied a fair trial.)

The following summer, Anglo soldiers and sailors in Los Angeles rioted for days, beating any pachuco they found on the streets and going into restaurants, bars, and theaters to find more. Local police looked aside, and the press blamed the pachucos for the unrest, which was quelled only when military police stepped in. Eventually, downtown Los Angeles was declared off-limits to off-duty military personnel. Zoot suit riots spread across the country and did not die down until they had racked not only the Los Angeles suburbs but Chicago, Philadelphia, and Detroit as well.

Yet despite these unsettling incidents, the war proved to be a turning point for Mexican Americans and indeed for all Latinos. The fight against Germany's racist regime, and the revelation of what it had wrought, affected American attitudes, official and otherwise, toward racism at home. An economic boom, fueled in part by the contribution of women in the economy, was under way, allowing the country to feel it could now afford to be a little more generous to its disadvantaged elements. And the progressive thrust of the New Deal had been forged during the war into a new, wider liberal consensus.

One result was that the federal government began to recognize Latino problems and do something about them. In 1941 the Fair Employment Practices Committee had been created to end discrimination in war industries. In response to the zoot suit riots, the government established a Spanish-Speaking Peoples' Division in the

State Department's Office of Inter-American Affairs to address prejudice and discrimination against Latinos.

More significant than the change in how America saw Latinos, however, was the change in how Latinos saw themselves. When the war was over, Latinos returned from the battlefields and emerged from the armament factories. They had fought in a war to make the world safe for democracy and won. It now seemed only appropriate that victory would mean a safer and better life for them. Throughout the late 1940s and 1950s, especially as Mexican Americans became increasingly acculturated through their public school educations and exposure to U.S. mass media, the prejudice they experienced grated more and more acutely—and they said so. The definitive moment would be the civil rights movement of the 1960s, resulting in revolutionary gains in the economic, political, legal, social, and even cultural spheres.

Latinos in World War II

As they had in World War I, Latinos volunteered for duty in World War II at a higher rate than any other ethnic group—and earned disproportionately more Medals of Honor than any other group as well. Approximately 500,000 Hispanic GIs (including 400,000 Mexicans and 65,000 Puerto Ricans) served their country, even as their families at home continued to be treated as second-class citizens.

Nor was the shabby treatment reserved solely for civilian Latinos: Sergeant Macario García was one of 17 Mexicans who won the Congressional Medal of Honor in this conflict. He was cited for his single-handed destruction of two enemy machine-gun nests. Wearing his uniform, with the medal pinned on his chest, he was nonetheless denied a cup of coffee at a café in his hometown of Sugarland, Texas. Other—Anglo—soldiers and sailors came to García's defense, and the ensuing brawl had to be broken up by the local sheriff. The incident even brought a protest from the Mexican government.

Puerto Rican Horacio Rivero (see page 297) received the Distinguished Service Medal, the Legion of Merit, and the Navy Commendation Medal for his exemplary service in the Pacific. (He eventually rose to four-star admiral, the first Hispanic since David Farragut to achieve that rank.)

Fully one-quarter of the men that endured the Bataan Death March were Mexican Americans.

■ ■ ■

THE STRUGGLE FOR CIVIL RIGHTS

ROOTS OF MOBILIZATION

The elements that coalesced into 1960s Latino activism had been in place for a century or more. The social bandits, mutual aid societies, and unions and other strike groups all represented faces of heightened Latino social consciousness. So, too, did the handful of Latino rights groups that had begun to spring up starting around the turn of the century, such as the *Congreso Mexicanista* (Mexican Congress) in Texas, the *Asamblea Mexicana* (Mexican Assembly), and the *Liga Protectora Mexicana* (Mexican Protective League) as well as the much more durable *Alianza Hispano Americana* (Hispanic American Alliance), started by Civil War veteran Santos Benavides (see also page 295) in 1894.

Still, probably the first truly effective organization founded specifically to fight for Latinos' civil rights was the League of United Latin American Citizens, or LULAC. Established in Corpus Christi, Texas, in February 1929 by middle-class professionals who valued their heritage but stressed their American identities,

LULAC's agenda was ending anti-Latino bias and discrimination, ensuring equal education and employment opportunities for Latinos, and securing adequate political representation. The organization, which quickly came to have chapters in 21 states, was at the forefront of Latino civil rights litigation, winning (often in conjunction with the Alianza Hispano Americana) court orders that forbade segregation of Mexican American students in a range of municipalities in the Southwest.

The American GI Forum, another powerful rights organization, was formed in 1948 by a group of Mexican American World War II veterans in response to the refusal of a Texas funeral home to conduct a reburial of the remains of a Mexican American war casualty, Félix Longoria. The Longoria incident brought to a head the mounting indignation Mexican Americans felt over their treatment in the Southwest. Despite their overwhelming participation and heroism in the war, on return they continued to be subjected to demeaning restrictions. Now the Longoria case dramatized how, even in death, Mexican Americans were denied equal status. (Longoria was ultimately interred in Arlington National Cemetery, with full military honors.)

The GI Forum's initial goal was to publicize the benefits of the postwar GI Bill to Latino veterans and provide assistance in helping them apply for its housing, education, and other benefits. But the organization, headed by veteran Dr. Héctor Pérez García (see pages 311–312), soon expanded its aims to general political and social reform, including antidiscrimination lawsuits and voter registration. By the end of 1949, there were more than 100 GI Forum chapters; a few years later the number increased by half again — most of them in the Southwest, particularly in Texas.

Many other organizations, both local and national, fought the lonely battles for Hispanic rights in the first half of the century. Luisa Moreno's (see page 310) *El Congreso de los Pueblos de Habla Español* (The Spanish-Speaking Peoples' Congress) included Latinos from Florida, New York, Pennsylvania, Illinois, and Indiana, as well as the Southwest. At the end of the 1930s, the group pressed for the right of urban workers to organize and targeted civil rights violations, police brutality, and mass deportations until it collapsed under accusations of communist influence (a not-uncommon fate in this era for many rights organizations, Latino and non-Latino alike).

The Community Service Organization (CSO), originally established to support the election of Edward R. Roybal (see page 305) to the Los Angeles City Council in 1947, expanded its agenda to all kinds of mistreatment of Latinos. It eventually grew to more than 50,000 members across the country. A 1962 effort to elect Roybal to the U.S. Congress was the defining moment for another political organization, the Mexican American Political Association (MAPA), founded in 1959 by Eduardo Quevedo, Bert Corona, and Roybal himself; a Texas chapter was formed soon after.

All these groups, and numerous (often short-lived) others—such as New Mexico's *Asociación Nacional México-Americana* (ANMA) and southern California's Civic Unity League—represented the first concrete steps toward Latino empowerment. Quite a few would continue their good work through the 1960s. But perhaps more important, they generated the mind-set, and many of the leaders, for the mass movement to come.

■ ■ ■

Latinos in Korea and Vietnam

Thousands of Hispanics fought in the Korean War, including nine who received the Congressional Medal of Honor. Most impressive perhaps was the contribution of Puerto Rican islanders. The newly created commonwealth's citizens volunteered in huge numbers—and accordingly saw losses far out of proportion to the island's population. One all–Puerto Rican infantry regiment arrived at Pusan on September 30, 1950, and participated in nine major campaigns over the next three years, earning a string of citations. Among the Puerto Rican heroes in Korea was flyer Colonel Manuel J. Fernández, whose multiple air victories made him one of the country's all-time top aces.

Although there were no all-Hispanic units in Vietnam, Latinos distinguished themselves in that conflict as well. Everett Álvarez Jr., a navy pilot, was the first American prisoner of war held by North Vietnam. Shot down in 1964, Álvarez spent more than eight years in a Viet Cong prison. Ironically, another Latino, Juan J. Valdez, was on the last helicopter to leave Vietnam in 1975. Latinos had a high casualty rate in Vietnam as well; though they represented less than 14 percent of military age males in the Southwest, nearly a fifth of all casualties from the region were Latino.

Mass Movement

The early 1960s were years of extraordinary social ferment in the United States. Perhaps the most remarkable phenomenon of the period was the African American civil rights movement. For the first time in their history, large numbers of black Americans, mostly from the South, agitated actively for the fair treatment the country had always denied them. In a series of boycotts, marches, sit-ins, and legal actions, they demanded an end to racial discrimination in public accommodations, jobs, housing, voting, and a range of other areas—and saw their actions bear fruit in such unprecedented legislation as the Civil Rights Act of 1964 and the Voting Rights Act of 1965. Federal open-housing legislation would follow in 1968.

The success of this movement was not lost on Latinos. On an immediate level, they found themselves to be the beneficiaries of many of the very same victories that African Americans had won. The civil rights legislation forbade discrimination in public accommodations, unions, employment, and all federally funded programs against anyone on the basis of their skin color, Hispanics as well as blacks. Mexican Americans, for so long excluded from stores, barbershops, restaurants, movie theaters, swimming pools, even churches in the Southwest, were suddenly excluded no more. In a single stroke, a world of job opportunities was, if more in principle than in practice, thrown open. (Though encouraging, the Voting Rights Act—which outlawed poll taxes, literacy tests, and other exclusionary gimmicks and guaranteed enforcement on behalf of African Americans—would not deliver specific benefits to Hispanics until the 1970s.)

But beyond the obvious legislative payoff, Hispanics found in the African American movement a source of inspiration. Clearly it was not impossible for the victims of prejudice, standing together, to fight for their rights. It was in the wake of these early monumental victories of the civil rights movement that Latinos began to rise en masse.

The epicenter of Latino civil rights agitation was the Mexican American community of the Southwest. Constituting almost all of the 3.5 million Latinos in Texas, southern California, New Mexico, Arizona, and Colorado in the early 1960s, Mexican Americans had long felt the sting of oppression most acutely. Puerto Ricans, though disproportionately poor and victimized by prejudice, were— in the northern urban centers in which they lived—free of the more severe forms of discrimination. At any rate, compared to Mexican Americans, they were relative newcomers to the mainland and lacked the organizational and social base of the Mexican Americans. Cubans, only beginning to arrive in the United States in significant numbers, were still by far the best off of the three groups in both economic standing and treatment by the Anglo population. For these reasons, Puerto Rican and Cuban involvement in the movement was quite limited.

Probably the principal agent of the Hispanic awakening was César Chávez (see pages 312–313), the emblematic hero of the movement. A migrant worker from Yuma, Arizona, Chávez was the general director of California's Community Service Organization (CSO) before deciding in 1962 that his calling was to organize the tens of thousands of Mexican American migrant workers of the Southwest. For decades the most downtrodden segment of the Latino population, migrant workers—most of them legal U.S. residents but few of them U.S. citizens—had never been protected by minimum-wage laws or guaranteed the right to organize. Living in grim camps, they worked long days for below subsistence wages and were exposed to pesticides, holding little hope that their children would have it better.

Encouraged by the end of the *bracero* program in 1964, which lowered the supply and therefore raised the demand for Mexican American pickers, Chávez started his National Farm Workers Association (NFWA) in Delano, California, and by 1965 had organized 1,700 families. In September of that year, the union joined several hundred Filipinos under the banner of the AFL-CIO in a *huelga* (strike) against grape growers in the San Joaquin Valley, demanding better working conditions and higher wages. Chávez soon formalized the NFWA relationship with the AFL-CIO and changed his organization's name to the United Farm Workers Organizing Committee (UFWOC, or simply UFW).

For the migrant workers involved, striking was an unimaginably bold step. Few had any savings to draw upon; the union had no money to support them. And the growers showed no signs of a willingness to make concessions. They threw the migrant workers out of their camps, secured injunctions against and continually harrassed union picketers, and brought in busloads of replacements from around the region. Nevertheless, within a matter of weeks, thousands of Mexican Americans were on strike on dozens of farms in the San Joaquin Valley. The strike would ultimately last five years.

In 1966, Chávez called for the first of what would come to be a series of consumer boycotts of grapes, targeting two major growers, Schenley and DiGiorgio. Chávez's charismatic personality soon transformed the *huelga* into a national movement, which came to be known as *La Causa*. His nonviolent tactics attracted the attention, and the support, of politicians, student activists, and civil rights and labor groups. In 1966, Senator Robert Kennedy headed up an investigation into the treatment of California migrant workers. In the spring of that same year, Chávez led a 25-day, 250-mile march from Delano to California's capital, Sacramento, to publicize the strike; 10,000 people joined the march. It was during the march that Chávez learned of the union's first victory: Schenley had decided to come to terms with the UFW.

Still, other growers refused to negotiate, and Chávez began to push for a boycott of all California table grapes that did not bear the UFW's black eagle insignia. Little by little, powerful allies began to come aboard. The AFL-CIO officially took up their cause. Dockworkers in several European countries refused to unload California grapes. And grape orders from the big cities began to creep down. Indeed, by 1970, an estimated 17 million Americans had joined the boycott and shipments to the top markets were down 22 percent and falling. On April 1, 1970, the vast Freedman ranches signed a contract with the UFW securing better wages, pesticide control, and meeting other demands. By the end of the summer, the rest of the San Joaquin Valley's growers had followed suit.

Despite its success in California, the United Farm Workers did have difficulty extending its influence to other migrant-worker centers such as Texas. A 1966 march from Rio Grande City to Austin failed to rouse the troops; it lacked organization, outside support, and internal unity. Chávez was also undermined by the virtually unlimited supply of undocumented Mexicans willing to supplant striking workers, harrassment by the Texas Rangers, the antagonism of Texas judges, and the state's antiunion right-to-work laws. Yet nothing could diminish the significance of Chávez's accomplishment in California. Chávez had created the nation's first effective agricultural union, and for the first time in their long history, the state's Latino migrant workers had stood up to the economic powers and won.

"The Road to Our Liberation"

"We, the striking grape workers of California, join on this International Boycott Day with the consumers across the continent in planning the steps that lie ahead on the road to our liberation. . . .

"If this road we chart leads to the rights and freedoms we demand, if it leads to just wages, humane working conditions, protection from the misuse of pesticides, and to the fundamental right of collective bargaining; if it changes the social order that relegates us to the bottom reaches of society, then in our wake will follow thousands of American farm workers. Our example will make them free."

—BOYCOTT DAY PROCLAMATION OF THE UNITED FARM WORKERS, MAY 10, 1969

RAISING THE STAKES

Disparate voices, some of them quite radical, began to make themselves heard as the decade went on. Quite a few focused on the issue of Latino pride. The assertive term "Chicano" came into currency as the way Mexican Americans referred to themselves. Mirroring the black movement, some Latinos rejected what they considered the assimilationist tendencies of earlier activists and pushed for a sort of Hispanic self-determination.

One of the more impassioned of these voices was Rodolfo "Corky" Gonzales (see pages 313–314). A former featherweight boxer, an active community organizer (through his Crusade for Justice organization), and a stirring writer and speaker, the Denver-based Gonzales began in the mid-60s to advocate Chicano *nacionalismo* — nationalism, or self-determination — in his newspaper, *El Gallo* (the *Rooster*). He rejected accommodation and assimilation in favor of ethnic pride and economic and political autonomy. Gonzales's philosophy was magnificently expressed in his epic poem, *Yo soy Joaquín/I Am Joaquín* (see pages 211, 212). A clarion call to Mexican Americans, the 1964 bilingual poem was often read aloud at rallies. Gonzales himself later wrote in an introduction to the poem that it "became a historical essay, a social statement. . . . It is a mirror of our greatness and our weakness, a call to action as a total people, emerging from a glorious history, traveling through social pain and conflicts. . . ." The poem's impact was wide, crystallizing the hopes and dreams of a people and inspiring thousands in the *movimiento* (movement).

In 1968, Gonzales joined in the Poor People's March in Washington, D.C., where he issued his manifesto, *Demandas de la raza* (The Race's Demands). *Demandas* urged better education and housing for Chicanos, as well as civil rights and land reform. A year later, Gonzales and his Crusade for Justice convened the first National Chicano Youth Conference, attended by almost 1,500 activists from some 100 organizations. There, he outlined his *Plan Espiritual de Aztlán* (Spiritual Plan of Aztlán). This 15-point nationalist plan — which looked for spiritual grounding in the great Indian cultures of Aztlán, the mythical homeland of the Aztecs — called for separate Chicano institutions, including schools and a political party. (Its preamble was a poem by Alurista [see pages 212–213].) The plan was overwhelmingly adopted by the assembled group. At the end of the conference, participants marched to the capitol building in Denver, raised the Mexican flag, and declared the independence of the Chicano nation.

As with the African American movement, the Latino call to ethnic pride found a particularly receptive audience among high school and college students, who served as shock troops in some of the more heated confrontations with the authorities. Many student organizations flourished during the period, none more visibly than the Mexican American Youth Organization (MAYO), begun by Texas

A&I University student José Ángel Gutiérrez (see page 315) and others in 1964, three years before its formal founding. Other groups that sprung up in the same period included the Mexican American Students Association (MASA) in East Los Angeles, the United Mexican American Students (UMAS) at Los Angeles's Loyola Marymount University, and the Chicano Association of Student Organizations (CASO) in New Mexico.

The groups' agendas principally focused on school-related matters, such as segregation in dormitories; discrimination in college admissions; English-only instruction; the scarcity of Latino teachers, counselors, and administrators (in both secondary and higher education); rundown, overcrowded facilities; and curricula that offered little mention of Hispanic contributions. But they were occasionally broadened to cover issues such as racism and police brutality, and even the high rate of Latino casualties in Vietnam.

The student groups' tactics included so-called blowouts or student strikes in the high schools, and sit-ins, mass demonstrations, and even vandalism at the universities. The rhetoric was often fiery. "We are going to move to do away with the injustices to the Chicano," Gutiérrez proclaimed at one rally, "and if the 'gringo' doesn't get out of our way, we will stampede over him."

In the spring of 1968, approximately 10,000 Mexican American students walked out of 16 Los Angeles high schools, inspired in large measure by local teacher Sal Castro and student organizations in the area. In the weeks leading up to the walkout, student leaders had appealed to the school board to improve education for Mexican Americans in order to reduce their dreadful dropout rate. But their demands had been ignored. With students picketing school buildings to shouts of "Chicano power" and blocking entrances, school authorities called in the police, who made mass arrests and, in some cases, brutalized the protesters. Still the walkout continued—only now it had won the support not only of Senator Kennedy, but of the students' own parents, many of whom had until then held mixed feelings about the walkout. And indeed it was the vigorous pressure of the parents who finally prevailed upon a reluctant school board to begin addressing the students' concerns. By June, the walkout was over.

Los Angeles authorities did not forgive and forget easily, however. That summer, a grand jury indicted 13 strike leaders, including Sal Castro, on (felony) charges of conspiracy to disrupt a public school. Although the case was later thrown out on Constitutional grounds, it took another prolonged protest by parents to persuade the school board to allow Castro to return to work.

Meanwhile, protests were spreading to other high schools, colleges, and universities throughout the Southwest. Thousands walked out in Denver, Phoenix, San Antonio, Crystal City (Texas), and Santa Clara (California). By 1970, the authorities in these and other districts had agreed to meet many of the students' demands. New Mexico moved particularly aggressively, not only adding multicultural choices to the curriculum in high schools and colleges but appointing the nation's first Mexican American university president. A year later, the various student groups would unify under the *Movimiento Estudiantil Chicano de Aztlán* (MEChA), a group that continues on various campuses across the country today (though with a much lower profile).

One of the most radical agendas, and some of the most radical tactics, were embraced by Reies López Tijerina (see also page 312)—known as "El Tigre," or "The Tiger." Tijerina was a one-time fundamentalist preacher and founder of a failed utopian community in Arizona called *Valle de la Paz* (Valley of Peace). As early as 1960 he had begun an effort to focus attention on the issues of land grants and Chicano property rights, particularly in New Mexico. As Tijerina saw it, many of the Mexican American lands that Anglos had acquired in the past had originally been *ejidos*, that is, grants made to whole communities for public use. As such, individual Mexican Americans simply had not had the authority to pass these along to anyone. Therefore, any takeover of *ejidos* by Anglos was, in fact, illegitimate. Pointing to the property rights guarantees in the Treaty of Guadalupe Hidalgo, Tijerina demanded them back.

The organization that came to be called the *Alianza Federal de*

Pueblos Libres (Federal Alliance of Free Towns) was founded in 1963 and claimed 20,000 members. Whatever the actual number, enough of them were present in a march from Albuquerque to Santa Fe to draw attention to the Alianza's claims. They won even more attention on October 15, 1966, when 350 *aliancistas* occupied the Echo Amphitheater campgrounds of the Kit Carson National Forest — land they claimed to be on the *ejido* of San Joaquín de Chama Pueblo. Two U.S. forest rangers at the site were captured by the Alianza, and then "tried" and "convicted" for trespassing. (Luckily for all involved, the "sentence" was suspended.) Within a week, however, state police came and removed the protesters, and Tijerina was arrested and charged with conspiracy and assault.

Tensions rose between *aliancistas* and state authorities over the following months. Forest services fences were being cut and haystacks and barns burned, and Tijerina's organization was regarded as the culprit. In anticipation of further disturbances, police broke up an Alianza meeting and arrested several participants. It was this action that provoked one of the more notorious incidents of the Chicano movement, an incident memorialized in a *corrido*. Angered at what they saw to be a violation of their rights of assembly by the district attorney for northern New Mexico (himself Hispanic), Tijerina and a group of *aliancistas* attempted a citizen's arrest of the D.A. in the small town of Tierra Amarilla. Violence and gunfire erupted as they descended on the county courthouse; a state patrolman and a jailer were shot, and two reporters and a deputy sheriff were held captive. Eventually, the National Guard was called in to put an end to the siege. Tijerina himself spent 10 days on the run before turning himself in.

The pending charges still did not slow him down. Tijerina continued giving incendiary speeches on campuses and with Corky Gonzales led a Chicano contingent during the 1968 Poor People's March. There he sought to meet with Secretary of State Dean Rusk to press the land issue. He and his group also attempted more citizen's arrests on the likes of Supreme Court nominee Warren Burger and New Mexico governor David Cargo.

Tijerina was finally tried and sentenced to two years on the assault charges—but was paroled after a year in prison on condition that he not act as an Alianza officer. The government strategy ultimately worked at blunting Tijerina's edge, but not before he had raised consciousness on the issue across the country.

"What Is My Real Crime?"

"What is my real crime? As I and the poor people see it, especially the Indo-Hispanos, my only crime is UPHOLDING OUR RIGHTS AS PROTECTED BY THE TREATY OF GUADALUPE HIDALGO . . . [and] demanding the respect and protection of our property, which has been confiscated illegally by the federal government. . . .

"Because I know WE ARE RIGHT, I have no regrets as I sit in my jail cell. I feel very, very proud and happy to be in jail for the reason that I am. . . . While others are free, building their personal empires, I am in jail for defending and fighting for the rights of my people. Only my Indo-Hispano people have influenced me to be what I am. I am what I am, for my brothers."

—LETTER FROM REIES LÓPEZ TIJERINA FROM THE
SANTA FE JAIL, AUGUST 1969

The Brown Berets represented yet one more manifestation of Chicano radicalism. Composed principally of barrio youths in cities across the Southwest, the Brown Berets were a self-styled paramilitary organization modeled loosely on the African American Black Panthers. Like the Black Panthers, their stated intention was to defend the community from police brutality—by force if necessary.

They were established in East Los Angeles as a community service club called the Young Citizens for Community Action and first attracted public attention during the Los Angeles 1968 school walkout. Although involved in the protest in only a limited fashion, their belligerent front made the Brown Berets targets for official harrassment. Of the 13 figures arrested during the walkout, seven were Brown Berets. In the years afterward, the Brown Berets grew more radical, demanding food, housing, jobs, and education for barrio residents. But they never became more than marginal players in the Chicano movement—the result to some degree of constant police infiltration and their own failure to produce a charismatic central leader.

Although a widespread movement never took hold in the Puerto Rican community—just as one never took hold among the North's African American community—frustration and resentment did at times boil over. In 1966, Puerto Ricans took part in riots that tore through Chicago. In the wake of this emerged the Puerto Ricans' own answer to the Brown Berets: the Young Lords. An established street gang before the riots, the Young Lords in 1967 reorganized themselves as the Young Lords Organization under the leadership of José "Cha Cha" Jiménez.

Addressing each other as *compañeras revolucionarias* (revolutionary comrades) and advocating "power to the people," the Young Lords conducted sit-ins and boycotts and organized strikes at service agencies and churches in an effort to coax the government and private institutions to start serving their communities better. A Young Lords chapter soon opened in New York, where in 1970 the members took over a rundown hospital in a Puerto Rican neighborhood, demanding better health care. Although their successes were few, they did accomplish part of what they had set out to do: instill a sense of pride in their people.

END OF AN ERA

By the early 1970s, the various Latino civil rights organizations could point to some impressive victories for all their efforts: improved conditions for Mexican American migrant farmworkers; increased Latino presence — in terms both of teachers and curricula — in the classrooms; the 1968 Bilingual Education Act (which provided federal aid for public schools to teach immigrants in their native language); the establishment in 1969 of a cabinet-level Committee on Opportunities for Spanish-Speaking People; improved public services in some Hispanic neighborhoods; and a general heightening of ethnic pride. These gains came on top of the end of legal segregation, the promise of more open voting, and the repudiation of housing and employment discrimination enshrined in the civil rights legislation years earlier — as well as the soon-to-be widespread affirmative action programs in jobs and school admissions.

But the Latino civil rights movement was running into the same dilemma as the African American movement. Now that some of the more straightforward issues had been addressed, stubborn problems of urban poverty — the source of so much Latino suffering — and other residual effects of the decades of discrimination remained. At this juncture, *el movimiento* fractured as leaders and rank-and-file alike bickered over which direction to take.

In 1970, Corky Gonzales organized the Colorado branch of La Raza Unida Party (LRUP), an independent Chicano political party, first begun by José Ángel Gutiérrez and other activists in Texas earlier that same year. Gonzales's insistence at the party's first convention two years later in El Paso that the LRUP press a radical agenda outside the two-party system, however, failed to win many hearts. A more moderate view, voiced by the much mellowed Gutiérrez, argued successfully for cooperation with the existing system. For his part, he had actually won election as an LRUP candidate to the Crystal City (Texas) School Board. The squabble in effect was the beginning of the end of Gonzales's career as a national activist; the following year, his Crusade for Justice all but evaporated after a clash with Denver police that saw one person killed, others shot, several arrested, and many members grow disenchanted with the organization. The embrace of Gutiérrez's position was really an acknowledgment that activism had reached its limits. (Indeed, the LRUP would be pretty much rendered obsolete in the next few years, as Hispanic candidates took their place in the Democratic and Republican parties.) Even Chávez's UFW, although by 1973 affiliated with the powerful AFL-CIO, grew increasingly weak in the face of a flood of undocumented workers, conflicts with the California Teamsters, automation, and the urbanization of Mexican Americans.

Radicalism, too, was marginalizing the movement. Otherwise sympathetic Anglos and even established Latinos had become alienated by the more aggressive tactics and extreme demands of some elements of the movement. Their apprehension was only heightened when a 1970 anti-Vietnam rally of 20,000 to 30,000 Chicanos in Los Angeles turned into a melee with 1,200 police officers; three people died (including popular Latino *Los Angeles Times* reporter Rubén Salazar), 60 were wounded, and more than 200 were arrested. The violence in Los Angeles, as well as destructive demonstrations in East Los Angeles and Albuquerque that same year, unsettled many both inside and outside the Hispanic community. It also convinced a nation already rattled by the upheaval of the 1960s and early 1970s to once and for all move the priorities of Latinos and other minorities to the back burner—and brought an end to the organized Latino civil rights movement.

THE NEW AGE

The struggle for rights did not end with the mass movement. But it did shift to a new arena—or, rather, back to an old one. For decades before the civil rights movement, Latinos had looked to the courts and, to some degree, the government to secure what justice they could. But if the satisfaction they found in those bodies had been minimal then, circumstances now were vastly changed for the better.

The 1965 Voting Rights Act had had a revolutionary impact on the African American community. In guaranteeing access to the ballot in the South, it had resulted in soaring numbers of black registered voters and the consequent election of more black officials than at any time since the post–Civil War Reconstruction era. The significance of this change was very clear to Hispanics, who had themselves been systematically discriminated against in voting — through the same devices that stymied blacks, such as poll taxes and literacy tests. The standard practice of providing English-only ballots also served to disenfranchise many Hispanics. But if the Voting Rights Act was to be made to work for Latinos, it required some judicial and legislative fine-tuning.

The leading force in this drive was the Mexican American Legal Defense and Education Fund (MALDEF), established in 1968 with the mission of using the legal and political systems to ensure protection of Hispanic rights. Its president during the crucial years of 1973 to 1982 was Mexican American attorney and rights leader Vilma Martínez (see page 314). Also joining in MALDEF's campaign to open the vote was the Puerto Rican Legal Defense and Education Fund (PRLDEF), established in 1972 with a similar agenda.

The original Voting Rights Act had offered a range of federal ballot access guarantees specifically to areas with large black populations whose representation in Congress appeared not to reflect the region's racial makeup. Almost immediately after its founding, MALDEF began gathering evidence to demonstrate that Hispanics in Texas were also being systematically denied ballot access and proper congressional representation, and demanded that they receive the same protections. In 1975, Congress responded to MALDEF's efforts and amended the act to apply to areas with large Latino populations.

MALDEF won more such victories in the following years. Encouraged by an early 1970s court ruling that English-only ballots in New York had discriminated against Puerto Ricans, MALDEF pushed to make bilingual ballots available. In 1982, new amendments to the Voting Rights Act extended it to include such provisions. (The ballots were made even more accessible by the 1992 Voter Assistance Act.)

But the 1982 amendments were notable for even more significant changes. For the first time, the law took notice of the fact that congressional districts seemed to have been drawn by state legislatures specifically to divide minority communities and thereby prevent minority officials from winning office. Reacting to a series of court rulings that supported this claim, the amendments required that election districts be designed to make sure minorities were winning adequate representation. The result was a major series of often stormy redistrictings, as state legislatures carved out districts that were almost certain to create Latino and African American seats in Congress.

Latinos encountered similar devices to prevent the election of minorities at the state and local levels: not only questionably drawn districts but also at-large and multimember districts designed to dilute minority voting strength. Locality by locality, Latinos, often in alliance with African Americans, challenged these devices and won and the results affected bodies as diverse as state senates and school boards, the Los Angeles County Board of Supervisors and the Dade County (Florida) Metropolitan Commission.

The rise in accessibility of the political system has gone hand in hand with aggressive efforts to get Latinos to *use* the political system—both as candidates and as voters. The lead in raising Latino political consciousness was taken by established groups such as the Mexican American Political Association (MAPA) and the Texas-based Political Association of Spanish-Speaking Organizations (PASSO), established in 1961. Both groups sought to encourage and support Latino candidates for office. The brief flourishing of La Raza Unida Party in the early 1970s convinced many Hispanics to register. Other groups have worked aggressively to expand the number of Latino voters. The massive Southwest Voter Registration Project, aimed at Mexican Americans; the Spanish American League Against Discrimination (SALAD), aimed at Cubans; the Community Development Project, established in 1965 and aimed at Puerto Ricans; the National Association of Latino Elected and Appointed Officials (NALEO); and the influential National Council of La Raza (NCLR) all have participated in this mission: increasing registration, raising political awareness, and encouraging noncitizens to become citizens and get in the game.

To be sure, increased political involvement has not been the only focal point for ongoing action. MALDEF, PRLDEF, LULAC, NCLR, SALAD, and a host of other local and national organizations have taken aim at other forms of discrimination, as well as social and economic problems facing Latinos. In a 1970 school discrimination case, *Corpus Christi Independent School District* v. *Cisneros,* LULAC for the first time led the federal courts to acknowledge that Mexican Americans were in fact "an identifiable ethnic minority with a past pattern of discrimination"; this acknowledgment would give them legal standing to demand the same special protections granted to African Americans in schools, voting, employment, and other areas. Education-related victories followed: In 1974, Latinos won crucial amendments to the Bilingual Education Act, including a provision for the encouragement of cultural education. And in the following years, bilingual education was mandated in close to 500 school districts and expanded in many others.

■ ■ ■

Notable Latinos in Government

The considerable voting strength of Latinos has been reflected in recent years in the election of numerous Hispanics at the national, state, and local levels as well as the appointment of many others to cabinet posts and other federal positions. Although there has been no Hispanic U.S. senator since the defeat of New Mexico's Joseph M. Montoya in 1976, Congress currently has 18 Latino members, from Arizona (1), California (4), Florida (2), Illinois (1), New Jersey (1), New Mexico (1), New York (2), Texas (5), and Puerto Rico (1).

President Clinton brought two Latinos into his cabinet, as did President Bush before him. Florida, Arizona, and New Mexico have all recently had Hispanic governors and Miami, Denver, San Antonio, El Paso, and even Hamilton, Ohio, have recently had Hispanic mayors. The Latino members of state assemblies and senates, county and city councils, and school boards are too numerous to mention. Among the many notable political figures of the last 25 years:

TONEY ANAYA
Democratic governor of New Mexico from 1982 to 1986.

JERRY APODACA
Democratic governor of New Mexico from 1974 to 1978, and the first Hispanic in the post since Octaviano A. Larrazolo left office in 1920.

HERMAN BADILLO
Democratic member of Congress from New York from 1971 to 1978, and the first mainland Puerto Rican in Congress (see also page 306).

ROMANA ACOSTA BAÑUELOS
Treasurer of the United States from 1971 to 1974 and the first Mexican American in the post.

JOSÉ A. CABRANÉS
Federal appeals court judge for the second circuit since 1994, and before that a federal district court judge (eventually Chief

Judge) in Connecticut—the first Puerto Rican to hold a federal judgeship on the mainland.

RAÚL HÉCTOR CASTRO
Democratic governor of Arizona from 1974 to 1977, and later the U.S. ambassador to Argentina.

LAURO F. CAVAZOS
Secretary of education from 1988 to 1990, and the first Mexican American (and first Hispanic) in the cabinet.

HENRY CISNEROS
Secretary of housing and urban development since 1993, and before that the first Mexican American mayor of San Antonio in modern times (1981–89).

LINCOLN DÍAZ-BALART
Republican member of Congress from Florida since 1993, and the first Cuban American (and first Hispanic) to sit on the House Rules Committee (1995–).

HENRY GONZÁLEZ
Democratic member of Congress from Texas since 1962—the first Mexican American (and first Hispanic) representative from Texas—and before that the first Hispanic in the Texas Senate in 110 years (1956–61).

EDWARD HIDALGO
Secretary of the navy from 1979 to 1981, and the first Mexican American (and first Hispanic) in the post.

MANUEL LUJÁN
Secretary of the interior from 1989 to 1993, and before that a Republican member of Congress from New Mexico (1969–89).

ROBERT MARTÍNEZ

Republican governor of Florida from 1989 to 1991—the first Hispanic governor of Florida (under the U.S. flag)—and later director of the Office of National Drug Control Policy, aka "drug czar" (1991–93).

GLORIA MOLINA

Democratic member of the Los Angeles County Board of Supervisors since 1991, and before that a member of the California State Assembly (1982–87) and of the Los Angeles City Council (1987–91)—in all three cases the first Mexican American (and first Hispanic) ever elected to those bodies.

JOSEPH M. MONTOYA

Democratic U.S. senator from New Mexico from 1965 to 1977, and before that a member of Congress (1957–65).

ANTONIA C. NOVELLO

U.S. Surgeon General from 1990 to 1993—the first Puerto Rican (and first Hispanic), as well as first woman, in the post.

FEDERICO PEÑA

Secretary of transportation since 1993, and before that mayor of Denver (1983–91).

LUCILLE ROYBAL-ALLARD

Democratic member of Congress from California since 1993, and the first Mexican American woman in Congress (and daughter of former congressman Edward R. Roybal).

ILEANA ROS-LEHTINEN

Republican member of Congress from Florida since 1989, and the first Hispanic woman and first Cuban American in Congress.

NYDIA VELÁZQUEZ
Democratic member of Congress from New York since 1993, and before that a member of the New York City Council—in both cases the first Puerto Rican woman ever elected to those bodies.

THE CUBAN MIRACLE

CASTRO'S REVOLUTION

Along with the Mexican American civil rights movement, one of the most remarkable phenomena of the past four decades of Latino history has been the rise of the Cubans in America. From a total of about 40,000 Cuban Americans in 1959, the community has grown to more than 1.1 million today, a full 5 percent of all Latinos. More significant than their size, however, has been the Cubans' great success. That success has been economic, of course. But the Cubans have also succeeded at building a community that is largely self-sufficient, politically powerful, and culturally influential. Their success has been called "the Cuban miracle."

The immediate impetus for the dramatic increase in the Cuban American population—and indeed for its success as well—was Fidel Castro's overthrow of Cuban dictator Fulgencio Batista in 1959. As head of the Cuban army then legitimate president of the nation, Batista had been Cuba's dominant political figure in the prosperous decade leading up to 1944, before stepping aside in accordance with his own liberal, democratic 1940 constitution. Batista's next legal opportunity to run for the presidency came in 1952; but when he saw he might well lose, he tossed aside the constitution and reestablished a complete dictatorship—and in so doing quickly lost the high regard in which he had long been held. Only a year later, Castro, a lawyer and former major-league baseball prospect, launched a rebellion against the government with a July attack on an army barracks. Although soon captured and imprisoned, Castro, along with his brother Raúl and Ernesto "Che" Guevara, renewed the movement upon his release in 1955, decamping to Cuba from his base in Mexico and waging a campaign of guerilla warfare from hideouts in the Sierra Maestra. Batista's brutal attempts at suppression—combined with ongoing widespread disapproval of his generally corrupt and autocratic ways— soon won Castro and his movement considerable support, not only among the Cuban masses but among the professonal and middle classes, and even many of the rich.

But shortly after Batista fled the island in 1959, leaving Castro to fill the power vacuum, the new leader disappointed many of his followers. He quickly dispensed of his promise of free elections and established a Soviet-style dictatorship. The opposition was silenced through government control of all media, and often by firing squads and prison. Foreign and domestic property of all kinds was nationalized, and the middle and upper classes lost their property; bank accounts, homes, furniture, and other assets were confiscated. Castro's destruction of Cuba's economic base soon resulted in serious food and consumer goods shortages.

Castro's establishment of close ties with the communist leaders of the Soviet Union only slightly compensated for the crumbling economy. Moscow began to provide billions of dollars in subsidies to the island. But in return, Cuban youngsters found themselves fighting as Soviet proxies in remote battlefields in places such as Ethiopia, Somalia, and Angola; thousands of Cubans shed their blood advancing the cause of worldwide communism. The ties with the Soviet Union also earned Cuba the hostility of its powerful northern neighbor, the United States—a hostility that has made itself felt in decades of attempted overthrows, assassination plots, showdowns, and blockades.

Almost from the beginning, then, great numbers of Cubans began looking for the opportunity to escape Castro's rule, and, not surprisingly, they generally turned to the United States, where

Cubans had long before established a beachhead in southern Florida. Targeted by the communist regime, the middle and upper classes—using what they could salvage of their resources—made up the bulk of the first wave of post-Castro Cuban immigration. From Castro's takeover until his suspension of flights to the United States in 1962 (during the Cuban Missile Crisis, one of many U.S.-Cuban confrontations during the decade), nearly 250,000 Cubans entered the United States. Most stayed in and around the Miami area, founding the neighborhood known as Little Havana.

The second wave of immigration began in September 1965 when Castro used it as a safety valve for internal problems and announced that Cubans in the United States could pick up friends and relatives in the port of Camarioca. That year the U.S. government granted refugee status to Cuban émigrés, enhancing their ability to enter and settle in the country. Nearly 5,000 Cubans came in the Camarioca boatlift until the U.S. and Cuban governments negotiated an orderly immigration agreement. In the years leading up to April 1973, Cuban "freedom flights" between Varadero, Cuba, and Miami brought almost 300,000 Cubans to U.S. shores. By 1971, there were half a million Cubans in America, mostly in Florida but also in Los Angeles, New York, New Jersey, and Chicago.

MIRACLE MAKING

This first and, to an only slightly lesser degree, second wave of immigrants formed the core of the Cuban miracle. Though the Cubans who arrived in the late 1950s and early 1960s had been stripped of all their property, they came as a virtual Noah's Ark— complete communities of professionals and clients, businesspeople and customers, employers and employees. And the welcome America gave them could hardly have been warmer. To underline its opposition to communism in an increasingly polarized world, and to further needle the Cuban regime, the U.S. government offered considerable aid to Castro's exiles: Financial support, educational loans, and other transitional services, provided through offices such as the Cuban Refugee Center, ensured that the refugees would transplant well.

Cubans also brought a strong entrepreneurial spirit along with their skills. Cubans with access to capital were willing to lend money to other Cubans based on little more than reputation—so-called character loans, an unheard-of practice in major U.S. cities. Cuban businesspeople were comfortable in Miami, a city that had been part of the Cuban commercial orbit for centuries. And English-language skills, as well as other education, were high among the Cuban newcomers. Needless to say, the relative freedom from racial discrimination (Afro-Cubans excepted) to which they had long been accustomed also made success in their new home that much more possible.

Finally, the Cubans were motivated to succeed not just for the usual reasons but as a reply to Castro, who characterized the early emigrants as "worms" and "parasites." Their wealth, plus their political power and influence throughout the areas they inhabit, well known among the Cuban populace, was and is a shining reproof to the struggling socialist regime across the water.

The Cubans built such a strong community in southern Florida—an area lacking the kind of powerful Anglo establishment present in immigrant centers such as New York and Los Angeles—that, rather than being subject to the pressures of assimilation, they have caused what has been called acculturation in reverse. They have spread their language, culture, and institutions throughout the region. "English only" diehards have either left Miami or retreated to isolated pockets.

Los Polacos

One of the most curious aspects of the waves of Cuban immigration that followed Castro's rise was the presence among the newcomers of a sizable number of Jews.

Jews had actually lived in Cuba since the earliest days of Spanish settlement, having been officially expelled from Spain itself in 1492—the year that Columbus (who some claim was himself a secret Jew, or *marrano*) made his famous voyage to the New World. But no noteworthy quantity of outsiders joined this small Jewish community until after World War I, when Jews began fleeing Europe to escape the rising tide of nationalism and anti-Semitism. Cuba became one of their many destinations—particularly for the much beleaguered Polish Jews.

Even before Hitler's September 1939 invasion of Poland, which would lead to the murder of 3 million Polish Jews by 1945, fascist influence had made life in Poland virtually intolerable for Jews. For a time, Cuba, along with other Latin American countries such as Argentina, responded to U.S. pressure to open the door to Jewish refugees from Europe—a door that had been slammed shut by the United States itself. Thousands of Jews, mainly from Poland, sailed into the aptly named port of Havana (*La Habana,* meaning "haven"), during the 1930s. Regarded in Poland as strangers and a foreign element, the Jews were ironically known in Cuba as *polacos* (Poles). At their peak in the late 1930s, the Jews of Cuba numbered 16,500.

Most of the Cuban Jews lived in and around Havana. Their original intention was usually to emigrate as soon as possible to the United States where there were large and well-established Jewish communities. But many ended up loving what, as new arrivals from dismal, cold Eastern Europe, they could only have seen as a tropical paradise. Trading their dark woolen garb for traditional guayabera shirts and other accoutrements of Cuban life, the Jews became an important segment of the Cuban middle and merchant classes. Cuban Jewish life often perpetuated religious and cultural institutions left behind in Europe. The Cuban Jews' existence was by and large a satisfying one.

Castro's revolution changed all that. While overwhelmingly progressive and anti-Batista, the Jewish community in Cuba found Castro's turn toward the Soviet Union ominous. Well attuned to impending disaster, and feeling vulnerable again (if only for their bourgeois class identities), the Jews left Cuba en masse—ultimately leaving no more than a thousand behind.

As politically acceptable Cuban refugees, the Cuban Jews gained easy entry into the United States. Many joined Cuban enclaves in Florida, feeling more Cuban than Jewish. Others joined family members who survived the Holocaust, living in Jewish communities throughout the United States. With their uniquely Yiddish-accented Cuban Spanish, the Cuban Jews settled into the second exile of their lifetimes. Their families carry a legacy of hardship and sadness that all Latinos can appreciate but that is uniquely theirs.

◼ ◼ ◼

CUBA LIBRE

As much as economic success has been a defining characteristic of the Cuban American community, so, too, has vehement anti-Castro sentiment. This is hardly surprising. To many Cuban Americans, Castro is the man who effectively forced them into exile. In their eyes, he has led their country to economic ruin and established a totalitarian government that continues to oppress those friends and family members who have not been lucky enough to escape. Indeed, quite a few Cuban Americans themselves spent time in Cuban prisons or saw their family members imprisoned or worse. For many Cuban Americans, until Castro is gone—and the system he instituted replaced—there can be no question of returning or even visiting their former homeland.

Almost from the beginning, then, these exiles have done their part to bring an end to Castro's regime, and, especially at the height of the cold war, their desires have often dovetailed with those of the U.S. government, which had little use for a hostile nation 90 miles off American shores. On April 17, 1961, 1,400 CIA-trained Cuban fighters (the so-called Brigade 2506) stormed Playa Larga and Playa Girón, two beaches along the island's Bay of Pigs, in the hope of stirring a general revolt against Castro. Promised heavy U.S. air and naval support, however, failed to materialize; fearing a public outcry and the Soviet reaction, President John F. Kennedy had got cold feet. After three days of heavy fighting along the shoreline, Castro's 20,000-man military forced the invaders to surrender. (The 1,189 prisoners were ransomed to the United States on Christmas, 1962.)

Since then, although no further substantial attacks have been launched, Cuban Americans have continued actively to pursue their goals. They have engaged in propaganda warfare, transmitting anti-Castro radio broadcasts to the island and dropping leaflets. Cuban Americans were instrumental in persuading Congress to establish Radio Martí and TV Martí, which transmit the kind of uncensored news currently unavailable in Cuba. They have made daring airplane and boat rescues of those forbidden to leave. And they have pressed for a hard line in U.S. policy toward Cuba: increased sanctions, a tighter trade embargo, and aggressive denouncing of the Castro regime's human rights record, especially in international forums. Indeed, it is largely because of the Republican Party's adherence to these policies that the GOP has won the lion's share of Cuban American support. As its economic and political muscle has increased, the Cuban American community has become a decisive voice in the shaping of U.S. policy toward Cuba, much to the dismay of the Castro government. Today, no political candidate who hopes to win Florida can afford to ignore them.

To be sure, not all Cuban Americans take a hard line on Cuba; some push instead for "constructive engagement" with the Castro regime, arguing that contact with the United States will lead Cuba to become a more open country. Indeed, in 1977, a small group of young Cuban Americans calling themselves the Antonio Maceo Brigade went to Cuba to do service work and try to open up a dialogue with the government. The group, however, took heavy criticism from others in the Cuban American community, and for the most part, the constructive engagement approach has been little welcome.

TROUBLED WATERS

The strength of the Cuban American community, and of the United States' longtime hospitality toward Cubans, was tested by a third wave of immigration beginning in 1980. When nearly 11,000 Cubans forced their way into the Peruvian embassy demanding asylum, Castro—needing another escape valve—angrily invited all Cubans who so desired to sail to the United States via the port of Mariel. Among the 125,000 Cubans who joined the Mariel boatlift in three months of that year were a special surprise gift from Castro: inmates of prisons and psychiatric hospitals whom Castro loosed on the United States. While most of these were subsequently reimprisoned and reinstitutionalized in the United States (Cuba has refused their repatriation), the presence of this mixed multitude, as well as a new group of working-class and black Cubans, was the cause of the first substantial backlash against previously welcome Cuban immigrants. Rioting by refugees in some U.S. internment camps only further soured Americans on their open-door policy.

The new attitude really started to make itself felt when—following the disintegration of the Soviet Union in 1989 and the end of Castro's huge annual bailout from the Soviets—a fourth wave of

Cuban immigrants began crashing on U.S. shores. A trickle of *bal-seros*, or rafters, who began crossing the Straits of Florida in 1990, grew into a torrent, encouraged by increasingly permissive noises about immigration from Castro. But now, with the cold war over, the United States no longer had use for Cuban immigrants, especially the impoverished newcomers.

Beginning in 1994, Cubans picked up by the U.S. Coast Guard in the straits were returned to the (still U.S.-controlled) naval base at Guantánamo, Cuba (see pages 122–123). Eventually, 30,000 detainees were being housed in a facility not built for the purpose, resulting in riots over the deplorable conditions. Finally, the United States and Cuba agreed in May 1995 that although the Cubans at Guantánamo would be permitted into the United States, new *bal-seros* would be returned to Cuba, bringing an end to a 36-year-old asylum policy. (The two countries did also agree to allow 20,000 Cubans to come legally to the United States each year.)

The policy change was met with widespread anger in South Florida, and sparked protests and civil disobedience—including a 10,000-person march in Miami and blockades of the city's critical expressways. But the policy remains in place: In January 1996, the last group of *balseros* was allowed in, and the refugee camps at Guantánamo were shut down.

What do Cuban Americans envision for the much anticipated post-Castro era? A generation ago, Cuban exiles sang a song called *"Cuando volveremos"*—"When We Return." But returning permanently is no longer the goal of the majority of Cuban Americans. They have built new lives, families, and enterprises in their American diaspora—still primarily in the "magic city" of Greater Miami, where 700,000 live. Despite their abiding concerns about their homeland—or the homeland of their parents—a solid majority, as indicated by surveys, do not intend to return to a free Cuba.

Living in the U.S.A.

Mexican America

Since 1960, the number of Mexican Americans has risen from about 4 million to at least 12 million (a full 64 percent of all Hispanics in the country) and most likely several million more if undocumented immigrants could be counted. Although some of this increase has been a function of the high Mexican American birthrate, the highest of all Latino groups, most of it can be credited to immigration. The reasons for all this immigration are simple: a consistently poor Mexican economy, in contrast with which the opportunities in the United States seem fantastic. Even though such opportunities do exist elsewhere, only the United States has a vast, porous border with Mexico.

But if business interests have welcomed the low-wage workers, Mexican immigration has met with considerable resistance from other quarters—especially U.S. workers (including even some Mexican Americans) who regard the immigrants as a threat to their own wages or jobs. However, widespread concerns that the mostly poor immigrants simply add to the ranks of the dependent population and overtax the country's already stretched social services, from schools to welfare to medical care, have also raised cries of alarm. And, of course, there's the matter of simple prejudice, which grows stronger as the presence of Latinos increases so visibly. All these factors have led to efforts to stem immigration that, though couched in more general terms, have clearly been targeted principally at Mexicans.

The 1930s had its repatriation drives, and the 1950s its federal Operation Wetback, which deported almost 4 million illegal Mexican immigrants even as the *bracero* program continued to thrive. But in 1968, the United States for the first time went beyond "cleanup" campaigns to introduce, through amendments to the 1952 Immigration and Nationality Act, a cap on Western Hemisphere immigration. While the law permitted foreigners to join any family members who were legal residents of the United States, it otherwise instituted a strict annual limit of 20,000 immigrants per country—unless, as in the case of Cuba, there were special considerations. (In 1990, the per-country limit was raised to 25,000.)

The main effect of the new restrictions has not been to stop the flood of Mexicans into the United States; immigration has continued apace, only now most of it is considered illegal. Instead of simply applying for entry, Mexicans have had to turn to more creative methods of getting into the United States. Some obtain "dailies," 72-hour permits to visit the country, and then once here just disappear into Mexican American communities. Others slip across the ill-protected border in broad daylight with no visa at all. Still others come in truckloads in the dead of night, seeking to avoid the often frustrated U.S. Border Patrol. Even if caught in the act, the immigrants are usually just sent back across, and then they simply try their luck again a few days later. So although the government has only documented a few hundred thousand entrants into the United States in the last few decades, the true but unofficial figures have been in the millions.

Recognizing the general inefficiency of existing laws, Congress in 1986 tried again with the Immigration Reform and Control Act. It granted amnesty to those potentially many millions who could prove they had been in the country since before 1982. At the same time, in an effort to undermine the relationship of convenience between illegal Mexican immigrants and many businesses, it imposed new penalties for those who hired undocumented workers. Again, the law had only a marginal effect on immigration. For many businesses and even individuals seeking cheap domestic help, it remained a worthwhile, and miniscule, risk to hire illegals—and they kept right on coming. Meanwhile, quite a few Mexicans who otherwise would have qualified for amnesty couldn't prove residency. And many legal Mexican residents ended up being denied jobs despite their lawful status, turned away by nervous businesses that simply "didn't want any trouble."

Nuyo- and Other Ricans

Although the success of Operation Bootstrap and its ongoing effects considerably slowed the pace of Puerto Rican migration to the United States mainland by the beginning of the 1960s, it did not put an end to it completely. The attraction of economic opportunities on the mainland was just too great for many to resist. Furthermore, even some of the island's efficient new industries actually put more people out of work than they employed. And because Puerto Ricans are U.S. citizens, no immigration laws apply; they are free to move anywhere in the country they wish.

Added to a birthrate second to Mexican Americans among Latinos, the resulting migration (especially the influx following an economic downturn on the island in the 1980s) has brought about a rise in the mainland Puerto Rican population from 900,000 in 1960 to 1.5 million in 1970 to 2.5 million (or slightly more than 10 percent of all mainland Latinos) today. Puerto Ricans have spread throughout the country—to New Jersey, Connecticut, Michigan, and Illinois, the last with a Puerto Rican population of 125,000. But by far the great preponderance of Puerto Ricans remain in New York City, the home of around one million. Concentrated largely in the neighborhood known as Spanish Harlem, where they have built a politically and culturally active community, New York's Puerto Ricans have taken to calling themselves "Nuyoricans" to reflect their dual national identity.

Although now under U.S. rule for almost a century, Puerto Rico itself retains its distinct cultural identity. The steadily rising population of just under 4 million still speaks Spanish almost universally; only a small minority speaks English fluently. (Both Spanish and English are the island's official languages.) This in itself has been a barrier to the infiltration of U.S. culture. Still, Puerto Rico's unique commonwealth status has brought change to the island. Mainland investment in Puerto Rico has turned a formerly rural, agricultural economy into one based on manufacturing and tourism; the one-time rural population has little by little made its way to the island's larger cities or to New York. Although its per-capita income and employment figures are lower than those of any state in the union, Puerto Rico is the economic powerhouse of the Caribbean. And with considerable travel back and forth to the island by Puerto Rican mainlanders, it remains the cultural touchstone of the Nuyorican population.

■ ■ ■

Commonwealth, Statehood, or Independence?

Ever since Puerto Rico was made a commonwealth in 1951—indeed ever since the island was brought under the U.S. umbrella in 1898—the debate has continued over its status.

A vocal minority population of advocates of complete independence has never stopped making itself heard, insisting that the debilitating dependence on the United States is holding Puerto Rico back economically and culturally. In 1950, two so-called *independentistas* made headlines when they tried to assassinate President Harry Truman; in 1954, four *independentistas*, headed by Lolita Lebrón fired shots from the gallery of the House of Representatives and injured five congressmen. Another militant group, called the *macheteros* (machete-carriers), has engaged in sporadic terrorism, including a 1983 robbery of $1.7 million from a Connecticut armored-car company. For the most part, though, the advocacy is carried on more sedately by the Puerto Rican Independence Party (PIP).

A considerably more widely accepted alternative is statehood. Statehood would mean sending two senators and seven representatives to Congress, and would undoubtedly give more power to Latinos in the United States. But it would also mean an end to commonwealth status. Currently, mainland companies operating on the island are exempt from most federal taxation; if the exemption were to be repealed, as it would be with statehood, those companies would likely move their operations to Mexico or other third world countries.

In several critical referenda over the decades, a majority of Puerto Rican islanders have supported maintaining commonwealth status. In 1964, 61 percent voted for the commonwealth against 39 percent for statehood. (Independence was not a ballot option.) In a 1993 referendum, the results were a bit tighter: 48 percent voted for commonwealth status against 46 percent for statehood and 4 percent for independence. An opinion poll taken the same year among mainland Puerto Ricans showed 68 percent in favor of the commonwealth, 27 percent for statehood, and 4 percent for independence.

■ ■ ■

NEWER IMMIGRANTS

While the largest, and best-established, Latino groups in the United States are Mexicans, Puerto Ricans, and Cubans, other Hispanic populations—hailing from the Caribbean islands, Central and South America, and even Spain—have made their presence felt, some in a big way, in recent decades. Indeed, the population of "other Hispanics" has surged from 57,000 in 1950 to at least 1.4 million in 1985 to more than 3.5 million today, and as with Mexican Americans, this figure is no doubt low, since so many undocumented immigrants go uncounted.

By far the largest "other Hispanic" group in the United States comes from the Dominican Republic (which shares the island of Hispaniola with Haiti). In 1993, there were more than 800,000 Dominicans in the New York City area alone; few doubt that the number is now near a million. Although some have settled in New Jersey, Florida, and Puerto Rico, the largest concentration of

Dominicans is in Manhattan's Washington Heights—known to Dominicans as Quisqueya, the name given by the Taíno Indians to Hispaniola.

The Dominican exodus began after the fall of the dictator Rafael Trujillo in 1961. Four years later, the Organization of American States authorized the introduction of U.S. and Latin American troops to the Dominican Republic to avert a Communist takeover. The political turmoil and poverty were spurs to large-scale immigration, legal and otherwise, to the United States.

Each year thousands of Dominicans risk their lives crossing the 80-mile channel known as the Mona Passage between their Hispaniola and Puerto Rico. Small boats carrying thousands have capsized in the strait, drowning innumerable Dominicans. But the trip is worth it for those who survive, estimated at 20,000 a year. Once on Puerto Rican soil, they are in the United States, free to travel— even by air—to any other point in the country without showing a passport. On top of the 20,000 undocumented Dominicans estimated to settle here each year, an additional 20,000 visas are granted to Dominicans seeking legal entry to the country.

As many as a third of the Dominican immigrants who are granted visas are college-educated or know a skilled trade. Skilled or otherwise, many Dominicans are blacks, making their reception in the United States all the more difficult. Most are poor, though there has been a smattering of small Dominican business growth on U.S. soil.

The unrest and civil strife in Central America have resulted in thousands of other immigrants flocking to the United States as well. In the 1970s and 1980s, the government war against the mountain guerrillas in Guatemala sparked the emigration of 150,000 Maya Indians and other Guatemalans to Mexico and the United States (mostly Florida and California). Following the overthrow of Nicaraguan dictator Anastasio Somoza Debayle in 1979, a vicious civil war raged between the Cuba- and Soviet-backed Sandinista government and the U.S.-backed Contras.

The decade-long war, during which countless civilians were

murdered by death squads of one side or the other for giving real or suspected sympathy or aid to the "wrong" side, led tens of thousands of Nicaraguans to emigrate. Because the émigrés were, like the Cubans, fleeing a communist government, it was U.S. policy to be generous in granting refugee visas; many came without permission as well. Even since the end of the war in 1990 and the establishment of a democratically elected government, miserable economic conditions have kept refugees flowing north, despite the fact that—also like the Cubans—they are no longer valuable political trophies. They have established themselves primarily in South Florida, home to some 100,000 Nicaraguans. The town of Sweetwater in the Greater Miami area has earned the name Little Managua (for Nicaragua's capital).

A similar situation resulted in a large emigration from El Salvador, where a U.S.-backed military government fought a bitter civil war against Cuba- and Soviet-backed guerrillas. Tens of thousands of civilians were killed by death squads through the 1970s and 1980s, resulting in substantial immigration to the United States. (These immigrants did *not* have political cachet for the U.S. authorities, and so were not given refugee status.) By 1990, more than half a million Salvadorans lived in Los Angeles, home to numerous Guatemalans and Nicaraguans as well. Thus Los Angeles came to be known as the Central American capital of the United States.

Latino Moneymakers

As Latinos have become more and more welcome at every level of the U.S. economy, quite a few individuals have emerged as powerhouses. There are some 20 Mexican Americans, at least five Puerto Ricans, and a remarkable 23 Cuban Americans with a net worth of $25 million or more—as well as eight from Spain and one each from Chile, the Dominican

Republic, and Ecuador. Among the most noteworthy business figures (families included) are:

JOSEPH A. UNANUE
Owner of Goya Foods, and the country's wealthiest Puerto Rican (and wealthiest Hispanic), with a net worth of $340 million.

JOHN ARRILLAGA
Commercial real estate developer in San Francisco, and the wealthiest Spanish American ($330 million).

ROBERTO GOIZUETA
Chairman of the board of Coca-Cola, and the wealthiest Cuban American ($300 million).

AMIGO AND MAX SORIANO
Founders of Western Pioneer Shipping and Delta Western fuel distributors ($95 million).

JORGE MAS CANOSA
Head of publicly traded Mas Tec Company, which lays telephone cables ($65 million).

ANTONIO R. SÁNCHEZ
Head of International Bancshares Corporation and Sanchez-O'Brien Oil and Gas Company, and the wealthiest Mexican American ($55 million).

CARLOS Y. BENAVIDES
Owner of 120,000 acres in south Texas ($45 million).

IGNACIO E. LOZANO JR.
Former publisher of Los Angeles–based *La Opinión,* largest Spanish-language daily newspaper ($40 million).

LINDA AND ROBERT ALVARADO
Owners of Alvarado Construction of Denver and part owners of the Colorado Rockies baseball team.

GLORIA AND EMILIO ESTEFAN
Pop music stars ($40 million).

OSCAR DE LA RENTA
Fashion designer ($35 million).

BELIA BENAVIDES DE MUÑOZ
Owner of a 10,000-acre ranch in south Texas ($30 million).

GERALDO RIVERA
Television reporter and producer ($25 million).

■ ■ ■

LATINO RISING

It has been almost a century and a half since the first distinguishable population of Latinos found itself resident in the United States, a century and a half during which both Latinos and the United States have come a long way. From a tiny and oppressed minority, Latinos have become a sizable and influential segment of the American community. And the United States, in finally throwing open the doors of opportunity—not, of course, without a great deal of prompting—has brought itself more in line with its own basic ideals.

Rising numbers tell only part of the story, but an important part. At 27 million accounted for, and many millions more that the census has missed, Latinos today constitute 10 percent of the U.S. population, up from 15 million (6.4 percent) as recently as 1980. (California alone saw its Latino population jump by almost 70 percent, from 4.5 million to 7.6 million, in the 1980s.) Hispanics are a visible presence not just in California and the Southwest (where some 63 percent now live) but in Florida, New York, New Jersey, and Illinois (collectively, home to 26 percent of all Latinos) as well as many other places, in smaller quantities, across the country.

It is these numbers, coupled with the hard-won enhancement of Latino voting rights, that have turned a once disenfranchised community into vital power brokers. With Latino voting rates increasing at five times the rate of the general public, they have elected hundreds of Latino lawmakers at the national, state, and local levels, with California, Texas, Florida, New York, and New Mexico leading the way. The mere 20 or so Latino elected officials in 1950, which had increased to almost 3,200 by 1985, now stands at more than 4,600, including over 1,100 Latinas. The U.S. Congress boasts 18 Hispanics. In some states—such as Florida, which George Bush would not have won in 1992 without Cuban American support, and Colorado, which Mexican Americans have made a marginally Democratic state—Latinos' status as the swing vote has given them a particular importance. Now that candidates and legislatures can no longer afford to ignore the votes of Latinos, it is hardly surprising that more and more Latinos are being appointed to high offices, such as judgeships, ambassadorships, and cabinet posts. Clearly, Latinos have won their place at the political table.

But the influence of the Latino community is more than political. The growth of the Hispanic population has also dovetailed with widening economic opportunities, and the result has been both an expanding middle class and an overall increase in buying power. Indeed, Latino buying power has almost tripled in the past 25 years to more than $200 billion. (By the end of the century, it is expected to hit $300 billion.) These dollars help sustain the now considerable stable of Hispanic businesses, which today number well over 600,000, employ hundreds of thousands of people, and pull in annual revenues close to $30 billion. The increasingly broad financial base of the Latino community has also caught the eye of mainstream producers, whose marketing savvy has been turned to winning over these potential consumers.

The strength of the Latino community is evident in less measurable ways, too. It takes no more than a quick glance over the nation's cultural and professional landscape to become aware of the high profile of Hispanics. In movies and on television, in bookstores and in music shops, on playing fields and in sports arenas, in laboratories and in boardrooms, Latino names are now almost as common as those of any of the more established ethnic groups. In a more anonymous if no less substantive manner, the rich Hispanic cultural heritage has left its stamp on everything from the food Americans eat to the language they speak. Meanwhile, the great bulk of Latinos live their lives as most Americans do: raising families, holding jobs, and making their contributions, big and small, to the country's well-being.

The picture is not, to be sure, uniformly rosy. Latinos still contend with lingering prejudice and the legacy of long years of maltreatment. In income, employment, and education, Hispanics as a whole lag far behind the overall U.S. population. One-quarter to one-third of all Latinos live below the poverty line, and even those that do not often lack good housing, health care, and social services. Especially in the urban areas where 90 percent of Latinos now live, they suffer disproportionately from the many problems associated with economic and social alienation, such as drug use, crime, and juvenile delinquency. Although among (and, of course, within) the various Latino communities there is considerable disparity along these lines—with Cuban Americans the best off and Puerto Ricans the worst off—even the status of Cuban Americans is notably below that of the U.S. population as a whole.

There are still, then, important battles to be fought. But they are battles that Latinos can now enter with a strong and justifiable sense of confidence.

Chronology of Events

1849 At the California constitutional convention, a sixth of the delegates are of Mexican descent, and they ensure that Mexican Americans retain the right to vote.

1850 As part of the Compromise of 1850, California is admitted as a free state and Texas gives federal control to parts of present-day New Mexico, Oklahoma, Colorado, and Wyoming.

The Foreign Miners Tax Law is designed to keep Mexicans out of the California gold mines, and lynchings threaten even native Californios.

1851 The California Land Act facilitates the Anglo takeover of ranchos owned by Mexican Americans.

1853 The Gadsden Purchase is negotiated, letting the United States buy the southern areas of New Mexico and Arizona from Mexico.

1856 California stops translating its legislation into Spanish.

1857 In the Cart War in Texas, Anglo teamsters attack Mexican and Mexican American porters.

As a mestizo, Manuel Domínguez, a former delegate to the California constitutional convention, is not allowed to testify against a white man in court.

1859 Juan "Cheno" Nepomuceno Cortina takes over Brownsville, kills several Anglos accused of brutality toward *tejanos,* and later escapes from federal troops into Mexico.

1861 The Civil War breaks out, lasting to 1865. About 10,000 Hispanics fight in the war, including David Glasgow Farragut and

Manuel Chaves on the Union side and Santos Benavides on the Confederate side. Texas joins the Confederacy.

1862 The Homestead Act accelerates the "land grab" of Mexican American property in the West.

1863 Arizona is separated as a territory from New Mexico.
The Emancipation Proclamation frees all slaves in the rebelling states.

1865 The 13th Amendment abolishes slavery in the United States.
President Abraham Lincoln is assassinated.

1866 Farragut, who captured New Orleans in 1862, becomes the first four-star admiral in the United States.

1867 The United States buys Alaska from the Russians.

1868 Inspired by exiled independence leader Dr. Ramón Emeterio Betances, Puerto Rican rebels issue their *Grito de Lares* and begin an uprising on the island, which the Spanish quickly crush.
In Cuba, Carlos Manuel de Céspedes issues a cry for Cuban independence *(Grito de Yara)*, leading to an unsuccessful 10-year war against the Spanish.
In the United States the 14th Amendment guarantees citizenship to anyone born in the United States and due process and equal protection under the laws to all residents.

1870 The 15th Amendment ensures that the right to vote shall not be denied because of color.

1873 Puerto Rico abolishes slavery.

1875 Lieutenant Governor Romualdo Pacheco takes over as the first Mexican American governor of California and later serves as a U.S. representative.

1876 The Southern Pacific Railroad arrives in Los Angeles, making it a predominantly Anglo town.

1877 In the El Paso Salt War, riots break out when Anglos try to charge *tejanos* for salt from a salt lake; federal troops arrive to restore order.

The Santa Fe Railroad opens.

In New Mexico, Juan José Herrera organizes *las Gorras Blancas* (the White Caps) to cut fences and keep Anglos from appropriating public lands.

1894 Civil War veteran Santos Benavides starts the *Alianza Hispano Americana* (Hispanic American Alliance) in Arizona.

1895 Led by José Martí, Cuban insurgents issue the *Grito de Baire* and rise up against the Spanish, who send some 200,000 troops and set up concentration camps. Martí dies at the Battle of Dos Ríos.

1897 Spain grants limited autonomy to Puerto Rico and Cuba, but the Cubans continue their revolt.

1898 Sent to Cuba to protect U.S. interests during the rebellion, the USS *Maine* is blown up, leading to the Spanish-American War. After 113 days, the Spanish surrender. As a result, Cuba gains independence (although U.S. forces remain) and the United States gains possession of Puerto Rico, the Philippines, Guam, and Wake.

1900 Under the Foraker Act, Puerto Ricans can elect the lower house of their legislature, but the upper house and the governor are appointed by the U.S. president.

1901 Gregorio Cortez becomes a folk hero in a fight for justice after he kills a Texas sheriff in self-defense.

The Platt Amendment to Cuba's constitution gives the United States the right to intervene in Cuban affairs.

1902 U.S. occupation forces leave Cuba, which elects its first president.

1910 In Mexico, Francisco Madero leads a revolt against Porfirio Díaz's dictatorial rule; Díaz resigns, and Madero becomes president in 1911 but is assassinated in 1913. The Mexican Revolution continues until 1920, with bands led by such rebels as Francisco "Pancho" Villa and Emiliano Zapata roaming the land. With the unrest in Mexico, there is a mass migration to the United States (1910–30).

Luis Muñoz Rivera becomes Puerto Rico's delegate to Congress, where he lobbies for reform of the Foraker Act.

1912 New Mexico and Arizona become states. New Mexico's constitution guarantees Mexican Americans the right to vote, run for office, serve on juries, and use Spanish in public documents.

1914 Backed by U.S. troops, Venustiano Carranza wrests power from the autocratic general Victoriano Huerta in Mexico.

World War I begins in Europe, lasting to 1918.

1916 Ezequiel Cabeza de Baca is the first Mexican American governor of the state of New Mexico but dies a few months after taking office and is succeeded by Octaviano A. Larrazolo.

1917 The Jones Act gives Puerto Ricans U.S. citizenship and the right to elect the upper house of their legislature but not the governor.

The United States enters World War I, and many Puerto Ricans and Mexican Americans serve in the U.S. forces.

Some provisions of the Immigration Act ease the way for Mexican workers, especially farm laborers, during World War I.

1920 The 19th Amendment is ratified, giving women the right to vote.
General Álvaro Obregón deposes Carranza and is elected president of Mexico.

1921 The first immigration quotas do not restrict Latinos.

1925 Congress sets up the U.S. Border Patrol.

1926 Anglos attack New York's Puerto Rican barrio.

1928 Octaviano A. Larrazolo of New Mexico is appointed the first Hispanic to serve in the U.S. Senate.

1929 The League of United Latin American Citizens (LULAC), a civil rights group, is founded in Texas.
The Great Depression begins.

1930s During the depression anti-immigrant sentiment leads to a mass deportation of not only Mexicans but also Mexican Americans who are U.S. citizens.

1933 President Franklin D. Roosevelt implements his New Deal.
Mexican American strawberry pickers unionize and hold a successful strike in El Monte, California.

1934 In Cuba, the Platt Amendment is revoked.

1936 Dennis Chávez of New Mexico is the first U.S.-born Hispanic elected to the U.S. Senate (Larrazolo was born in Mexico).
The Spanish Civil War erupts.

1938 Led by Emma Tenayuca and Luisa Moreno, pecan shellers hold a major strike in San Antonio.

Luis Muñoz Marín sets up the *Partido Popular Democrático* (Peoples' Democratic Party) in Puerto Rico, with the slogan "Bread, land, liberty."

1939 World War II breaks out in Europe.

1941 The United States enters World War II, and about 500,000 Latinos serve in the American forces before the war ends in 1945.

1942 In the Sleepy Lagoon murder in Los Angeles, 22 *pachucos* are charged, forced to stand trial in their zoot suits, and convicted; the verdicts are later overturned.

The United States and Mexico agree to the *bracero* program, bringing Mexican migrant farmers to the United States to help during the World War II manpower shortage; the program lasts until 1964.

1943 Anglos beat up *pachucos* in Los Angeles and other cities in the zoot suit riots.

1946 President Harry S. Truman appoints Jesús T. Piñero as Puerto Rico's first native-born governor.

1947 Puerto Ricans gain the right to elect their own governor.

The Community Service Organization (CSO) forms to back Edward R. Roybal for the Los Angeles City Council and goes on to fight discrimination in its many guises.

1948 Led by Héctor García, Mexican American war veterans start the GI Forum, a civil rights group.

In its first gubernatorial elections, Puerto Rico chooses Luis

Muñoz Marín, who initiates Operation Bootstrap, designed to industrialize and improve the island's economy.

1950 President Truman signs the Puerto Rican Constitution Act, allowing Puerto Ricans to write their own constitution.

Many Hispanics fight in the Korean War, and nine earn the Congressional Medal of Honor.

1952 Puerto Rico officially becomes a commonwealth.

1954 Operation Wetback, a federal program to send back illegal Mexican immigrants, is instituted.

The Supreme Court rules that segregation in public schools is unconstitutional.

1959 Eduardo Quevedo, Bert Corona, and Edward R. Roybal form the Mexican American Political Association (MAPA).

Fidel Castro overthrows Cuban dictator Fulgencio Batista; soon disappointment in his regime leads tens of thousands of Cubans to flee to the United States.

1961 CIA-trained Cuban fighters invade the Bay of Pigs in hopes of sparking a revolt against Castro but are forced to surrender.

Dominican dictator Rafael Trujillo is assassinated, and the ensuing turmoil increases immigration to the United States.

The Political Association of Spanish-Speaking Organizations (PASSO) is formed in Texas to support Latino political candidates.

Henry González, in a special election, is the first Mexican American from Texas elected to the U.S. House of Representatives.

1962 César Chávez starts the National Farm Workers Association (later the United Farm Workers, or UFW) to protect Mexican American migrant workers.

Joseph M. Montoya of New Mexico is the third Hispanic elected to the U.S. Senate.

President John F. Kennedy thwarts a Soviet plan to build atomic missile bases on Cuba, ending the Cuban Missile Crisis.

1963 Following Reies López Tijerina, the *Alianza Federal de Mercedes*, later to be called the *Alianza Federal de Pueblos Libres* (Federal Alliance of Free Towns), forms to reclaim Mexican American property illegally acquired by Anglos.

1964 Congress passes the Civil Rights Act, forbidding discrimination in public accommodations, education, and employment.

The Tonkin Gulf Resolution allows the president to take military action in Vietnam, and many Latinos fight and die in the Vietnam War before U.S. involvement ends in 1973.

Chicano rights activist Rodolfo "Corky" Gonzales issues a clarion call to Mexican Americans in his epic poem *Yo soy Joaquín/I Am Joaquín.*

José Ángel Gutiérrez organizes a protest group in Texas that will come to be called the Mexican American Youth Organization (MAYO); many similar student civil rights groups form at this time.

1965 Chávez begins a successful five-year strike against California grape growers, which expands into a national boycott.

Castro allows Cubans with U.S. relatives to leave, leading to the Camarioca boatlift and later the "freedom flights," which continue until 1973.

Congress passes the Voting Rights Act.

1966 Protesting barrio conditions, Puerto Rican youths riot in Chicago.

1967 Chicano youths start the militant Brown Berets in California. Puerto Rican youths in Chicago organize a similar group, the Young Lords, which soon spreads to New York.

1968 The Mexican American Legal Defense and Education Fund (MALDEF) is set up to fight for civil rights in the courts.

Mexican American high school students in Los Angeles walk out of schools to protest conditions; similar demonstrations spread to the Southwest.

An amendment to the Immigration and Nationality Act goes into effect, setting a cap on Western Hemisphere immigration.

Congress passes federal open-housing legislation.

1969 Corky Gonzales issues his *Plan Espiritual de Aztlán* (Spiritual Plan of Aztlán).

1970 José Ángel Gutiérrez starts La Raza Unida Party (LRUP) in Texas, which wins offices in Crystal City elections; Corky Gonzales organizes a Colorado branch of the party.

During an anti-Vietnam rally of Los Angeles Chicanos, TV reporter Rubén Salazar and two others are killed; violent demonstrations take place in East Los Angeles and Albuquerque.

1971 Herman Badillo of New York is the first mainland Puerto Rican representative in the U.S. House.

Romana Acosta Bañuelos is the first Mexican American treasurer of the United States.

1972 At the first national LRUP convention, participants back José Ángel Gutiérrez's stand favoring coexistence with the two-party system over Corky Gonzales's more radical alternative.

The Puerto Rican Legal Defense and Education Fund (PRLDEF) is formed.

1974 Strengthening the 1968 Bilingual Education Act, new amendments guarantee bilingual education in public schools.

Raúl Héctor Castro is the first Hispanic governor of the state of Arizona.

Jerry Apodaca is the first Hispanic governor of New Mexico in more than 50 years.

1975 An amendment to the 1965 Voting Rights Act provides greater access to ballots for Latinos.

1977 The Antonio Maceo Brigade does service work in Cuba, hoping to inaugurate a peaceful rapprochement between the United States and the Castro regime.

1979 José A. Cabranés is the first Puerto Rican federal judge on the mainland, as a district court judge in Connecticut.

Edward Hidalgo is the first Mexican American (and Hispanic) secretary of the navy.

Rebels overthrow Nicaraguan dictator Anastasio Somoza Debayle, but the ensuing civil war between the Sandinista government and the U.S.-backed Contras causes many Nicaraguans to flee to the United States. Also, civil unrest in El Salvador and Guatemala increases immigration from those countries to the United States.

1980 The Mariel boatlift brings 125,000 Cubans, including some convicts, to the United States.

1981 Henry Cisneros is the first Mexican American elected mayor of San Antonio in modern times.

1982 At the urging of MALDEF, the Voting Rights Act is amended to make bilingual ballots available and to ensure that district lines give Latinos adequate congressional representation.

Toney Anaya becomes governor of New Mexico.

Gloria Molina is the first Mexican American (and Hispanic) in the California State Assembly.

1986 The Immigration Reform and Control Act grants amnesty to "illegal" aliens who can prove they have been in the United States since before 1982.

Franklin Chang-Díaz is the first Latino in space.

1988 Appointed secretary of education by President Ronald Reagan, Lauro F. Cavazos is the first Hispanic in the cabinet.

1989 Manuel Luján is the first Hispanic secretary of the interior.

Robert Martínez is the first Hispanic governor of the state of Florida.

Ileana Ros-Lehtinen of Florida is the first Cuban American and first Hispanic woman in Congress.

1990 Appointed by President George Bush, Antonia C. Novello is the first woman and first Hispanic U.S. Surgeon General.

1991 Gloria Molina is the first Mexican American (and Hispanic) on the Los Angeles County Board of Supervisors.

1992 Puerto Rico's delegate to the U.S. House of Representatives is given a vote on the floor.

1993 President Bill Clinton's cabinet includes Henry Cisneros as secretary of housing and urban development and Federico Peña as secretary of transportation.

1993 Lucille Roybal-Allard of California is the first Mexican American woman and Nydia Velázquez of New York is the first Puerto Rican woman in Congress.

Ellen Ochoa is the first Latina in space.

Congress authorizes the North American Free Trade Agreement (NAFTA).

1994 Proposition 187, denying education and social services to all undocumented immigrants, is passed in a California referendum; skeptical courts immediately put a stay on the measure.

1995 Lincoln Díaz-Balart of Florida is the first Cuban American and Hispanic on the House Rules Committee.

The United States agrees to admit Cubans in refugee camps at Guantánamo naval base but stipulates it will return any new rafters, ending its 36-year-old asylum policy.

1996 The Cuban military shoots down two private planes piloted by members of the Florida-based anti-Castro Brothers to the Rescue. In response, the United States passes the Helms-Burton Law, tightening the embargo on Cuba.

II
culture

THERE IS NO WAY in which the United States can be said more to resemble the famous "melting pot" than with regard to its culture. From egg rolls to blues music to Saint Patrick's Day parades to "gesundheit," the many diverse ingredients that constitute mainstream American culture — a complicated and ever evolving notion, to be sure — are a true reflection of the country's mosaic of racial, ethnic, and religious groups. To this smorgasbord Latinos have contributed at least as much as any group. In the long centuries of their presence in this land, during which they have come to represent an increasing proportion of the country's population, Hispanics have had an enormous influence on what their fellow Americans eat, read, listen to, speak — on the very texture, in other words, of their lives.

But as with so many of the nation's ethnic groups, even as Latinos have been adding their ingredients to America's general cultural stew, they have also continued to cultivate and preserve an independent culture of their own. It is a rich and sophisticated culture with age-old roots, embraced by different Latinos to different degrees.

The Hispanic contributions to the American mainstream really represent but the points at which that abundant culture has overflowed. *Quinceañera* celebrations and *música norteña*, for example, may never cross over, but they remain vital elements of Latino cultural life.

Of course, it is somewhat misleading to speak of Latinos in general without acknowledging the great diversity behind that label. After all, in many respects, Cuban Americans, Mexican Americans, Puerto Rican mainlanders, Colombian Americans, and so on have distinct cultures—and their contributions to the mainstream culture have been accordingly distinct. They brought these distinct cultures from their home countries when they first arrived on American shores, and each new wave of arrivals has provided reinforcement. At the same time, however, the original culture of each community has been shaped and molded by its experience in the United States. In fact, the same American mainstream that Latinos have influenced has in turn influenced them. So, by and large, Mexican Americans are not simply Mexicans who happen to live in America; they have a homegrown Mexican American culture all their own that includes Mexican, American, and entirely original elements. The same can be said of the other national groups.

And yet, there is still a unifying factor that makes it possible to speak about "Latino culture," even if one does so with many caveats. Cuban Americans, Puerto Ricans, and the rest may each hail from unique cultures, but those cultures all share a heritage in Spanish language, religion, and custom. Each of these communities has also shared the experience of having lived as minorities in a very race-conscious United States. These common threads bind America's Hispanics together and account for a distinctive flavor that bridges the separate communities. These common threads have been reinforced by the considerable degree of interaction among the Hispanic groups; indeed, there has been so much cross-fertilization that many Latino contributions to the mainstream cannot even be traced to any one community.

Given all the complexities of Hispanic culture and the multifarious nature of its influence on the American mainstream, it would be impossible to do justice to the subject even in a volume many times the size of this one. The best that can be hoped for here is a sampling, enough to encourage an appreciation of the richness of Latino culture and for its enhancements of American life.

SPANISH ENGLISH

American English would be a different animal entirely if not for its considerable Latino influences. Since it was first spoken on American shores almost 400 years ago, English has incorporated hundreds of Spanish words—more by far than the words of any other language. For the most part, these words were brought into American English through contact with Hispanics in the New World. Many of these words actually had their origins in the New World as Spanish variations on Indian words. Others already existed in Spanish before the conquest but were especially applicable to life in the Americas. Still others were coined by the explorers, conquerors, and settlers who found the mother tongue did not entirely equip them to speak about what they experienced in the colonies.

When the English-speaking settlers by and by began interacting with their Latino counterparts in the Spanish and later Mexican territories, they encountered this convenient terminology and adopted much of it as their own. The process continued as those territories were absorbed into the United States, and was reinforced as wave after wave of newcomers arrived. The process continues to this day.

Besides the new people and places that the Spanish encountered in their early decades of exploration, they were confronted with a whole range of plants, animals, and native products and practices that were entirely unfamiliar to them. Having no words of their own to describe these phenomena, they looked for ideas to the original Taíno, Nahuatl, Quechua, and other Indian languages in the vast territories of Spain's American empire.

They directly borrowed the Indian names or converted them into Spanish equivalents, thereby coining the terms by which the English-speaking settlers later came to know these phenomena. Often the English speakers would in turn Anglicize the now Spanish words before incorporating them into their own language. (Of course, the English would also coin their own words based on independent encounters with Native Americans.) Just a small sampling:

- alpaca (Spanish, from Aymara *allpaqa*)
- avocado (from Spanish *aguacate*, from Nahuatl *ahuacatl*, meaning testicle, referring presumably to the shape of the fruit)
- barbecue (from Spanish *barbacoa*, from Taíno, meaning the practice of cooking on a raised bed of sticks)
- cannibal (from Spanish *caníbal*, from Taíno *caniba* and *carib*, and from Carib *galibi*, meaning strong man—also the origin of the word "Caribbean")
- canoe (from Spanish *canoa*, from Taíno and from Carib *canaoua*)
- cassava (from Spanish *cazabe*, from Taíno *caçábi*)
- chili (from Spanish *chile*, from Nahuatl *chilli*)
- chinchilla (Spanish, from Quechua *sinchi*, meaning strong— that is, for a little rodent)
- chocolate (Spanish, from Nahuatl *xocoatl*)
- cocaine (from Spanish *coca*, from Quechua *kúka* plant)
- condor (from Spanish *cóndor*, from Quechua *kúntur*)
- coyote (Spanish, from Nahuatl *coyotl*)
- hammock (from Spanish *hamaca*, from Taíno)
- hurricane (from Spanish *huracán*, from Taíno *hurakán*)
- jaguar (Spanish, from Guaraní *yaguara* and from Tupi *jaguara*)
- llama (Spanish, from Quechua)
- maize (from Spanish *maíz*, from Taíno *mahiz*)
- mescal (Spanish, from Nahuatl *mexcalli*)

- mesquite (Spanish, from Nahuatl *mizquitl*)
- peyote (Spanish, from Nahuatl *peyotl*)
- poncho (Spanish, from Araucanian *pontho*, meaning woolen fabric)
- potato (from Spanish *batata*, from Taíno)
- puma (Spanish, from Quechua)
- quinine (from Spanish *quina* and *quinaquina*, from Quechua)
- savanna (from Spanish *sabana*, from Taíno)
- tamale (from Spanish *tamales* and *tamal*, from Nahuatl *tamalli*)
- tapioca (Spanish, from Tupi *typyóca*)
- tobacco (from Spanish *tabaco*, from Taíno, meaning a roll of tobacco leaves used for smoking)
- tomato (from Spanish *tomate*, from Nahuatl *tomatl*)
- vicuna (from Spanish *vicuña*, from Quechua *wikúña*)

Still, the vast majority of Spanish-inflected words in American English from colonial days to the present are not derived from Indian languages. They come from the mother tongue itself—the lingua franca of most of the Americas north to Mexico and, until far into the nineteenth century, much of the present United States as well—or from one of the Spanish dialects that sprang up in the New World in the centuries after the conquest. Some of these words, like tortilla (little cake) and sassafras (from *sasafrás*), were themselves new coinages for New World phenomena. Others were time-tested Spanish words (or local variations on them) that Anglo Americans, when they eventually came across them, simply preferred to homegrown alternatives. Still others traveled via England but only came into common usage once they found their way to America. Today, many of these words have become so completely integrated into American English, they barely betray their Spanish origin. Among them are:

- adobe
- aficionado
- alligator (a bit of an understatement: from *el lagarto*, the lizard)

- cabana (*cabaña*, hut)
- cafeteria (*cafetería*, coffeehouse)
- cockroach (*cucaracha*)
- embarcadero
- incommunicado (*incomunicado*)
- junta
- loco
- machete
- macho
- marijuana (*mariguana, marihuana*)
- mesa (literally "table")
- mosquito (a diminutive of *mosca*, fly)
- patio
- plaza
- pronto
- tornado (*tronada*, thunderstorm)
- vamoose (*vamos*, let's go)
- vigilante (guard)

Next to the Latino culinary arena—whose vocabulary (burrito, taco, jalapeño, enchilada, quesadilla, tequila, paella, *huevos rancheros, arroz con pollo,* and so on) has entered American English as Mexican and other Hispanic foods have become part of the the edible mainstream—there is probably no greater individual source of common nouns from Spanish than the cowboy culture. The Spaniards made cowboys possible by bringing horses and cattle to Florida, California, and the Southwest. Spain and Mexico developed ranching on this continent, building large *ranchos* (ranches) in the Southwest; Hispanic *vaqueros* (cowboys)—giving rise to the word "buckaroos"—spread the vocabulary. Some of the words that galloped into English:

- bonanza (fair weather)
- bronco (wild)
- buffalo (from *búfalo*)

- burro
- calaboose (from *calabozo,* dungeon)
- lasso (from *lazo*)
- mustang (from *mestengo,* stray)
- pinto (spotted)
- rodeo (from *rodear,* to surround)
- stampede (from *estampida*)

Other Spanish words that have entered the American vernacular retain a distinct association with the language of their origin. They have nonetheless been used and understood in American English for generations. Among them are:

- adios
- amigo
- arroyo
- bodega
- conquistador
- fiesta
- hacienda
- hombre
- mañana
- padre
- playa
- señor, señorita, señora
- siesta
- sombrero

Among the truly hip, use of other, less common Spanish phrases, such as *¿que dice?* (What are you saying?) and *oye* (listen), are much in vogue. And at the heights of American culture, what could be more apple-pie than a muscle-bound Austrian saying, *"Hasta la vista,* baby!"?

■ ■ ■

On the Map

Probably the most obvious examples of the infiltration of Spanish into American English are geographical. As a glance at any good map of the United States will show, the long period of Spanish rule left its mark on hundreds of place-names that the English adopted with few changes, save for taking out the accent marks and sometimes shortening. Five, and perhaps six, of the state names are purely Spanish coinages:

- California, likely selected by explorer Fortún Jiménez, inspired by the name of a legendary island of griffins and gold, ruled by Amazon women, in the popular 1508 Spanish romantic novel *Las sergas de Esplandián* by Count Ordoñez de Montalvo
- Colorado, from the Colorado River, from a Spanish word for "red," presumably referring to the water's hue
- Florida, from *La Florida*, so named by Juan Ponce de León because he discovered it during *Pascua Florida* (Easter) and perhaps also because the land was indeed *florida*, or filled with flowers
- Montana, from *montaña*, meaning "mountain," for obvious reasons
- Nevada, from the bordering white-capped Sierra Nevada, Spanish for "snow-covered"
- Oregon, from *oreja*, meaning "ear," because the Spaniards thought the local natives had big ones (though in the spirit of full disclosure, it should be said that alternative explanations for this name do exist)

The names of three other states—like quite a few towns, mountains, bodies of water, and other natural phenomena—

are Spanish adaptations of Indian words: Arizona, a Spanish mutation of the Papago *Arizonac,* meaning "land of few springs"; New Mexico (from the Spanish *Nuevo México*), which, minus the "New," takes its name from the Nahuatl *mexihco;* and Texas, from the Spanish *Tejas,* which itself comes from *techas,* meaning "friends," with which the resident Hasinai Indians greeted the first Spaniards.

On a more local level, Spanish-derived place-names are everywhere, in every state of the union. California has about 400 (including 80 that are the names of saints), New Mexico and Texas have about 250 each, and Arizona has 100. Los Angeles, San Francisco, Las Vegas, Palo Alto, Sacramento, San Jose, Santa Fe, Santa Monica, El Paso, Monterey, San Antonio—these are just some of the more prominent such place-names scattered across the West. There are numerous ones in Florida, including the city of Saint Augustine (originally *San Agustín*) and four of the state's counties.

Even New England retains a few of the names given by Esteban Gómez when he sailed up the New England coast in 1525: Casco Bay (from *casco,* "helmet," likely alluding to the shape of the inlet), Madrid, East Peru, West Peru, Carmel, and Mexico in Maine, as well as Ayer (yesterday) in Massachusetts. And the largest single "place" on earth—the Pacific Ocean—was named *Océano Pacífico* by the Portuguese sailor Ferdinand Magellan, at the time circumnavigating the globe on behalf of the Spanish.

READING MATERIAL

Individual Hispanics have been writing as long as they have been in the New World. The earliest decades of settlement saw such classic works as Álvar Núñez Cabeza de Vaca's *La relación* (1542) (see page 14) and Gaspar Pérez de Villagrá's *Historia de la Nuevo México* (1610) (see pages 56–57). In later centuries, Hispanics in the United States (especially Mexican Americans) published a string of memoirs, poems, novels, and histories. Political unrest in the late nineteenth and early twentieth centuries brought many intellectuals from Cuba, Puerto Rico, and Mexico to the United States, where they wrote some of their best work. But Latino literature truly gained momentum in the middle of this century, when many writers consciously began to address the unique difficulties and pleasures of being Hispanic in a predominantly Anglo nation.

Since then, Latino writers have flourished, generating an extraordinary body of work—in Spanish, English, or a combination of the two—that constitutes a thoroughgoing and compelling account of the contemporary Hispanic experience. This work has won not only critical acclaim but also the ultimate compliment of wide, general readership. Today the work of Latino writers must be included in any serious reckoning of contemporary American literature. (Their work is to be distinguished from the widely read translations of such Latin American writers as Gabriel García Márquez, Carlos Fuentes, and Laura Esquivel. Yet this distinction is occasionally blurred, as in the case of writers such as the Chilean émigré Isabel Allende.)

Latino literature can best be appreciated by looking at it not as a single undifferentiated genre but rather as a collection of national subgenres. Each of the principal national groups (Mexican Americans, Puerto Ricans, Cuban Americans) has its own story to tell and preferred modes of expression. Yet although the literature of each national group has evolved independently, that development has not been without cross-fertilization. All good writers, after all, are readers of good writing, no less of good writing on "their" topic. Thus the authors of the respective national literatures have kept an eye on each other along the way. Of course, genre or subgenre notwithstanding, each writer also brings his or her own particular vision to bear; this is what ultimately gives the great works of Latino literature their value.

MEXICAN AMERICAN LITERATURE

The 1960s civil rights movement in the Southwest (see pages 147–157) ushered in a golden age in Mexican American literature; during this period Chicano literature found a clear and powerful voice, and took its place as a tool in the struggle for equality. The sterling example of this era is Rodolfo "Corky" Gonzales's epic poem *Yo soy Joaquín/I Am Joaquín*. Read at marches and dramatized at rallies, *Joaquín* was the literary clarion call to Chicanos, raising their consciousness and self-esteem and stirring them to action. A prevalent theme in this and other work of the time was the challenging of the long-held emphasis on assimilation into Anglo American society.

Many Chicano works were first disseminated in Spanish-language newspapers. But numerous literary journals, such as the influential *El Grito*, and small publishing houses, such as Quinto Sol, were founded in the late 1960s to provide other outlets for the groundswell of Chicano writing. An independent theater movement also came into being to provide forums for the new Chicano drama. Most celebrated was the *Teatro Campesino* (Farmworkers' Theater) founded by Luis Valdez, considered the father of Chicano theater; the Teatro performed political one-act pieces (*actos*) in community buildings, churches, and even open fields. Although many of these institutions no longer exist, the voices they articulated are now part of the nation's mainstream.

The confrontational tone of much civil rights–era literature has been moderated. But many of the themes remain the same: the cultural heritage of Mexican Americans, including the Aztec and Maya legacies; growing up in the barrio; the current struggles of everyday life; Mexican American *carnalismo*, or solidarity; protest and political action.

It would be impossible to give full due to the many works (and authors) of the past few decades of Mexican American literature. Where, for example, does one place John Rechy's best-selling *City of Night* (1963), an autobiographical novel with only a few references to the author's Mexican heritage, but a classic of gay literature that portrays the neon-lit culture of drag queens and hustlers? Inevitably any list of significant works has a degree of arbitrariness. But certainly the serious reader of Mexican American writing should be familiar with these works:

• *Pocho* (1959) by José Antonio Villareal (see page 335) is considered by many to be the first Chicano novel. It is the story of Richard Rubio, the son of fugitives from the Mexican Revolution, who grows up as an assimilated Mexican American (*pocho*) in depression-era California. The novel describes the painful experience of the family's adjustment to a new society and the conflict of the Mexican culture with that of the new country, as well as Rubio's struggle to become a writer.

• *Yo soy Joaquín /I Am Joaquín* (1964 English; 1967 bilingual edition), an epic poem by Rodolfo "Corky" Gonzales (see pages 313–314), is the most famous example of Chicano verse. It is an expression of pride in Mexican American culture, history, and heritage, what Gonzales calls "a mirror of our greatness and of our weakness." The official poem of the 1960s Chicano rights movement, it was ultimately made into a film by Luis Valdez.

• *. . . Y no se lo tragó la tierra (. . . And the Earth Did Not Swallow Him)* (1971, bilingual) by Tomás Rivera is a lyrical, poetic semiautobiographical novel about a nameless young southern Texas Chicano's struggle for identity. As the youth tries to recall the previous year, he reconstructs events and overheard conversations that portray the hardships of migrant farmworkers in the mid-1940s to mid-1950s. The book was made into a 1994 film.

• *Floricanto en Aztlán (Flower Song in Aztlán)* (1971, mixed

Spanish/English) by Alurista, aka Alberto Urista, is a collection of politically charged poems that celebrate the Indian heritage of Mexican Americans. "When *raza?*" urges Chicanos to act today and not *"mañana"* to claim their freedom; *"Mis ojos hinchados"* ("My Swollen Eyes") reflects on the pain of enjoying personal freedom while one's people remain oppressed. Throughout these poems Alurista combines Spanish and English in innovative ways, helping to initiate the bilingualism prevalent in much contemporary Latino poetry.

• *Tierra Amarilla: Cuentos de Nuevo México (Stories of New Mexico)* (1971, bilingual) by Sabine R. Ulibarrí is a collection of short stories that draws on the author's own boyhood experience in the New Mexico town of Tierra Amarilla. He records a world of vanishing customs and traditions threatened by the encroaching Anglo American culture.

• *Barrio Boy* (1971) by Ernesto Galarza traces the author's childhood journey with his family from a mountain village in Mexico to the streets of Sacramento. Staying at first within the familiar world of the barrio, where everybody speaks Spanish, the family eventually moves into a bordering neighborhood, where Anglo culture dominates. (Although Galarza's autobiography ends with this transition, he later became known as a champion of migrant workers and vice president of the National Farm Labor Union.)

• *The Autobiography of a Brown Buffalo* (1972) by Oscar "Zeta" Acosta (see also pages 335–336) is an irreverent, semiautobiographical novel describing the madcap coming-of-age adventures of a crusading Chicano lawyer-writer from a small town in California. Taking on the identity of "Zeta," a self-styled freedom fighter mixing elements of the *bandido* and Don Quixote, Acosta continues his tale in *The Revolt of the Cockroach People* (1973).

• *Bless Me, Ultima* (1972) by Rudolfo Anaya is a lyrical novel about a boy's coming of age. His mentor, a *curandera* (healer) named Ultima, gives advice and reveals mystical truths to him as he chooses between his Spanish ranching heritage and his Indian farming heritage. The book is a rich exploration of *nuevomexicano* Chicano/Indian culture, not least the mythical Aztec home called

Aztlán. (*Bless Me, Ultima* received the ultimate literary blessing: It is available in Cliffs Notes.)

• *Estampas del valle y otras obras (Valley Sketches and Other Works)* (1973, bilingual) by Rolando Hinojosa is based on the author's personal experiences growing up in Texas's Rio Grande Valley. While describing an existence marked by racism and cultural misunderstanding, Hinojosa vividly conveys both the Chicano and Anglo cultures of southern Texas. *Estampas* and the interrelated works *Klail City y sus alrededores (Klail City and Its Surroundings)* (1979), *Mi querido Rafe (My Dear Rafe)* (1981), and *Claros varones de Belken (Fair Gentlemen of Belken* [County]) (1986) constitute what the author calls the "Klail City Death Trip."

• *Rain of Scorpions and Other Writings* (1975, revised 1993) by Estela Portillo Trambley is one of the first major examples of the new Chicana literature. The collection, including the title novella and nine short stories, features strong women characters who refuse to be victimized; they challenge and rise above the *machista* Mexican American culture.

• *Zoot Suit* (1978) by Luis Valdez (see page 336) mixes fact and fiction in its dramatic staging of the Sleepy Lagoon murder trial (see page 142). Narrated by El Pachuco, a rebellious young zoot suiter, the play condemns the racism and press hysteria that led to the mass arrests of young Chicanos and their railroaded convictions. The first Chicano-produced play to reach mainstream audiences, it had runs both in Los Angeles and on Broadway, and was later made into a movie.

• *Hunger of Memory: The Education of Richard Rodriguez* (1982) by Richard Rodriguez (see pages 336–337) is an autobiographical account of a Mexican American who willfully rejects Spanish and embraces assimilation—and in so doing becomes distanced from his parents. The author, who began school in Sacramento with only 50 words of English, stresses that success requires immersion in the dominant language and culture. His ardent opposition to bilingual education earned him strong criticism as a *pocho*.

• *The House on Mango Street* (1984) by Sandra Cisneros is a series of vignettes portraying a young Mexican American woman's coming of age and finding her own personal space. For Esperanza, the tiny, crowded red house on Mango Street doesn't come close to the idealized home of her dreams. But she recognizes that however far from the Chicago barrio she may hope to travel, she will always "belong" to Mango Street, rooted in her Latino culture.

• *The Last of the Menu Girls* (1986) by Denise Chávez, also author of such plays as *The Flying Tortilla Man* (1975), is another coming-of-age story, set in southern New Mexico. The seven intertwined tales portray the experiences of Rocío Esquibel, from a teenager delivering menus to hospital patients to an aspiring novelist, finding her stories among the people and culture she knows best.

• *A Summer Life* (1990) by poet Gary Soto (see page 337) is a collection of vignettes about growing up in Fresno, California. Vividly conveying the world as seen through a child's eyes, he recreates the magic of such delights as exploring the sounds and sparks of the taps on his shoes.

• *Rain of Gold* (1991) by Victor Villaseñor is the epic saga, the first in an anticipated trilogy, of the author's family history. It follows his mother's and his father's stories from their life in Mexico during the Revolution through their flight to the United States and the racism they encounter there to the happiness of their eventual marriage. Wanting to tell his own children about their roots, Villaseñor not only interviewed his parents over several years but traveled to Mexico to verify some of the seemingly fantastic tales he had heard.

• *Songs My Mother Sang to Me* (1992) by Patricia Preciado Martin collects 10 oral histories of elderly southern Arizona women who represent the generation that made the rancho to barrio transition. Theirs is the last testimony of the lost rancho world, a world of fiestas, religious pageants, and age-old customs.

• *Always Running* (1993) by Luis J. Rodríguez reflects on the author's coming-of-age amid the gang warfare, murders, beatings, and arrests in East Los Angeles during the 1960s. With this autobiographical account, Rodríguez, now a successful poet, hoped to dissuade his son and others from continuing the craziness and senseless slaughter.

Puerto Rican Literature

The first Puerto Rican literature to take root in the mainland was the work of René Marqués, the best-known Puerto Rican playwright. In the 1950s, his dramas—most notably *La carreta (The Oxcart)* —urged the preservation of Puerto Rican history and culture among mainlanders, and even their return to the island.

Return, however, was not a realistic consideration for many Puerto Ricans, and the literature of the next decade reflected the reality of the Puerto Rico–New York axis. During the 1960s—at the time Chicanos were rejecting assimilation—Puerto Ricans in New York City began to use the term Nuyorican to assert their own unique culture of synthesis. Inspired by the civil rights movement, Nuyorican poets and writers clustered around New York's Lower East Side, notably at poet Miguel Algarín's Nuyorican Poets Cafe, where the likes of Víctor Hernández Cruz, Miguel Piñero, Sandra María Esteves, and Tato Laviera read their works. The voice of this transplanted nation has continued to flourish in the decades since. Some of the vital Puerto Rican works are:

• *La carreta (The Oxcart)* (1951 Spanish; 1969 English translation) by René Marqués (see pages 333–334) dramatizes the story of a *jíbaro* (peasant) family that leaves the mountains of Puerto Rico for the streets of New York. First staged in New York in 1953, the play conveys the poverty, oppression, and alienation of the Puerto Rican experience on the mainland.

• *A Puerto Rican in New York and Other Sketches* (1961) by Jesús Colón (see page 333) is a collection of newspaper columns and essays reflecting on the author's experience as a black Puerto Rican who came to the mainland during World War I and worked as a cigar maker. He attacks racial and class discrimination, condemns the exploitation of Latin music, outlines the needs of the working poor, and argues for increased political awareness.

• ***Down These Mean Streets*** (1967) by Piri Thomas (see page 335) is an autobiographical account of the poverty and prejudice the author faced as a New York City youth; of his involvement with gangs, drugs, and crime, with the inevitable jail time; and of his escape from that life through writing. Among the initial "mean streets" works, it is the first Puerto Rican one. The *New York Times* has dubbed this one of the best books to be written about life in New York.

• ***Spiks*** (1970 Spanish; 1973 English translation) by Pedro Juan Soto, an island writer, is a collection of 13 short works that portray the sordid reality of Puerto Ricans' daily life in New York City. Much like Marqués, Soto underlines the displacement of Puerto Ricans on the mainland, the illusoriness of their dreams, and their constant battle against oppression.

• ***Nilda*** (1973), an illustrated book by Nicholasa Mohr, deals with the life of a young Puerto Rican girl growing up in Spanish Harlem during World War II amid prejudice and economic hardship. It was selected Outstanding Book of the Year by the *New York Times* and a Best Book of 1973 by the American Library Association.

• ***Short Eyes*** (1974) by Miguel Piñero is a prison drama that addresses the tensions and prejudices of life behind bars, particularly for Puerto Ricans and African Americans. Feelings explode when a white man charged as a child molester ("short eyes" in prison slang) is thrown into a cell block. Begun by Piñero when he himself was serving time, the play won an Obie and the New York Drama Critics Award for the best American play of the 1973–74 season. It was later made into a movie.

• ***La Carreta Made a U-Turn*** (1979) by Jesús Abraham "Tato" Laviera is the definitive poetic answer to René Marqués's *La carreta:* Laviera champions the Puerto Rican culture of New York, proclaiming there is no need to return to the island. At the same time he deplores the oppression and other social problems facing Puerto Ricans on the mainland.

• ***Yerba buena*** (1980) by Sandra María Esteves is a collection of poems reflecting on the author's status as a woman of Puerto Rican and Dominican heritage. The poems touch on her political activism, including her participation in the Puerto Rican Socialist Party and the women's liberation movement.

• *The Comeback* (1985) by Ed Vega, born Edgardo Vega Yunqué, is a satirical novel about a half–Puerto Rican, half-Eskimo ice-hockey player who participates in an underground revolutionary movement seeking Puerto Rican independence. As the main character flounders in his identity crisis, Vega pokes fun at everyone from the "professional" revolutionaries of the barrio to the high-minded psychiatrists and slick undercover cops of mainstream culture.

• *Rhythm, Content and Flavor* (1989) by Victor Hernández Cruz, an Afro–Puerto Rican "jazz poet," combines new work with selections from four earlier volumes—including *Snaps* (1968), the first Latino poetry collection strongly promoted by a major U.S. publisher. Drawing on the rhythm of Latin music, Cruz mixes Spanish and English as he reveals the Hispanic presence in U.S. culture.

• *The Line of the Sun* (1989) by Judith Ortiz Cofer, a Pulitzer Prize nominee, is a novel based on the author's own experience of the pull between her native island culture and her barrio home on the mainland. As the young woman narrator recollects her uncle's life, she describes the transition from a rural Puerto Rican village to a New Jersey housing project and the acceptance of a new culture without rejecting the old.

• *When I Was Puerto Rican* (1993) by Esmeralda Santiago is an autobiographical account of growing up in rural Puerto Rico with numerous siblings and then adjusting, as an eighth grader with little English, to the confusing new world of New York.

CUBAN AMERICAN LITERATURE

Although José Martí (see pages 119–120) and other early Cuban exiles began the Cuban American literary tradition as far back as the nineteenth century, most Cuban American literature is a product of the post—Cuban Revolution (see pages 166–168) period. Indeed, numerous Cuban-born writers, such as Reinaldo Arenas and René Ariza became Cuban *Americans* precisely because of their writing while in Cuba—having left the island after stints in prison for criticizing Castro's government. (Perhaps the most notable contemporary Cuban-born writer, Armando Valladares, now lives in Spain but remains an important voice in the Cuban American community; his 23 years in Castro's jails are dramatically related in *Contra toda esperanza [Against All Hope]*, published in 1985 in Spanish and 1986 in English.)

The unique experience of this first generation of Cuban American writers underlies a sharp thematic distinction from later generations. While the older writers generally wrote (and still write) in their native Spanish and take Cuba and the Cuban Revolution as their subject and setting, today's Cuban American writers focus on their American experience. Some of the major Cuban American works:

• *Los primos (The Cousins)* (1971) by Celedonio González (see page 334) focuses on three Cuban cousins: One decides to return to the island after 10 years in Miami; one chooses to remain in the States; and the third, initially pro-Castro, is disillusioned and heads for Florida. In Spanish, the title is slang for someone who is readily deceived, whether by the American dream or by communist ideology.

• *Fefu and Her Friends* (1977) by María Irene Fornés, a pre-Castro immigrant to the States, is an Obie-winning drama about eight women who gather for a weekend retreat and review their loves and losses, dreams and setbacks. In another Obie-winning play, *The Conduct of Life* (1985), Fornés features a Latin American man who carries the violence of his job as a government torturer into his life at home.

• *El portero (The Doorman)* (1987 Spanish; 1991 English translation) by Reinaldo Arenas is the author's first novel set in the United States. Its central character, a Cuban refugee working as a doorman in New York, joins up with the pets in his apartment building to revolt against the inhumane humans. In a posthumously published memoir, *Antes que anochezca (Before the Night Falls)* (1992 Spanish; 1993 English translation), Arenas recounts his own journey, from his Cuban childhood, through his stint as pro-Castro rebel and imprisonment as a homosexual, to his flight to the United States in 1980 and his subsequent battle against AIDS.

• *We Were Always Afraid* (1987) by Leopoldo Hernández is a play about a Cuban living in Los Angeles who visits his sister in their homeland after 20 years. The siblings condemn each others' supposed cowardice—one for living passively under dictatorship, the other for abandoning the ship altogether—and sadly realize you can't go home again.

• *The Great American Justice Game* (1987) by Miguel González-Pando is a satirical drama about life in 2005, when María Libertad is put on trial for speaking Spanish and thereby violating the "English and English Only Act." González-Pando clearly takes aim at proponents of "Official English," notably in southern Florida.

• *Raining Backwards* (1988) by Roberto G. Fernández is a novel satirizing Miami's Cuban community. A family epic, told through letters, news clips, narratives, recipes, and advice to the lovelorn, it features an enterprising plantain chip–manufacturing mother, her doomed lovesick daughter, a fervent revolution-fighting son, and his saintly brother, who becomes the pope.

• *Latin Jazz* (1989) by Virgil Suárez centers on a Cuban American musician and other family members, expressing their different views of life in the States, as they wait for a relative to arrive with the Mariel boatlift. The shifting voices of the novel tell of places that have been lost forever, of departure and arrival.

• *The Mambo Kings Play Songs of Love* (1989) by Oscar Hijuelos (see page 337) focuses on the struggles in New York City during the 1950s of two Cuban musicians whose ambition leads them so far as to appear on "I Love Lucy" with America's favorite Cuban, Desi Arnaz. The first Hispanic novel to receive strong backing from a major publisher, it vindicated that judgment by becoming the first to receive the Pulitzer Prize. It was also made into a movie.

• *Exiled Memories: A Cuban Childhood* (1990) by poet Pablo Medina is a sensitive, insightful memoir of the author's early years in Cuba, before the revolution, and his readjustment, as a shy 12-year-old, to life in America.

• *Dreaming in Cuban* (1992) by Cristina Garcia interweaves fantasy and reality to contrast the lives of three generations of Cuban women: the grandmother, a firm supporter of Castro, volunteering for work on the island; her two daughters, one a deluded member of a Santería cult in Cuba, the other a strongly anti-Castro bakery owner in New York; and the granddaughter, an Americanized punk artist.

• *Next Year in Cuba: A Cubano's Coming-of-Age in America* (1995) by poet and essayist Gustavo Pérez Firmat is a compelling memoir of the author's early years in the insular world of Little Havana in Miami, where each Christmas brought the refrain "Next year in Cuba." For Pérez Firmat, the life of the exile is one of seesawing between two cultures rather than a true synthesis.

OTHER LATINO LITERATURE

Although Cubans, Puerto Ricans, and Mexicans have had the most time to develop a culture reflecting their American experiences, other Latinos have contributed important works to American letters as well. Among these works is *How the García Girls Lost Their Accents* (1991) by Julia Alvarez; based on the author's own experiences, it is the story of the adjustments of a physician, his wife, and four daughters to life in New York City, where they settle after fleeing the Dominican Republic's Trujillo regime in 1960. Although their work does not directly address the Latino experience in America, two other important figures are Carlos Castañeda (see pages 334–335), a Peruvian-born anthropologist whose mystical explorations of the nature of reality produced a string of best-sellers (including *The Teachings of Don Juan: A Yaqui Way of Knowledge* [1968]);

and Chilean American Isabel Allende (see page 337), whose Spanish-language novels (including *La casa de los espíritus [The House of the Spirits]* [1982; 1985 English translation]) have made her one of the most respected writers of the age.

Hispanic Hollywood

Hollywood has not had a very honorable record when it comes to representing Latinos and Latino life. From the early silent films, whether played by Hispanics or Anglos in makeup, Latino characters have mostly been limited to a narrow range of stereotypes. Men might appear as dapper Latin lovers, sleazy villains, charming Cisco Kid–type caballeros, comic layabouts, or big city hoodlums, while women were generally seen only as sexy spitfires or exotic dark ladies. To be sure, such stereotyped roles sustained the careers of the likes of Ramón Novarro (see also page 320), César Romero (see also page 322), Dolores del Río (see also pages 321–322), Lupe Velez, and other Hispanic actors. And a few Latino actors—notably, Anthony Quinn (see also page 323) and Rita Hayworth (see also pages 324–325)—managed to step out of typecast parts and win acclaim for their portrayals of non-Latino characters.

A memorable exception to the usual screen fare was Herbert Biberman's now classic *Salt of the Earth* (1954). Although written and directed by non-Hispanics, the film was based on an actual strike by mostly Mexican American miners in New Mexico and featured Hispanic actors, including a local labor leader and many union members.

Yet it is only in the last two decades, with increasing ethnic consciousness and sizable Latino audiences, that the portrayal of Hispanics on the silver screen has begun to change considerably, encompassing the variety of real life. More and more Latino writers, directors, actors, and even film executives are gaining experience in the industry, particularly through the making of the less expensive documentaries and independent films. Among the more intriguing feature films on Latinos in the last two decades are:

- *El Súper* (1979, directed by León Ichaso, based on Iván Acosta's play) focuses on a Cuban refugee in Manhattan trying to make it as a building superintendent.
- *Short Eyes* (1979, directed by Robert Young, based on Miguel Piñero's play) is a prison drama about a child molester.
- *Zoot Suit* (1981, directed by Luis Valdez [see also page 336], based on Valdez's play) comments on the Sleepy Lagoon murder case (see page 142). The first commercial Chicano film released by a major Hollywood studio, it starred Edward James Olmos (see pages 329–330) as the zoot-suited narrator, El Pachuco.
- *The Ballad of Gregorio Cortez* (1983, directed by Robert Young) is based on the story of a nineteenth-century Mexican American (played by Edward James Olmos) who becomes the subject of a Texas manhunt after he kills a police chief in self-defense (see pages 101, 310). Sentenced to life in prison when he finally turns himself in, he is pardoned only after serving 12 years.
- *El Norte* (1983, directed by Gregory Nava) tells the story of a Guatemalan brother and sister who flee the persecution of their homeland, scramble through an underground tunnel into the United States, and struggle to survive in California. Touches of magic realism are used to sharpen the contrast between the old values and the new.
- *Crossover Dreams* (1985, directed by León Ichaso) traces the rise of a salsa artist (played by Rubén Blades [see page 330]), who distances himself from the barrio to suc-

ceed in the English-speaking record industry but then realizes how much he has given up and returns to his community.

- *La Bamba* (1987, written and directed by Luis Valdez) is a romanticized account starring Lou Diamond Phillips of real-life Chicano rock and roller Ritchie Valens's fulfillment of the crossover dream, only to die with Buddy Holly in a plane crash while on tour.

- *Born in East L.A.* (1987, written, directed by, and starring Richard "Cheech" Marin) humorously but pointedly recounts the adventures of a third-generation Chicano who can hardly speak Spanish and is "caught" without papers while visiting a factory and summarily deported to Mexico as an undocumented worker. In attempt after hilarious attempt, he struggles to be "accepted" by his native country.

- *Stand and Deliver* (1988, directed by Ramón Menéndez) is based on the true story of Jaime Escalante, a tough but loving math teacher in the L.A. barrio. When his students pass the grueling Advanced Placement calculus exam, the testing authorities can't believe it and insist on a retest to rule out cheating. Edward James Olmos's performance as Escalante won him an Oscar nomination.

- *Hangin' with the Homeboys* (1991, directed by Joseph P. Vásquez) is a night on the town in Manhattan with two Puerto Rican and two African American adolescent males out to prove themselves to each other and the world.

- *American Me* (1992, directed by and starring Edward James Olmos) is a grim, violent memoir of a former drug gang member from the L.A. barrio who is trying to make a life for himself after 18 years in prison.

- *The Mambo Kings* (1992, directed by Arne Glimcher, based on the novel by Oscar Hijuelos [see page 337]) follows two Cuban brothers who come to New York to hit it big in the music business.

- *El mariachi* (1993, written and directed by Robert Rodríguez in Spanish) is a mistaken-identity adventure in which an aspiring mariachi player in a border town is confused with a hit man. After winning the audience award at the Sundance Film Festival, the movie was a hit on the independent film circuit, leading to Rodríguez's big-budget English-language sequel, *Desperado* (1995).
- *My Family* (1994, directed by Gregory Nava), starring Edward James Olmos, Esai Morales, and Jimmy Smits, recounts a Mexican family's struggles in Los Angeles from the father's arrival in the 1920s to the contemporary barriers faced by his sons.
- *Nueba Yol* (1996, written and directed by Ángel Muñiz in Spanish) is a comic fable about the misadventures of a young Dominican widower trying to make it in New York—or *Nueba Yol* in Dominican slang. The movie was a major hit in its home country, where the principal character has for years been a popular television figure.

Like Robert Wise and Jerome Robbins's *West Side Story* (1961, based on the 1957 musical play)—about two young lovers caught in the crossfire between Anglo and Puerto Rican gangs—several recent films about Latinos by non-Hispanics are also of interest, although not without their problems. Robert Redford's *The Milagro Beanfield War* (1988), coproduced by Moctesuma Esparza, uses magic realism to tell the story of a New Mexico town's opposition to development. Mira Nair's *The Perez Family* (1994) is a lighthearted farce about the Mariel boatlift to Miami, while Allison Anders's *Mi Vida Loca* (1994) focuses on a Latina gang in Los Angeles's Echo Park.

LATIN RHYTHMS

Ever since early Anglo settlers in the Southwest were wowed by the lively fandango, the music and dance of the Spanish-speaking Americas—from Buenos Aires to Havana to Spanish Harlem— have been finding their way into the United States' cultural mainstream. Indeed, this rich and vital "Latin" heritage has, in both subtle and not-so-subtle ways, been one of the greatest influences on popular music and dance throughout the century. Latin rhythms, arrangements, and instruments have become part of the standard toolbox for jazz, country, pop, and rock artists from Anglo George Gershwin to African American Bo Diddley to Latinos Freddy Fender (born Baldemar Huerta) and Jon Secada. Whole Latin music styles like the tango, mambo, and cha-cha have (along with their associated dances) established themselves as classics, and newer varieties such as salsa and *tejano* are doing the same. Such Latin standards as *"Babalú," "Guantanamera," "La bamba,"* and *"Oye como va"* have made regular appearances on the pop charts.

For this solid contribution, the United States largely has its own Latino communities to thank. Not only have receptive Latino audiences encouraged Cuban, Mexican, and other Latin American musicians and singers to perform regularly in this country, but Latinos have formed their own bands and served as front-line cultural ambassadors for these sounds. Most important, Hispanics have continuously generated their own homegrown music, from the hero *corridos,* or ballads, of the nineteenth-century Texan Mexicans and the later *rancheras,* or ranch songs, to the more contemporary *tejano* sounds of Emilio Navaira and Selena. In the late nineteenth century, Mexican and Mexican American musicians helped bring the Cuban beat to New Orleans, where it contributed to the nascent jazz phenomenon. The sounds of Latin music were well rooted in American soil long before the dance crazes of the twentieth century.

All Latin music share a common ancestry in three distinct traditions: that of the Spanish (and, through the Spanish, Europeans as a whole); that of the indigenous peoples, with their curious instruments such as the *güiro* (a notched gourd, played by scraping its side with a stick); and that of the African slaves in Spain's American colonies, with their rhythmic, drum-based music. Over the centuries, these ingredients have combined and recombined in varying degrees to create a range of sophisticated and colorful styles and regional variations.

In Cuba, with its sizable African population, this mix produced a variety of strongly syncopated music styles known as *son*, built on a rural nineteenth-century conga- and bongo-based drum rhythm, supplemented by maracas, claves (wooden sticks), and other percussion instruments. Of all the Latin styles to which the United States has been exposed, these Afro-Cuban forms, featuring what has come to be called simply "Latin rhythm," have had the greatest impact. Although contemporary salsa is a hybrid form, with many antecedents, its main roots are in the *son*, with its insistent beat and strongly African call-and-response song structure.

It is, of course, almost impossible to consider Latin music apart from Latin dance. The two have mostly been created simultaneously and for one another's sake. Like Latin music, Latin dance has drawn on Spanish, Indian, and African traditions. Again, it is the Cuban dance forms that have most influenced the American mainstream. At the heart of these dance forms, the physical counterpart to the *son*, is that certain gracefully sensuous hip and foot movement dubbed the "Cuban motion."

To trace the many varied influences of Latin music and dance, Cuban and otherwise, would be a superhuman task. Identifying some of the major Latin styles that have crossed over into mainstream acceptance, however, is a start. Among them are:

• **Afro-Cuban jazz:** During the 1940s Afro-Cuban jazz, or Cubop, brought together Afro-Cuban sounds with jazz in one of the century's most revolutionary and sophisticated fusions of two popular musics. A product of years of experimentation and cross-fertilization across the whole landscape of jazz and Latin music, the final development of Cubop was fueled by the new bebop movement and led in part by jazz greats Dizzy Gillespie and Stan Kenton. But probably the principal roles were played by Cubans Machito (né Frank Grillo) (see page 323), maraca-shaking founder of the Afro-Cubans in 1940, and Mario Bauza (see pages 322–323), the Afro-Cubans' musical director. This wildly successful band, which for some time featured future "Mambo King" Tito Puente (see page 325), released a string of Afro-Cuban jazz hits throughout the decade, most notably Bauza's 1949 "Tanga." The Cubop style began to fade in the 1950s, but its influence can still be felt in today's "Latin jazz."

• **Bolero:** Related to the lively, castanet-clacking music of the Spanish dance, with its sharp turns and foot stomping, the romantic Cuban bolero had a brief surge of popularity in the United States in the 1950s. The love song "Maria" in *West Side Story* (staged 1957), for example, was based on this form.

• **Bossa Nova:** The bossa nova has Brazilian roots and is therefore not technically Hispanic (Brazil was a Portuguese, not a Spanish, colony). Yet Brazil's musical development is so intertwined with that of its Spanish-speaking neighbors, it cannot be ignored. A combination of traditional Brazilian rhythms and jazz that creates a light, flowing line, bossa nova flourished in the United States in the 1960s, along with its accompanying "dance of love"—slower than the samba and more fluid than the rumba. Brazilian Antonio Carlos Jobim's "The Girl from Ipanema," recorded by Stan Getz with Brazilians João and Astrud Gilberto, is a classic bossa nova tune.

• **Bugalú:** The creation of New York City Latino musicians in the 1960s, bugalú music—with its brashly sung English-language lyrics—fused the familiar mambo sound with rhythm-and-blues and early rock and roll. The music and its dance were especially popular among both Hispanics and African Americans. Before it faded away at the end of the decade, bugalú had a string of hits, including the million-selling "Bang Bang" by Joe Cuba and "Boogaloo Blues" by Johnny Colón.

• **Cha-cha:** Known to Latinos as the *chachachá,* the music and dance, with its punctuating triple beat, began in Cuba with the work of Enrique Jorrín before sweeping the United States in 1954—not least because it was easier to dance than the then popular mambo. The dance played a starring role in the movie *Cha Cha Cha Boom* and others, and today it remains a ballroom basic.

• **Conga:** Named after the tall, narrow drum so fundamental to the Afro-Cuban sound, the familiar conga dance, in which dancers form a winding line, started as a Cuban carnival entertainment. The relatively simple rhythm, with its heavy percussive accent on the fourth beat of every measure, invites everyone to join in. Cuban Desi Arnaz (see page 324)—who played in the celebrated Xavier Cugat (see page 320) orchestra before going on to become a star in his own right—may not deserve the credit he claims for having introduced the conga to the United States in 1937 (the conga song "Havana Is Calling Me" had already appeared the year before), but he was certainly responsible for popularizing it.

• **Latin Jazz:** Drawing on the Cubop tradition, Latin jazz covers a range of music. During the late 1960s and 1970s Brazilian-born percussionist Airto (Airto Moreira), Argentine-born tenor sax player Leandro "Gato" Barbieri, and American pianist Chick Corea, with his influential Return to Forever group, created their own idiosyncratic fusions of Latin music and jazz. In recent years musicians like Jerry Gonzalez and the Fort Apache Band have added bits of reggae, salsa, bossa nova, and calypso to create an original sound that has won a considerable following, especially among New York City Latinos.

• **Latin Rock:** While Latin music formed its first clear relationship with rock and roll when Ritchie Valens (see also page 328) turned a traditional Mexican wedding song into the rollicking number "La Bamba," it was Carlos Santana (see also page 330) who began to give Latin rock a distinct identity. In the late 1960s and early 1970s, Santana and other California musicians, such as the group Malo, incorporated Latin instruments and grafted salsa rhythms and melodies onto more familiar rock-and-roll sounds. In the process Santana created a string of fresh-sounding hits, including a version of Tito Puente's *"Oye como va"* (from the album

Abraxas) and "She's Not There." More recently the East L.A. band Los Lobos—which recorded most of the soundtrack for the film *La Bamba*—has introduced the accordion-based sound of *música norteña,* the traditional folk music of the borderland, to rock.

• **Mambo:** Although the tango and rumba had earlier sparked dance crazes all their own, neither could compare to the mambo in the 1950s. Throughout the decade, the mambo not only dominated the dance halls (especially in New York), it permeated the movies (making appearances in *Mambo* and *Underwater!,* starring Jane Russell, to name two), Broadway shows (*West Side Story, Damn Yankees*), television, and advertising. Its precise origins are murky, having developed from the so-called *son montuno,* a sound that Cuban Antonio Arcaño created in the 1930s by adding percussion and a bass line to the island's traditional European-based *danzón,* a ballroom dance. Although its critics sneeringly called it by the nonsense word *"mambo," son montuno* was embraced and reshaped in the coming years by other Latino musicians, including Orestes López and Israel "Cachao" López (from Arcaño's band) (see page 324)—both of whom have been called fathers of the mambo.

Credit for finally popularizing the music and its fluid, energetic, tough-to-master dance, however, goes to Cuban Dámaso Pérez Prado (see page 325). It was his big 1949 hit, *"Qué rico el mambo"* ("What Fun the Mambo Is") that really started the craze. The mambo, with its contrasting brass and sax riffs, was quickly added to the repertoires of Xavier Cugat and Desi Arnaz, and Puerto Ricans Tito Rodríguez and Tito Puente. (Puente's still at it today and only increased his bookings with his appearance in the film *The Mambo Kings.*) With the rising popularity of rock and roll, mambo fever receded at the end of the 1950s, but the fast-paced courtship dance, which has been described as a "rumba with a jitterbug accent," remains a dance hall standard.

• **Merengue:** A Dominican dance with roots in the early nineteenth century, the traditional country form uses the sounds of the accordion, *tambora* drum, *güiro,* and human voice. The authentic merengue sound was introduced to the United States in the 1950s following a few watered-down variations the decade before. The snappy dance, with its dragging foot movement, proved relatively easy to master.

• **Miami Sound:** American pop, salsa, jazz, and samba ingredients are brought together in the Miami sound, a fresh musical trend that appeared in the 1980s, spearheaded by Gloria Estefan (see page 331) and the Miami Sound Machine with such albums as *Conga* (1985).

• *Pachanga:* A fast, energetic dance, set to a syncopated ta-tum ta-tum beat, the *pachanga* had a short-lived popularity among New York Latinos in the early 1960s. Believed to be Cuban in origin, it was associated with *charangas*, Cuban dance orchestras that used flutes, violins, piano, bass, and timbales.

• **Rumba:** It was with the sensuous rumba that the percussive, hip-shaking Cuban *son* was first introduced to a mainstream American audience. The 1930 appearance of Don Azpiazú's Havana Casino Orchestra in New York started a rumba music and dance craze that lasted until well into the 1950s—and provided the opening wedge for the many waves of Latin music and dance to follow. While Latina Rita Hayworth and others danced the dance in a string of movies (including the aptly named *Rumba*), the soundtrack for the rumba era came from Azpiazú's band (especially with its classic recording of *"El manicero"* [The Peanut Vendor]), the revered Cuban Ernesto Lecuona's (see page 319) Rumba Boys, Xavier Cugat, and others. The fast, syncopated, percussive music drew on the sounds of such Cuban instruments as maracas, claves, *timbales, güiros*, bongos, and conga—which were new at the time to most Americans. The dance, mimicking a mating ritual, gave the men a chance to show their stuff and the women a chance to lure them in. Today, the rumba is an established ballroom classic.

• **Salsa:** With its steady Afro-Cuban beat and touches of jazz, pop, and even Puerto Rican *plenas* (satirical, socially aware songs), salsa is one of today's most popular musical styles within the Latino community and beyond. Its name, referring to that familiar spicy condiment, gives a sense of its punch. Rooted in the Cuban *son*, with the same alternating call-and-response structure, emphasis on brass and percussion, and marked syncopation, salsa takes its cue from the barrios in both the United States and the Caribbean. Although most of its elements were in place in the work of Machito, Tito Puente, and Tito Rodríguez in the 1950s, the form did not fully crystallize until the later 1960s. Popularized by such giants as New York–born Willie Colón and Cuban-born Celia Cruz (see page 326), the once and future "Queen of Salsa," it still attracts new artists like the youthful Puerto Rican–born La India (aka Linda Caballero) and Marc Anthony (aka Marco Antonio Muñiz).

• **Samba:** An Afro-Brazilian music and dance with a strong drumbeat, different in accent from the Cuban rhythm, the samba is closely associated with the Rio de Janeiro carnival. It probably developed from another Brazilian dance, the *maxixe*, before landing in the United States in the late 1930s. Following the success of "Brazilian Night," with English lyrics by American Marion Sunshine, the samba found a tremendous following, which it held until well into the 1950s. Like the tango, the rumba, and later the chacha, it made its appearance in Hollywood movies, often danced by Portuguese-born Carmen Miranda sporting her trademark fruited headdresses. Characterized by its quick bouncing dip, with knees bent, to each beat, the samba has become part of the ballroom repertoire.

• **Tango:** The tango, with its long gliding dance steps and dramatically clipped staccato music, has its origins in the Argentine *milonga* dance and the smooth Cuban habanera rhythm (a European-derived sound inflected with African elements, different from the percussive Afro-Cuban *son*). The flashy dance, set to music on guitar, flute, violin, and *bandoneón*, an instrument similar to the accordion, took over Buenos Aires in 1910. Vernon and Irene Castle caught the tango fever in France and introduced it to enthusiastic U.S. audiences in a 1913 Broadway show. By 1921, when Rudolph Valentino did his famous number in the silent film *Four Horsemen of the Apocalypse*, the tango was a full-blown craze. Early cries of outrage about the lewd nature of the dance (and Yale's refusal to permit it at the 1914 junior prom) gave way to a popularity that no dance would find until the mambo came along decades later. Although the tango did start to fade somewhat in the 1950s, today it remains one of the world's best-known dances, and Al Pacino's magnificent tango in his recent *Scent of a Woman* probably won it even more converts.

• *Tejano:* For years one of the most popular styles in the Mexican American Southwest, *tejano* music has its roots in traditional songs—*rancheras, cumbias* (folk tunes of Colombian origin), and Mexican polkas—to which are added elements of country, pop, rock, and Afro-Cuban sound. *Tejano* was already on the verge of finding mainstream success when its number-one star Selena (Selena Quintanilla Pérez) (see pages 331–332) was shot to death in 1995; her posthumous crossover album, *Dreaming of You,* then became the all-time fastest selling album by a woman. The *tejano* sound is carried on by Emilio Navaira, such groups as La Mafia and Mazz, and others.

Established music and dance styles—and the individual songs and performers associated with those styles—represent one aspect of the Latin influence. But, again, the influence does not stop there. Anglo performers have at times drawn heavily on Latin traditions, introducing some of its flavor to mainstream audiences. During the 1960s, for example, Herb Alpert, inspired by Mexican *mariachis* (traditional street bands), formed his Tijuana Brass group and brought the sound to the top-10 charts; at the same time Pete Seeger popularized the Cuban folk ballad *"Guatanamera."*

Hispanic singers also have done much to add a Latin inflection to mainstream styles. During the 1960s, for example, Trini López (see pages 326–327), added Mexican guitar rhythms to his folk song performances, and introduced "Lemon Tree" (from the Latin folk song "Hojita de limón"), while Freddy Fender blended the emotional pitch of the *ranchera* into rhythm-and-blues–country numbers. In 1968, José Feliciano (see also pages 328–329), with his flamenco-flavored singing, won best new artist and best male pop vocalist Grammys with his interpretation of "Light My Fire."

Several vocalists have had their initial successes in mainstream music and then brought in their Latin heritage. Mexican American Vikki Carr (see page 327), for instance, hit the charts with "It Must Be Him" but later won Grammys for her albums *Simplemente mujer* and *Cosas del amor.* Linda Ronstadt (see also page 329) first gained fame for such country-rock albums as *Heart Like a Wheel* but went on to record some of the Mexican *rancheras* she grew up with as a child. Other Latino successes in the music world range from folksinger Joan Baez (see also pages 327–328) to more recent bilingual pop successes as Lisa Lisa (Lisa Velez), the Cover Girls, the Barrio Boyzz, and others.

There are also many styles, songs, and performers that have been extremely popular within the various Latino communities, even if they have never quite crossed over. From the early nineteenth century, Mexicans in the Southwest have chronicled their history in *corridos* (see page 137), folk ballads set in polka, waltz, or march time and often sung as duets. One of these *corridos* became the basis for the movie *The Ballad of Gregorio Cortez.* And fresh *corridos* continue to appear, such as *"El corrido de César Chávez,"* reflecting new political and social concerns. Another influential form of Mexican American music—*música norteña,* or Chicano *conjunto*—featured an ensemble lead by an accordion, usually backed by a *bajo sexto* (a 12-string guitar) and, later, sometimes drums. Playing mainly polka music at first, the groups increasingly turned to *rancheras,* a Chicano equivalent of country. *La onda nueva* (new wave), also called *la onda chicana*—led by Little Joe (José María de León Hernández) and the Latinaires (later Little Joe y la Familia)—grew out of this tradition in the late 1960s. Using brass, saxophones, electric guitars, and even an electric organ, Little Joe's group blended *rancheras* with country, rhythm and blues, and rock. Accordionist Flaco Jiménez has also created his own contemporary version of *música norteña.*

Today, such Mexican American groups as Los Temerarios (The Daring Ones), Los Bukis, and Los Tigres offer a variety of pop Latin sounds. The ongoing importance of these and other performers of Latin music as a vital component of American music is attested to by four separate Grammy award categories, as well as by the well-stocked Latin sections in the music stores and the number of Spanish-language tunes heard on the airwaves throughout the country. Besides, the mainstream is an ever shifting one, and it may not be long before these styles, songs, and performers do cross over.

■ ■ ■

Crossover Sounds

Many Latin sounds have gained a wider audience via the movies or through somewhat altered versions by non-Latin performers. Few people realize, for example, that the song "What a Difference a Day Makes," recorded by singers as diverse as Dinah Washington and Bobby Darrin, is a translation of *"Cuando vuelva a tu lado,"* published in the United States in 1934 by Mexican-born María Grever (who also wrote *"Júrame"* and other hits). Often well-known jazz composers collaborated with Latin musicians, as in *Afro-Cuban Suite* (1948) by Dizzy Gillespie and conga player Chano Pozo or *"Desafinado"* (1962), a Grammy-winning recording by Stan Getz of the bossa nova composition by Antonio Carlos Jobim and João Gilberto. But there are also many Latino recordings that have brought the music to a wide audience, including:

- *"El manicero"*/"The Peanut Vendor" (1930), recorded by Don Azpiazú's Havana Casino Orchestra and sung in English by Azpiazú's sister-in-law Marion Sunshine when the group toured. Based on a chant by street vendors, this song became a national hit in 1931 and helped initiate the rumba era, introducing the Cuban *son*, with authentic Cuban instruments, to American audiences. One soda fountain in Los Angeles even honored it with a "Peanut Vendor" sundae.

- **"Babalú"** (1941), initially recorded by Xavier Cugat and Miguelito Valdez; popularized by Desi Arnaz in 1946. Addressed to a Yoruba deity, it became a major hit.
- **"Tanga"** (1949), written by Mario Bauza and recorded by Machito's Afro-Cubans. Considered a perfect synthesis of Afro-Cuban rhythms with jazz, this hit is notable for the riffs setting brass against sax, as well as Machito's vocals and Luis Miranda's conga beat. Another notable recording by this group is *Afro-Cuban Jazz Suite* (1951), composed by Cuban trumpeter Chico O'Farrill.
- **"Cerezo Rosa"/"Cherry Pink and Apple Blossom White"** (1953), recorded by Dámaso Pérez Prado, who started the mambo craze with his earlier hit *"Qué rico el mambo."* Popularized in the movie *Underwater!* starring Jane Russell, "Cherry Pink," with its lively syncopation and bolero-mambo beat, sold 4 million copies worldwide.
- **"La Bamba"** (1958), recorded by Ritchie Valens. Setting a traditional Mexican wedding song, with Spanish lyrics, to a rock-and-roll beat, Valens's path-breaking number was initially released on the B side of his top-five pop hit "Donna." In 1987, "La Bamba" hit number one on the pop charts, when it was rerecorded by Los Lobos for the film *La Bamba*.
- **Dance Mania** (1958), album by Tito Puente, featuring the singer Santos Colón. This big band recording exemplifies Puente's appeal as "King of the Mambo." His earlier "Abaniquito," played on many English-language radio stations, set the pace for mambo fever.
- **"Wasted Days and Wasted Nights"** (1959), recorded by Freddy Fender. Mixing *ranchera* and rhythm-and-blues, this song has been called "a classic of South Texas rock." Fender rerecorded it in 1975, when it went to the top 10 and backed his number-one pop hit "Before the Next Teardrop Falls."
- **"El Watusi"** (1962), recorded by conga player Ray Bar-

retto. A million-selling rhythm-and-blues hit, this single was just one of Barretto's crossover successes, which also included a variety of fusions of jazz, Afro-Cuban sounds, and New York salsa.

- **"Bang Bang"** (1966), recorded by Joe Cuba. The first bugalú single to top a million, this brash single was a hit among both Latino and African American teens, in part for its double entendre lyrics.
- *Abraxas* (1970), album by Carlos Santana. This second album by the leader of Latin rock transforms Tito Puente's *"Oye como va"* and other salsa numbers with an infusion of rock guitar and jazz organ. Santana went on to win a 1988 rock instrumental Grammy for his album *Blues for Salvador.*
- *The Good, the Bad, the Ugly* (1974), album by Willie Colón. Although grounded in Cuban salsa, this album is spiced with Brazilian, Panamanian, Puerto Rican country, and rock flavors. *"El cazanguero"* brings in samba and mambo sounds, while "EMC²" rocks with electric guitar.
- *Celia and Johnny* (1974), album by Celia Cruz and Johnny Pacheco. Joining the explosive salsa singer, known for her fast-paced scatting, with the celebrated salsa bandleader and flutist, this release went gold. By 1977 the *New York Daily News* was calling Cruz the year's best female vocalist.
- *Sun of Latin Music* (1974), album by Eddie Palmieri. Mixing salsa and disco, this release by one of New York's major bandleaders won the first Grammy award for Latin music.
- **"Conga"** (1985), recorded by Gloria Estefan and the Miami Sound Machine. Melding salsa to pop, this lively Miami-sound dance number not only sold more than a million copies but showed up on the pop, dance, black, and Latin charts at the same time. By 1988, Estefan and her group had a number one pop hit with the ballad

"Anything for You" (recorded in English, Spanish, and a mix). Estefan's *Mi tierra* (1993), which sold 2.5 million in the United States and another 5 million abroad, picked up a Grammy for best tropical Latin album.

• ***Canciones de mi padre/Songs of My Father*** (1988), album by Linda Rondstadt. Drawing on her Mexican heritage, mainstream pop sensation Ronstadt turned to traditional songs sung to her by her father, including a number of *rancheras*. She followed this Mexican American Grammy winner with two 1992 Grammy winners: *Frenesí* (for tropical Latin) and *Más canciones* (for Mexican American).

• ***Nothing but the Truth*** (1988), album by Rubén Blades (see also page 330). Collaborating with Sting, Lou Reed, and others, Blades—the star of the film *Crossover Dreams*—made his first English-language recording. In the same year he won the best Latin pop Grammy for another album (in Spanish), *Antecedente*.

• ***"La Macarena"*** (1993), recorded by Los Del Rio. A pop-Flamenco tune with an infectious accompanying line dance, it originated in Spain, soon caught on with Latinos in the U.S., and in 1996 hit number one in an English-language version.

• ***Dreaming of You*** (1995), album by Selena. Breaking records for first-day sales, this posthumous release, intended as the *tejano* star's crossover debut, contained passionate English- and Spanish-language songs and duets with David Byrne and the Barrio Boyzz. Two of the songs were used in the film *Don Juan DeMarco*, in which Selena appeared.

LATINO ARTS

It is no easy matter to put a finger on what constitutes Latino art. Museums and galleries that have tried to do so have come to widely differing conclusions. Some emphasize folkloric references, others focus on political declarations of identity. The fact is, Latino artists are, above all, individuals. To be sure, many Latino artists draw deliberately on their heritage (or heritages), but that is just one of their sources. Hispanic artists are not an isolated group. They figure in almost every major twentieth-century art movement in the United States, and in recent years several have been major players within these movements.

Marisol's (see pages 338–339) witty assemblages, for example, provided an intriguing counterpoint to pop art, and Rafael Ferrer's (see page 339) piles of autumn leaves and other works helped set the pace for the process art of the late 1960s and 1970s. Today, Andrés Serrano's huge Cibachrome religious icons and portraits expand notions of conceptual art; Arnaldo Roche Rabell's (see pages 340–341) self-portraits and Luis Cruz Azaceta's haunting figures exemplify expressionistic painting, and any consideration of political art comes up against the murals of Judy Baca (see page 340) and other Chicanos, the photographic installations of Alfredo Jaar, and the performances of Guillermo Gómez-Peña, to name just a few. The Latino contribution is part of the fabric of American art, although it is illuminating to look at a few traditions specifically associated with Hispanic culture—most notably, the religious art of the *santeros* and the politically driven Chicano murals.

THE ART OF THE *SANTEROS*

Some of the most beautiful and moving of all Latino art is the religious art that flourished in New Mexico in the nineteenth century—and to some degree continues today. A true folk art, these holy images came in the form of *retablos* (paintings, mostly in tempera on wood panels, created for church altars) and *bultos* (painted figurative sculptures, usually carved from cottonwood). The practitioners of the craft were a select and often anonymous group known as *santeros* (makers of *santos*, or "saints"). Their work was in demand not only for churches but also for devout Catholics who wanted their own pictorial reminders of their patron saints.

Many of the creations of the preeminent *santeros* from the golden age—the pioneering "Laguna Santero," the "Truchas Master," and José Rafael Aragón (see also page 338)—still adorn churches in New Mexico. Typically, the figures in the *retablos* are elongated and outlined in black or brown, with oval faces and prominent almond-shaped eyes. The sculpted figures are also usually tall and slender, with short chests and long legs; often the head and arms are carved separately and attached to the body with pegs.

Although the *santeros'* art declined in the later nineteenth century as plaster saints and cheap religious prints became available, a few committed artists continued to create. Miguel Herrera, for example, carved sometimes life-size figures, dressed in fabric, for the persecuted Penitente Brotherhood in the 1870s and 1880s, and José Benito Ortega (see page 338) traveled throughout northern New Mexico and created brightly colored *bultos* well into the twentieth century.

Bultos had a revival starting in the late 1920s, when Santa Fe hosted crafts shows featuring Hispanic works and gave birth to the Spanish Colonial Arts Society. Tourists in the Southwest began searching for "authentic" Hispanic art, although all too often Anglo collectors' tastes—for unpainted rather than gaily painted pieces, for example—influenced the market. Cordova, a small community between Santa Fe and Taos, became (and remains) a center for santo making, with entire families—including the well-known José Dolores López and his son George—practicing the art. Another noted *santero* of the 1930s and later was Patrocino Barela of Taos, who evolved his own surrealistic style.

Yet another revival coincided with the assertion of Chicano identity in the late 1960s. Young wood-carvers in northern New Mexico formed a loose-knit group, *La Escuela Artesana, SA,* which sponsored shows at fiestas. Contemporary master Félix López works in cot-tonwood and even uses the traditional natural pigments, mixing his own paints from crushed rock, boiled leaves, and the like. Today, major museums, from the National Museum of American Art in Washington, D.C., to the Taylor Museum in Colorado Springs, prominently display the work of both classic and more modern *santeros*. Their works are now accepted as a vital part of America's artistic heritage.

THE CHICANO MURAL MOVEMENT

In the late 1960s and 1970s, as proud assertions of Hispanic identity began to manifest themselves as much in the arts as in politics, no art form garnered more attention than the Chicano murals. Across the barrios of the urban Southwest, California, and Midwest, Mexican American artists (primarily) descended upon the walls of housing projects, post offices, cultural centers, schools, stores, and factories and—often with the assistance of dozens of community residents—covered them with colorful depictions of Latino-themed scenes.

Both in content and form, the murals are a true expression of Chicano identity. With their images of Mexican and Mexican American history, ranging from the pre-Columbian age through contemporary life in the barrio, they speak to a population not used to seeing their own images prominently honored in public. At the same time, the murals, as public art, reflect a typically Hispanic focus on the community, away from the individual.

The mural form itself draws directly on one of the most signifi-cant Mexican contributions to the course of twentieth-century art and American art in particular. During the 1920s in Mexico, in-spired by the revolution of 1910 (see pages 133–134), a group of artists was determined to forge an authentic Mexican art, helping to define the nation's identity. With government support, they began decorating the walls of schools and other public buildings. Muralist David Alfaro Siqueiros voiced the movement's goals in his call for "a monumental art, a human art, a public art, with the great and alive example of our great and extraordinary pre-Hispanic cultures of America." That this cry would be echoed, across the border, in the Chicano murals of the 1970s is no accident.

The three great Mexican muralists *(los tres grandes)* — Diego Rivera, José Clemente Orozco, and Siqueiros — all created works in the United States during the early 1930s. These murals and the controversies that swirled around them because of their strong political messages greatly influenced not only the U.S. muralists during the depression era (including such Mexican Americans as José Aceves, Antonio García, and Edward Chávez) but also the American school of social realism that emerged in the later 1930s. The Chicano artists of the 1970s did not have far to turn to find a precedent for their socially concerned art.

Hundreds of Chicano artists ultimately involved themselves with the mural movement, often forming groups committed to the enterprise. In Los Angeles, Los Four — Carlos Almaraz, Frank Romero, Gilbert "Magú" Luján, and Roberto de la Rocha (sometimes with a fifth artist, Judithe Hernández) — created some of the first spray-can murals; they were also the first local Chicano artists to show their work at the Los Angeles Country Museum of Art (in 1974). In San Francisco *Mujeres Muralistas* (Women Muralists) — Patricia Rodríguez, Graciela Carrillo, Irene Pérez, Consuelo Méndez, and others — provided positive images for Chicanas and all women. And in Santa Fe *Artes Guadalupanos de Aztlán* (Guadalupe Arts of Aztlán) — with brothers Samuel, Carlos, and Albert Leyba, as well as Gerónimo Guzmán, Pancho Hunter, and Gilberto Garduño — emphasized the state's multicultural heritage in murals on the State Records Center and other buildings. Just a few of the many important murals are:

• *The Great Wall of Los Angeles* (1978–83, Tujunga Wash drainage canal, San Fernando Valley), directed by Judy Baca. Representing California history from a multiethnic perspective, this half-mile-long mural depicts the first Native American culture, both

Spanish and Mexican rule, and the many subsequent waves of immigrants. Specific panels highlight struggles faced by different ethnic groups, such as the repatriation of Mexicans during the depression (see pages 138–140). More than 250 teenagers and 50 artists participated in the mural's creation.

• *Black and White Moratorium Mural* (1973, Estrada Courts Housing Project, East Los Angeles) by Willie Herrón and Gronk (Glugio Gronk Nicandro). Done mostly in black and white, this graphic mural features more than 20 vignettes, primarily of life in the barrio and protesters participating in anti-Vietnam demonstrations. A close-up of a screaming woman near a phalanx of policemen during the demonstrations is just one of the images decrying police brutality.

• *The Broadway Mural* (1981, Victor Clothing Company, Los Angeles) by John Valadez. Based on photographs the artist took of street life in the area and done in a photo-realist style, this interior mural re-creates the many faces of diverse backgrounds that populate downtown Los Angeles. Another of the many murals both inside and outside this building is *460 Years of Chicano History* by Gonzalo Plascencia.

• *Gerónimo* (1981, Centro Cultural de la Raza, Balboa Park, San Diego) by Victor Ochoa. Rifle ready, the Apache warrior Gerónimo, haloed by a blazing sun, symbolizes resistance. All around him are images of Chicano culture, such as an actor from El Teatro Campesino in a skeleton costume.

• *La raza cósmica* (*The Cosmic Race*, 1977, Pan American Center, Austin) by Raúl Valdez and others. Painted on an outdoor stage as well as nearby buildings, the images in this mural series range from a battle between the Aztecs and the Spanish, through figures from the Mexican Revolution, to vignettes of contemporary U.S. barrio life. Dominating the central stage area is the eagle that is the symbol of César Chávez's United Farm Workers (see pages 149–151).

• *History of the Mexican American Worker* (1974–75, Blue Island, Illinois, near Chicago) by Raymond Patlán, Vicente Mendoza, and José Nario. This controversial mural includes images of heroic former Mexican president Benito Juárez, blue-collar workers, the eagle of César Chávez's United Farm Workers, and others.

A DIVERSITY OF EXPRESSION

The mural movement is but one example of the strong political statements that have been made by Latino artists. Influenced by the earlier Puerto Rican poster movement, Jorge Soto and other Nuyorican artists formed the *Taller Boricua*, an artists' workshop, in 1969 to forge an art that spoke to the New York barrio and supply posters for the Puerto Rican Socialists, Young Lords (see page 157), and other community groups. Chicanos also created memorable poster art, such as Rupert García's (see also page 340) 1973 silk screen *¡Cesen deportación! (Stop Deportation!)* with three black bands of barbed wire set against a bloodred background.

Of course, Latino artists have created forceful works, conveying diverse visions of the world, in all the traditional media, from easel painting to sculpture. The only way to appreciate the range of Latino expression in the visual arts is to look at the many works on display in museums and galleries across the United States. A few works to start with include:

• *Lettuce Worker II, Salinas Valley* (1953) by Antonio Frasconi, a woodcut foregrounding a large bending picker working his way along seemingly endless rows of lettuce. Frasconi, who grew up in Uruguay, was called "the U.S.'s foremost woodcut artist" by *Time* magazine in 1953. His socially concerned prints can be seen in many books as well as museums.

• *Archaeological Find 3* (1961, Museum of Modern Art) by Ralph Montañez Ortiz, a burned mattress that the artist created by setting fire to an old mattress, soaking it in the ocean, tearing it, and further destroying it as it dried. A proponent of the destruction in art movement, Ortiz is also known for a televised performance piece in which he smashed a piano—a work that helped inspire Arthur Janov to develop his primal scream therapy.

• **Women and Dog** (1964, Whitney Museum of American Art) by Marisol, a witty ensemble of a girl and three women—with painted wood-block bodies—going for a walk with a dog, which wears a real collar and leash. The women's heads are all self-portraits of Marisol (one is actually a photograph on a rounded wood form).

• **Silueta Series (Silhouette Series,** 1973–80) by Ana Mendieta, pieces in which the artist literally left her own body imprint in the earth, recorded in photographs. At times she lined the dug-out cavity where her body had rested with gunpowder and then set it on fire, invoking Santería rituals of healing and transformation. In another series, the *Rupestrian Sculptures* (1981), Mendieta returned to her native Cuba to carve female body forms into the walls of limestone caves.

• **Sun Mad** (1981) by Ester Hernández, a silk screen mimicking the popular raisin box design but displays a skeletal woman as the grape-picking "maid" above the blurb "Sun Mad Raisins Unnaturally Grown with Insecticides-Miticides-Herbicides-Fungicides." This image was reproduced on T-shirts and postcards to protest the working conditions of Chicano farm laborers.

• **Death of Rubén Salazar** (1985–86, National Museum of American Art) by Frank Romero, a colorful, energetic painting showing a riot squad firing randomly into a barrio bar. A movie marquee at the side gives the painting title, a reference to the killing of a *Los Angeles Times* journalist during a protest march against the Vietnam War (see page 159).

• **Vaquero** (cast 1990, National Museum of American Art) by Luis Jiménez, a red-white-and-blue fiberglass sculpture portraying the original American cowboy, a pistol-waving Mexican victoriously straddling his bucking bronco. In this and other public sculptures Jiménez explodes the myths of popular culture and subverts racial stereotypes.

• **Untitled** (Death by Gun, 1990, shown at various museums) by Félix González-Torres, a poster documenting in relentless columns of photographs and captions the Americans killed by guns in one week. Hundreds of copies were stacked on the museum floor and viewers were invited to take one. A 1993 stack piece by this Cuban-born conceptual artist contained a black-and-white photograph, evocatively silhouetting a small bird against a vast, stormy sky.

■ ■ ■

Bricks and Stones

Spanish-influenced architecture may be the most immediately visible sign of this country's Hispanic heritage. Travel through Florida, the Southwest, or California, and the borrowings from the Spanish style are unmistakable. To speak of colonial architecture in these areas is to refer to *Spanish* constructions. Indeed, the oldest public building in the United States is Santa Fe's *Palacio de Gobernadores* (Palace of Governors), a flat-roofed adobe structure of 1610, mixing Spanish and Pueblo influences. Castillo de San Marcos in Saint Augustine, the oldest masonry fort in the continential United States, built between 1672 and 1695, was designed by Cuban Ignacio Daza to defend the settlement. Surrounded by a 17-foot-wide moat, it was fortified with 14-foot-thick towering walls made of resilient coquina, a local limestone formed by shells. Another imposing Spanish fort still standing today is Monterey's Presidio.

Most impressive of the early buildings created by the Spanish were (and are) the missions, constructed throughout the Southwest, from Texas to California, in the seventeenth through the early nineteenth centuries. (The missions in Florida, Georgia, the Carolinas, and Virginia are all long since destroyed and exist only as archaeological remains.) At times the only Spanish outpost along the frontier, these complexes generally included not only a church but also housing for the Catholic priests as well as the Mexican helpers and Indian converts. Initially, these missions followed the blend of Spanish architecture and indigenous styles that had evolved in Mexico in the sixteenth century, but variations took hold in different regions. In New Mexico, for instance, adobe was adopted from the Pueblo peoples as a building material, and flat-roofed buildings with exposed beams, or vigas, were common. More elaborate stone designs, with intricate portal sculptures and domed or vaulted roofs, can be found in Texas and Arizona. Today, tourists make special trips to see such specimens of mission architecture as:

- The various missions around San Antonio, Texas, including San Antonio de Valero, aka the Alamo (1718, but largely rebuilt); San Francisco de la Espada (1731), which has its own aqueduct; San Juan Capistrano (1731), noted for its *campanario*, a wall with arched openings for bells; the massive, domed Nuestra Señora de la Purísima Concepción (1731–55); and San José y San Miguel de Aguayo (1768–82), with its carved facade by the Spanish artist Pedro Huizar.
- The string of 21 California missions built by Father Junípero Serra and his followers (see pages 68–69), from the first and southernmost mission, founded in 1769 in San Diego, to the last and northernmost mission, founded in 1823 in Sonoma. A few highlights along this route are the low-lying *campanario* at San Juan Capistrano, a mission famed for its swallows; the imposing classic facade of Santa Bárbara; San Luis Obispo de Tolosa, the mission that introduced the tile roof to California; and the striking star-windowed San Carlos Borromeo de Carmelo, Father Serra's headquarters and burial site.
- The many adobe mission churches in New Mexico, including the elongated San Felipe (1601; rebuilt 1706 and circa 1801), with its walled plaza in front; San José de Gracia de Las Trampas (circa 1760) with its wooden towers and balcony; San Francisco de Asís (1813–15) in

Ranchos de Taos, known to many through Georgia O'Keeffe's paintings; and El Santuario in Chimayo (1816), a major pilgrimage site filled with mementos of those who have been healed here.

• One of the finest examples of the mission style, with an ornate sculpted facade: San Xavier del Bac, or the "White Dove of the Desert," founded by Father Eusebio Francisco Kino near Tucson, Arizona, in 1700 and later rebuilt by the Franciscans (1783–97).

The Spanish colonial style of the missions extended to domestic architecture. In the Florida territory, houses with whitewashed plaster walls, covered balconies, and grated windows were common, while in the Southwest, Spanish settlers built self-contained adobe haciendas with interior courtyards and corrals. During the nineteenth century, Spanish-influenced town houses with whitewashed adobe plaster walls, colorful red roof tiles, and decorative window grilles dotted the Southwest and California. Often they were built around a light-filled interior patio with a fountain at the center. In California especially, the new Monterey style, with its two-story colonnaded gallery, took hold, mixing Spanish, Anglo, and Greek Revival elements.

But it was in the early twentieth century that a major Spanish revival shaped the look of much of California and the Southwest, as well as parts of Florida. The popular mission style, as its name proclaims, mimicked elements of the colonial missions—from thick white stucco walls and red tile roofs to shaped parapets, arcaded entry porches, and even bell towers. Soon eclectic borrowings from Spanish models, as well as other Mediterranean styles, sprang up throughout the area. Fashionable residences in Florida, the Southwest, and California played with arched openings, quatrefoil windows, rounded towers, airy interior courtyards, ornate Moorish tilework, and elaborate grillwork. Whole middle-class neighborhoods took on a distinct Spanish-flavored stucco-and-tile design.

The infatuation with the Spanish look, especially in the warmer climates for which it is designed, continues. In recent years, Peruvian-born Bernardo Fort-Brescia, owner of Miami-based architecture firm Arquitectónica, has brought Spanish colonial elements into apartment and office buildings, resorts, and shopping centers across the country. On a less elevated level, the elements associated with the style have crept into everything from mini-malls to suburban developments, especially in southern California.

A related trend is the so-called Santa Fe style, popular in recent years, which goes beyond building architecture to interior decor. Drawing on a mix of Spanish and Native American sources, it infuses homes and other buildings with warm earth tones and the soft, rounded edges of adobe or stucco construction, at the same time flaunting colorful rugs and fabrics and decorative ceramic tilework. Throughout the country, people have turned to the Southwest and its Hispanic and Indian heritage to bring an inviting warmth, with a touch of romance, to their dwellings.

ON THE PLAYING FIELDS

Two American sports would be almost unthinkable without the Latino contribution: baseball and rodeo. After some U.S. sailors, according to most accounts, introduced baseball to Cuba in the mid-1860s, the sport quickly took hold on that island and soon spread to Puerto Rico, Mexico, and other Latin countries. When the first

U.S. professional league started in 1871, it included a Cuban player, Esteban Bellán, who later helped build up the sport in his own country. By the end of the 1800s, Cuba already was a mecca for ballplayers. In the twentieth century, U.S. players increasingly trained on the teams there, and major-league teams traveled to its warmer climate for off-season training. And in Cuba—in contrast to the United States before 1947—there was no color bar: white major-leaguers, African Americans from the Negro Leagues, and Latin players all took to the field together.

Hispanic players also continued to play on U.S. teams. A few—such as dark-skinned Cuban-born pitcher Adolfo "Dolph" Luque (see page 341), who played from 1914 to 1935, gained fame in the majors even before 1947. Others, such as Cuban-born Hall of Famer Martín Dihigo (see page 341), starred on Negro League teams. And it wasn't only the men who played pro ball. Several Cuban-born women were snapped up by the All-American Girls Baseball League in the late 1940s and early 1950s.

In the last 50 years, Latinos have figured among the greatest players on the field. No who's who of American baseball would be complete without such Hall of Famers as record-breaking shortstop and base stealer Luis Aparicio (see page 343); seven-time American League batting champion Rod Carew (see pages 344–345); four-time National League batting champion Roberto Clemente (see pages 342–343); two-time triple crown pitcher Vernon "Lefty" Gómez (see pages 341–342), with six World Series wins (and no losses); top-ranked catcher and manager Al López (see page 342); and Juan Marichal, 243-game winner, celebrated for his varied pitches. More recently, Latinos have set such records as:

• First rookie to win Cy Young Award: Mexican American pitcher Fernando Valenzuela, in 1981, when he was also Rookie of the Year.
• First (and only) player to hit the 40 mark in both home runs and stolen bases in the same season: Cuban American outfielder José Canseco with 42 homers and 40 stolen bases in 1988, when he

was also the American League's Most Valuable Player. In 1994, Canseco also tied three other players' record of most walks in a row (7).

• Most assists by first baseman in National League: Keith Hernández, with 1,662 between 1974 and 1989. He also set a record by leading the league in double plays for six years.

• Top baseball salary in 1994: outfielder Bobby Bonilla of the New York Mets at $6.3 million.

• American League batting champion for 1995: Edgar Martínez of the Seattle Mariners with a .356 average. He also led the league in 1992.

Also noteworthy: Willie Hernández in 1984 was only the seventh pitcher—and first Hispanic—ever to win both the Most Valuable Player and Cy Young Awards in a single season. Nicaraguan-born Dennis Martínez pitched a perfect game for the Montreal Expos in 1991, a feat accomplished only 14 times since 1880; Martínez was also the first Hispanic to do so.

Like the American cowboy, the American rodeo originated in the Mexican ranching culture. As early as the seventeenth century, mestizo *vaqueros* (cowboys)—also known as *charros*—held contests, or *charrerías*, to show off their riding and roping skills. By the nineteenth century these contests had become Mexico's national sport, and hundreds of spectators gathered for local cowboy fiestas, or *charreadas*, both in Mexico and what is now the American Southwest. One popular event was the *correr el gallo* (run the rooster), when a rider in the finest of *charro* attire quickly swooped down from his galloping mount to retrieve a coin or some other small object lying on the ground.

As Anglo Americans joined the cattle culture, they took on the challenge of these competitions and soon dressed up for their own local roundups, featuring many of the *charreada* contests. Today's main professional rodeo events—bareback riding, saddle bronc riding, bull riding, calf roping, and steer wrestling—all stem from the original Mexican competitions. And, especially in the Southwest, Mexican Americans continue to hold their own *charreadas*.

Among the many other sports in which Hispanics are prominent is boxing, which also attracts enthusiastic Latino spectators. Most of the lighter-weight classes have been dominated by Latinos or Latin Americans for years. Puerto Rican Sixto Escobar, for example, took the world bantamweight title in 1936, regained it in 1938, and was soon followed by Mexican American Manuel Ortiz, who held the title for almost eight years (1942–50)—except for a brief two-month period in 1947. One of the longer-reigning lightweight champs was Puerto Rican Carlos Ortiz, titleholder from 1962 to 1968, except for a seven-month period in 1965. A more recent lightweight boxer to watch is Oscar de la Hoya, the only U.S. boxing gold medalist at the 1992 Olympics and currently the WBC super lightweight champion.

Although soccer only occasionally draws major headlines in the United States, it is probably *the* top sport in the rest of the world and has many Latino fans. Uruguay bested Argentina to win the first World Cup in 1930. And in 1994, Brazil became the first to win four World Cup titles by beating Italy. With Major League Soccer just kicking off in the United States, many Latin and Latino stars may become familiar names to the American public.

A few of the other sports with top-ranked Latinos (past and present) include:

Football: Manny Fernández, leading defensive linesman for the Miami Dolphins (1968–77); Tom Flores (see pages 343–344), Super Bowl ring winner first as a quarterback (1967) and later twice as head coach of the Raiders (1981, 1984); Anthony Muñoz, three-time Pro Bowl player (1982–84); and Jim Plunkett (see page 345), 1971 American Football League Rookie of the Year and Most Valuable Player of Super Bowl XV (1981).

Golf: Nancy López (see page 345), four-time Ladies Professional Golf Association player of the year (1978–79, 1985, 1988) and member of its Hall of Fame; Juan "Chi Chi" Rodríguez (see page 343), one of only two players to ever score three consecutive wins on the Senior PGA tour (1987); and Lee Trevino (see page 344), two-time U.S. Open (1968, 1971) and PGA champ (1974, 1984) and three-time Senior PGA Player of the Year (1990, 1992, 1994).

Tennis: Rosemary Casals, five-time Wimbledon doubles champ with partner Billie Jean King (1967–73); Richard Alonzo "Pancho" González (see page 342), two-time U.S. singles champ (1948–49) and nine-time world pro singles champ (1954–62); and Puerto Rican Gigi Fernández and Cuban American Mary Joe Fernández, together the doubles gold medalists for the United States at the 1992 and 1996 Olympics.

EATING, DRINKING

Most Americans are unaware of just how much they owe to the Spanish and to the original Aztec inhabitants of Mexico for their daily diet. Bite into a hamburger or a juicy steak, and consider that it was Spanish and Mexican settlers who started grazing herds in what is now Texas. Slice some tomatoes for a salad, and ponder that the Spanish introduced this vegetable to Europe after learning about it from the natives of Mexico as well as Peru. Now move on to dessert—whether you choose something chocolate or vanilla, you are opting for a flavor that originated in pre-Columbian Mexico.

The Spanish and Mexican influence extends far beyond specific foods to dishes found in many general American cookbooks. What could be easier as an appetizer than mashing some ripe avocados, along with some garlic and lime and perhaps a jalapeño for added punch, into the popular dip called guacamole and filling up a bowl with store-bought tortilla chips? For a meat dish, you might look up a recipe for that Tex-Mex standby chili con carne, which some might say has become as American as apple pie. Among the common desserts that have found their way into U.S. hearts (and stomachs) via Spanish settlers and their descendants are rice pudding and the caramel-glazed custard known as flan.

Today, one of the most touted regional cuisines is southwestern cooking, especially the Santa Fe variety, which is rooted in the traditional dishes of Nuevo México, under Spanish and then Mexican rule until the mid–nineteenth century. Chile peppers are one of the essential ingredients of this cuisine, just as they are in Mexican cooking, and tortillas are commonly used for tacos, enchiladas, burritos, and the like.

The growing popularity of Latino foods—from traditional Mexican American dishes to the newer flavors introduced by Puerto Ricans, Cubans, and others—can be seen everywhere, from restaurant menus to supermarket aisles to cookbook shelves. Trendy urban restaurants now offer such hybrid treats as goat-cheese-and-mint burritos, and fast-food chains like Taco Bell are fixtures at many shopping centers. Tapas bars, featuring the snacks served in bars in Spain, are springing up in cities from coast to coast. Microwave aficiondos can pick up frozen enchiladas and similar entrées along with their other groceries, and supermarkets in several states, especially in the Southwest, display a dozen or more varieties of chiles for enterprising cooks. TV commercials proudly proclaim the punch of a particular brand of salsa. And in bookstores the eager learner can choose from dozens of volumes on southwestern and Mexican dishes, as well as introductions to the specialties of Puerto Rico and the Cuban-based flavors that underlie the hot new Miami cuisine. Latino foods are there for the tasting.

MEXICAN CUISINE

Mexican cuisine, as we know it today, is truly *mestizo* (of mixed blood), combining mainly Spanish and Indian influences. When the Spaniards arrived in Mexico and feasted at the table of the Aztec emperor Moctezuma II, they encountered and quickly adopted many new foods—not only tomatoes, vanilla, and chocolate but also corn, chiles, a variety of new beans (such as black and pinto beans), squash, avocado, and different tropical fruits (such as papaya). The Spanish settlers soon introduced the New World to olive oil and lard, wheat and rice, peas and globe onions, coriander (cilantro), citrus fruits, and bananas.

Over the years different styles of Mexican cooking evolved in different regions, depending on the vegetation and geography. Oaxaca and Puebla, for example, are known for their *moles,* or spicy sauces made with different kinds of chiles and often chocolate. Dishes from Veracruz, such as the famous Veracruz sauce used with red snapper and other fish, show a strong Spanish influence, using both olives and olive oil, as well as other Spanish staples. Although all these tastes have made their way into the United States, it is *norteño* cooking, from the north of Mexico, that extended strong roots into Texas as well as the Southwest, for until the mid-nineteenth century there was no border along the Rio Grande. Indeed, some Tex-Mex favorites, such as *menudo* (a tripe stew) and the flour tortillas (made from wheat) used for burritos, may be more popular now in the United States than in the northern Mexican states where they originated. And the art of making a flavorful chili—slowly cooking ground meat, chiles, liquid, spices, and often beans and tomatoes in a large pot—is a sine qua non of Texas cooking, and most communities there sponsor yearly chili cook-offs.

The chile peppers that give chili its name are an essential ingredient not only of Mexican but also of Tex-Mex and other southwestern cooking. Rich in vitamins A and C, they add both nutrition and flavor to a variety of dishes. There are well over 100 types, each with a distinct flavor, ranging from mild to very hot *(picante),* and many of these are grown in Texas and other parts of the Southwest, as well as California. For southwestern cooking some popular fresh chiles—usually used when they are still green, before ripening to red—are the Anaheim (mild to slightly hot), *güero* (also called the banana pepper, it's yellow and fairly hot), jalapeño (sometimes fiery), *poblano* (mild to fairly hot), and serrano (sometimes fiery). The hottest fresh chile is the *habanero,* used for sauces in the Yucatán and Campeche. Some dried (red) chiles to be found in the United States are the *ancho* (also called *mulato,* this is the dried poblano, mild to slightly hot), cayenne (very long and thin, it's often ground and can be fiery), *chipotle* (the smoke-dried jalapeño, often fiery), and *pasilla* (wrinkled and dark brown, resembling a raisin—*pasa* in Spanish—it's mild to fairly hot).

Some additional Mexican foods and dishes that have found their way onto American tables:

• **Burrito:** A wheat tortilla, wrapped around a warm filling—usually of rice, beans (refried or black), and chicken, beef, or cheese—and covered with red *(rojo)* or green *(verde)* chile sauce.

• *Ceviche:* Raw fish or other seafood marinated in lime juice and combined with onion, tomato, and avocado; depending on the recipe, Mexican oregano or chiles may be used.

• *Chile con queso:* Melted cheese with green chiles, served as an appetizer or light entrée. Fried tortillas are usually used to scoop it up.

• *Chiles rellenos:* Large, relatively mild chiles (usually *poblanos*) stuffed with cheese or meat; dipped in a batter of egg, milk, and flour; then fried.

• **Chimichanga:** Flour tortilla stuffed—usually with refried beans, meat, and cheese—then rolled up and deep-fried. It's served with red or green chile sauce, as well as such garnishes as lettuce, tomato, sour cream, and chopped onions.

• **Chorizo:** Pork sausage usually seasoned with ground chile and used in scrambled eggs, tacos, soups, and stews.

• **Enchilada:** Tortilla stuffed traditionally with cheese or chicken, then rolled and covered with red or green chile sauce. Beef enchiladas are a Tex-Mex innovation.

• **Fajita:** Strips of grilled marinated skirt steak *(fajita* in Spanish) served on a tortilla, usually with guacamole, onions, and salsa. Tex-Mex style, the meat may be marinated in anything from lime juice to pickled jalapeño juice to beer. Chicken and shrimp are also served fajita style.

• **Frijoles:** Beans. Pinto beans are most popular in northern Mexico and the American Southwest, while black beans top the list elsewhere in Mexico. Refried beans *(frijoles refritos)* are pinto beans that have first been cooked (boiled) and are then—as leftovers—partly mashed and fried, traditionally in lard or bacon drippings.

• *Huevos rancheros:* Ranch-style eggs, a Mexican breakfast dish popular throughout the Southwest. Essentially it consists of fried eggs placed on lightly fried tortillas and topped with red or green chile sauce and some grated Monterey Jack cheese.

• *Mole poblano:* Spicy chocolate sauce said to have been invented by nuns in Mexico's Puebla region. Chicken stock, chile peppers, almonds, garlic, onions, tomatoes, raisins, sesame seeds, cinnamon, cloves, cilantro, salt, and other flavors are all mixed in with the chocolate. It's often served over turkey.

• **Nachos:** Popular snack *(antojito)*, most basically consisting of a layer of *tostados* (tortilla chips) covered with shredded cheese and then broiled and often garnished with chopped jalapeño. Variations in many southwestern bars now include refried beans or shredded steak along with garnishes of lettuce, tomatoes, guacamole, sour cream, and salsa.

• **Quesadilla:** Snack made by filling tortilla dough with cheese and often jalapeños, then deep-frying.

• **Salsa:** Spanish for "sauce." In U.S. usage the term refers to uncooked sauces, used as condiments, essentially made from tomatoes (red) or tomatillos (green), chopped onions, and chiles. *Salsa fresca* is made with fresh raw ingredients. *Salsa picante* gets its kick from the fierier chile peppers.

• **Taco:** Most commonly, a crisp-fried corn tortilla folded in a half-moon shape, traditionally filled with spiced ground meat or chicken (though vegetarian versions are now available) and garnished with shredded lettuce, salsa, and sometimes cheese. Soft tacos are made with warm corn or flour tortillas rolled around shredded meat or chicken flavored with green chile or commercial taco sauce. *Flautas*, popular in the Southwest, are another variation, in which the tortilla is rolled around the filling into a tight cylinder and then fried until it is crisp.

• **Tamale:** Corn husk or other leaf wrapping folded around *masa*

(Mexican corn dough), usually combined with spicy meat or other fillings, to form a rectangular packet, then steamed. Used by the Aztecs in their celebrations, tamales in Mexico now come in innumerable varieties, from those wrapped in banana leaves to some baked in a barbecue pit. One of the first Mexican foods to be picked up by Anglo settlers in Texas, tamales were once commonly sold by street vendors there.

• **Tomatillo:** So-called green tomato native to Mexico—not related to the red tomato. In Mexico they're often used for green chile sauces.

• **Tortilla:** Soft, thin pancake, traditionally of ground corn, pressed or rolled, then baked. In northern Mexico and the United States, flour tortillas are popular. Cold tortillas are always reheated before being used to make burritos, enchiladas, or whatever.

Americans can also thank Mexicans and Mexican Americans for several popular alcoholic drinks. Originally from Spain, *sangría*—combining red wine and brandy with oranges and lemons or limes—gained popularity in the United States in Mexican restaurants and as a party punch. Today, one of the favored cocktails in the Southwest is the margarita, made with tequila (an alcoholic beverage from the agave tree), Triple Sec or Cointreau, and lime juice. Tequila, of course, can be sipped on its own; a more recent arrival is mescal, another agave drink, with a different taste because it comes from a different variety of the plant. And then there's Kahlúa, the tasty coffee liqueur.

PUERTO RICAN CUISINE

Combining the Spanish influence with native Taíno cooking and tastes introduced by enslaved Africans, Puerto Rican cooking has its own distinctive flavor. As Caribbean cooking in general gains in popularity, its specialties are becoming more widely known. New cookbooks focus on this cuisine, and most of the ingredients are available throughout the United States from mail-order suppliers.

Rice, often colored bright yellow with annatto oil, and beans, especially green pigeon peas and pink beans, are basic fare. Chicken is another, almost daily, ingredient — often, as on other Spanish Caribbean islands, prepared as *arroz con pollo* (chicken with rice), with everything combined in a single pot. A traditional holiday treat is roasted suckling pig, or alternatively, for Nuyoricans and other mainlanders who may have trouble finding a whole pig, roasted pork shoulder.

Two essentials to Puerto Rican cooking are *adobo,* a dry seasoning mix, and *sofrito,* a kind of puree underlying many sauces and stews. Available in bottled form, *adobo* combines garlic powder, oregano, black pepper, onion powder, and salt. The base for *sofrito* is made with cilantro, green bell pepper, sweet chile pepper, onion, and garlic, all blended with oil. This is then mixed and sautéed with tomato sauce, *alcaparrado* (a bottled mixture of capers, green olives, and pimientos), and sometimes cooking ham.

A few other Puerto Rican specialties:

• *Frituras:* Fritters, served as appetizers. One popular kind on the island is made with dry salted codfish, or *bacalao.*

• *Mofongo:* Fried green plantain mashed, then shaped into a ball; traditionally combined with garlic and pork cracklings but now often stuffed with seafood, vegetables, or chicken.

• *Pasteles:* Dumplings made from a vegetable dough (combining, for example, finely grated taro root, potato, unripe bananas, and green plantain), then stuffed with a pork, seafood, or poultry filling.

• *Tostones:* Double-fried green plantain slices, a kind of Puerto Rican equivalent to French fries. At some fancy restaurants this common treat has become a gourmet appetizer, stuffed with shrimp or other kinds of seafood.

For many Americans, however, probably the best-known Puerto Rican taste is a drink, the piña colada, combining the rum for which the island is famous with pineapple and coconut flavors.

CUBAN CUISINE

From its special black bean soup to its fried *maduros* (ripe plantains), Cuban cooking is finding its way into the American mainstream via Florida, where it has been an important influence not just since Castro's revolution brought tens of thousands of refugees to the United States (see pages 167–168), but as early as the mid-nineteenth century, when Cuban cigar workers arrived in the Key West and Tampa areas (see pages 123–124). In contrast to Mexican fare, Cuban cuisine is generally not hot, broadening its appeal to many Anglo Americans. The main flavorings are garlic, onion, cumin, and lime. Cuban cooking has been categorized under the rubric of "comfort food," with its warming soups and stews, its starchy root vegetables, such as sweet potato or yuca (also called cassava, the source of tapioca), and its custard desserts.

Cuban cuisine mixes ingredients and techniques from the original Taíno and Siboney inhabitants, the Spanish settlers, and the African slaves forced to harvest the island's sugarcane. The Indian contribution can be savored directly today in the earthy-tasting seasoning of annatto seeds and a healthful stew called *ajiaco* (including meat, plantain, yucca, potato, and other Cuban vegetables). The Spanish flavor is clearly preserved in Cuban-style *arroz con pollo* (a combination of chicken and yellow rice roughly comparable to the famed Spanish paella—minus the seafood), desserts like flan, and the widespread use of olive oil. Plantains, almost a staple now in Cuban meals, were initially popularized by Africans, for whom it was a native food.

As with Puerto Rican cooking, although in somewhat different versions, *sofrito* and *adobo* underlie many dishes. The Cuban *sofrito*— the base of many soups and stews—is sautéed with garlic, onion, and *cachucha* chiles (very mild and easily replaced with ordinary bell peppers). *Adobo* Cuban style is a marinade, blending sour orange or lime juice with garlic, cumin, oregano, and salt in a tangy paste. A related concoction is *mojo*, a cooked vinaigrette-type table sauce, combining sour orange juice and garlic along with olive oil, cumin, salt, and pepper. It jazzes up everything from grilled seafood to the multi-ingredient Cuban sandwich.

Some other Cuban tastes of note:

- **Lechón asado:** Roast suckling pig, the traditional dish on *nochebuena* (Christmas Eve). Caterers supply this in Florida, but some families now create their own version with half a fresh ham or pork leg.
- **Moros:** Soupy black beans ladled over rice, a common dish on the Cuban table. The name is short for *moros y cristianos* (Moors and Christians), a play on the mix of colors.
- **Picadillo:** Ground beef cooked with onion, bell pepper, garlic, raisins, olives, tomato, and other ingredients. *Picadillo* can be eaten on its own or stuffed in fritters.
- **Ropa vieja:** A kind of beef hash, combining skirt steak with onions, bell peppers, tomato sauce, and other ingredients. The name translates as "old clothes," referring to the torn strips of meat.
- **Vaca frita:** Fried beef, or literally "fried cow." Thinly shredded skirt steak is marinated in lime juice and garlic before being deep-fried.
- **Yuca con mojo:** Boiled yuca (a buttery-tasting root vegetable) served with a sauce of garlic and sour orange (or lime) juice.

Favorite Cuban drinks include a variety of rum concoctions, such as the daiquiri (rum, lime juice, and sugar) and Cuba libre (free Cuba). The latter, a mix of rum and Coke with sugar and lime juice, first took hold during the Spanish-Cuban-American War but has recently been renamed *mentirita* (little lie) by some Cuban Americans. *Café cubano* (Cuban coffee), a sugar-sweetened espresso, has become an official drink of Miami and is gaining in popularity elsewhere in the United States; served in a small cup with a splash of hot milk it becomes the *cortadita*. And there's always the popular Spanish standby favored by many Latinos and non-Latinos: *café con leche* (a blend of coffee and hot milk).

OTHER FLAVORS

Spanish cuisine was the first European food to find its way to the New World, and it remains popular among Latinos and non-Latinos alike. Not surprisingly, Spanish food shares many ingredients and flavors with its Hispanic descendants. But among the foods uniquely associated with Spain, some of the most well-loved include: *tapas*, a whole category of bite-size snacks—*tortilla* (Spanish omelet), olives, *pulpo* (octopus), and various cheeses and sausages—that are served à la carte in *tapas* bars; *gazpacho*, a chilled soup of tomatoes, cucumbers, vinegar, olive oil, garlic, and pimiento; paella, a mix of saffron rice with seafood that often includes chicken, meats, red pepper, green peas, and other ingredients; and the familiar *sangría*.

Nicaraguan, Honduran, Colombian, and Dominican dishes are among the newer arrivals on American shores. Restaurants and street fair booths featuring these cuisines appear wherever there are sizable immigrant populations. Miami residents, for example, can snack on *arepas* (fried cheesy cornmeal treats from Colombia, which might be compared to grilled cheese sandwiches) or *tajadas* (crunchy plantain chips from Nicaragua). Another Nicaraguan specialty fast entering the mainstream in South Florida is *tres leches* (three-milk cake), a sponge cake drenched with a creamy milk syrup and topped with meringue. Soon, no doubt, Americans across the country will be sampling these delights.

FIESTA TIME

Food, music, dancing, colorful flowers and decorations—all come to mind with the word "fiesta." It is a time for Latinos to celebrate, to honor, to come together and enjoy. The occasion may be a birthday party or a more complex, communal rite such as the Day of the Dead.

Most of the fiestas celebrated by Latinos in the United States have a long history, often incorporating both Indian and Spanish Catholic influences. Agricultural ceremonies, such as preparations to clear the land for spring planting, may be linked to Christian holidays, such as Candlemas in early February. Rites associated with such ancient Aztec gods as Tlaloc, the rain god, have long been merged with celebrations for such Christian saints as San Isidro, the patron saint of farmers.

Stemming from a rural tradition where priests were scarce is the notion of saints as personal intermediaries, linking ordinary people to God. Throughout the Southwest and California, many Mexican Americans continue to honor the patron saint of their local community. On the saint's feast day, there may be a colorful procession, embellished with an elaborate float, as well as a church mass, folk dances, traditional brass-and-guitar mariachi bands, and plenty to eat and drink. Puerto Ricans, Cuban Americans, and other Latinos also celebrate special saint days. At home, many Latinos build altars to their personal patron saints.

Most Latinos (like their Spanish forebears) are Catholic, so besides the many saint days, they observe the traditional church holidays, especially around Easter and Christmas. They also celebrate such rites of passage as baptisms and weddings. To honor the godparents of a newly baptized infant, for example, the parents may hold a luncheon or dinner party, sometimes hiring a band for dancing. At a wedding the celebrating may continue long after the church ceremony and reception (as it does among many other Americans), into the next day.

An elaborate affair among Cuban Americans, as well as Mexican Americans and Puerto Ricans, is the *quinceañera* or *fiesta de quince años* (feast of 15 years), honoring the transition from girlhood to womanhood. Traditionally, this ceremony includes a church mass for the young woman, who is attended to by as many as 14 female friends, who each choose a male companion. The feted young woman wears an ornate gown (often white), and afterward there is a large dinner and dance—much like a fancy coming-out party or even a wedding. This is *the* event for many young Latinas, and no expense is spared.

Alongside the Catholic fiestas are those stemming from the traditions of Santería (originally *lucumí*), a religion formed in Cuba by West African slaves, who fused their own Yoruba traditions with some of the trappings of Roman Catholicism. Forbidden to practice their African religion and worship their *orishas*, or deities, the slaves countered by "adopting" saints from the Catholic Church and assigning their images to various Yoruba gods. So when they appeared to be celebrating Catholic religious feasts or worshiping Catholic images, they were really praying to their own *orishas*. Today, a number of people of Cuban (as well as Dominican and Puerto Rican) descent continue to practice Santería, which has its own priesthood and rituals, many of which are guarded as religious secrets by initiates. A related practice is *santerismo*, a blend of Santería with Puerto Rican *espiritismo* (spiritism) but without priests.

Beyond the religious fiestas are the secular celebrations. Some holidays honor patriotic or historical events in Latinos' home countries that are so significant they continue to be celebrated by communities in the United States. Other fiestas are sporting events, such as *charreadas*, or Mexican rodeos, which include a variety of riding competitions as well as live music from mariachi or other traditional bands and food. A more recent Chicano phenomenon is the lowrider get-together, sometimes held in conjunction with another holiday. Car owners proudly display their "lowriders," which are literally close to the ground and often elaborately painted and decorated. After hopping competitions (with hydraulic lifters raising the cars' front ends) and cruising time, celebrants may gather for food and dancing.

Among the many traditions associated with fiestas, probably the best known is the piñata, featured at Mexican birthday and Christmas celebrations. Many Americans of all backgrounds have adopted this custom. Traditionally a clay or papier-mâché container, the piñata is usually colorfully decorated in an animal shape and filled with small toys, candies, and fruits. It is hung from a ceiling or under a tree, and blindfolded children (and playful adults) take turns trying to break it with a stick—until its contents fall to the ground and everyone scrambles to pick them up.

Some of the important fiestas celebrated by Latinos are:

January 6: *Día de los Reyes Magos* or *Día de los Tres Reyes* (Day of the Three Kings, or Epiphany). This Catholic holiday, commemorating the bringing of gifts by the Three Kings to baby Jesus, is the traditional day of gift giving for many Latinos and Latin Americans. Children receive gifts supposedly brought to them by the Three Kings (just like Santa Claus). Among Mexicans, a special bread is baked, filled with almonds, coins, and a doll of the baby Jesus. A more recent tradition is a parade in Little Havana, Miami.

January 11: Birthday of *Eugenio María de Hostos* (see also page 308), Puerto Rican educator and writer who advocated independence from Spain in the nineteenth century.

January 28: Birthday of *José Martí*, the poet and essayist who founded the Cuban Revolutionary Party and led the struggle for independence from Spain in the late nineteenth century (see pages 119–120).

February 2: *Día de la Candelaria* (Candlemas). This religious holiday celebrates the presentation of Christ at the temple and the purification of the Virgin Mary. Celebrants often take candles to the church for a blessing and then place them on the family altar. In some communities people also take seeds to be blessed, for this fiesta marks the beginning of the spring planting season.

February 24: *Grito de Baire* (Cry of Baire), commemorating the beginning of the 1895 Cuban war against Spain (see page 118).

March 21: Birthday of the great nineteenth-century Mexican president *Benito Juárez,* a courageous liberal reformer of Indian descent and a leader of the rebellion against French rule. (In 1864, Napoleon III had established a short-lived empire in Mexico under the Hapsburg prince Maximilian.)

March/April: *Ash Wednesday.* Marked by folk dancing in some places as well as traditional church ceremonies, this day signals the beginning of Lent, the 40 days of penance, prayer, and fasting in preparation for Easter Sunday. Before Ash Wednesday, people in Latin American countries and Spain (as well as Latinos) often celebrate at carnivals—sometimes lasting several days—since with the advent of Lent, dancing, drinking, and revelry are frowned upon.

March/April: *Holy Week,* including *Good Friday* and *Easter Sunday.* In addition to attending church services, some Latinos sponsor processions and other activities in their communities. In New Mexico and southern Colorado, *los Hermanos Penitentes* (Penitent Brothers), a lay religious group, reenact the 14 stations of the cross (the *vía crucis,* or "road of the cross") and then join with villagers on Good Friday for a restaging of the march to Calvary and the crucifixion. Afterward they celebrate the *tinieblas,* or earthquake ceremony, a ritual with 13 candles commemorating the death of Christ and the flight of the apostles. A more secular aspect of Mexican American Easter celebrations throughout the Southwest is the making of *cascarones* (hollow eggs decorated using crayons, paints, or tissue paper). Children hunt for these hidden eggs on Easter Sunday, much as in Anglo traditions.

April 17: Anniversary of the ill-fated *Bay of Pigs* invasion of 1961, celebrated in Cuba but considered a day of mourning among many exiled Cubans in the United States (see page 172).

May 3: *Día de la Santa Cruz* (Holy Cross Day). On this religious holiday celebrants adorn crosses and often statues of the Virgin with flowers. In some places it initiates a series of celebrations in honor of the Virgin Mary and the feminine role in the rites of spring. In Mexico this is also the day of the bricklayer, whose patron saint's symbol is the cross.

May 5: *Cinco de mayo,* celebrating the 1862 battle of Puebla, in which the Mexicans heroically defeated a French army force. (The French under Napoleon III were seeking to establish an empire in Mexico; they would succeed briefly two years later). In California and the Southwest, Mexican Americans honor their cultural heritage on this day with exuberant fiestas and parades. Many other Americans now join the eating, drinking, and dancing that commemorate this victory for independence.

May 15: Feast of *San Isidro* (Saint Isidore), patron saint of farmers. Especially popular in parts of Mexico, where livestock are decorated with flowers, this saint's day sometimes becomes a weeklong festival.

May 20: Cuba's Fourth of July, celebrating the beginning of the *Republic of Cuba* in 1902 (see page 125).

June 24: Feast of *San Juan* (St. John the Baptist), the patron saint of Puerto Rico. On the Sunday closest to this saint's day, New York Puerto Ricans hold a large-scale festival, including the famous Puerto Rican Day parade, with its elaborate floats, spirited dancers, and joyful marching bands. The huge event, combining religious and secular celebrations, attracts both Latinos and non-Latinos.

July 16: Feast of *Nuestra Señora del Carmen* (Our Lady of Carmen). This saint's day is of particular importance to seaside communities in Mexico and Puerto Rico.

July 17: Birthday of *Luis Muñoz Rivera* (see pages 302–303), Puerto Rican journalist and nationalist, who founded the San Juan paper

La Democracia, fought for independence from Spain, and later gained U.S. citizenship for Puerto Ricans.

July 25: Feast of *Santiago Apóstol* (Saint James). This saint's day may be honored with rodeos, feasts, and dancing in Mexico and Mexican American communities. In Puerto Rico villagers from Loíza celebrate with a religious procession and joyous dances by masqueraders. This tradition is carried on in New York's barrio, where dancers in traditional island costumes take to the streets, moving to a fast drumbeat. For all Puerto Ricans, this day has added significance, for it is their *Constitution Day,* commemorating the establishment of the Puerto Rican Commonwealth in 1952 (see pages 127–128).

September 8: Feast of *Virgen de la Caridad del Cobre* (Virgin of the Charity of Copper), the patron saint of Cuba, known affectionately as "Cachita." During colonial times, the Virgin is believed to have intervened directly during a violent storm, saving a boat of Cubans fleeing from the Spaniards as well as all the Cubans still on the island. She then moved into the mountains, to an area of copper mines, where she is honored with a much visited shrine. A symbol of Cuban identity, she is highly revered by Cuban Americans. Her feast day is marked by a special procession in Miami, where there is a church dedicated to her. On the same day practitioners of Santería pay homage to Ochún, their goddess of love, who is associated with Cachita.

September 16: *Grito de Dolores,* Mexico's Independence Day, commemorating the "cry" issued by Father Miguel Hidalgo y Costilla at his church in Dolores, marking the start of the Mexican war of independence (see pages 41–42). Today, Mexican celebrations are punctuated by a similar *grito,* or patriotic speech, as well as parades and picnics, featuring foods in red, white, and green (the color of the Mexican flag). In the United States the day is honored by the opening of celebrations for national Hispanic Heritage Month.

September 22: Feast of *Virgen de las Mercedes* (Virgin of Mercy), equivalent to the Santería god Obatalá. This saint's day is celebrated in parts of Cuba.

September 23: *Grito de Lares*, marking the start of the (ultimately abortive) Puerto Rican rebellion against Spain in 1868 (see page 117).

October 4: Feast of *San Francisco de Asís* (Saint Francis of Assisi). Particularly important in parts of Mexico and Puerto Rico, this saint's day is connected to harvest rituals.

October 10: *Grito de Yara,* commemorating the start of the Cuban Ten Years' War against Spain in 1868 (see pages 117–118).

October 12: *Día de la Raza* (Day of the Race), commemorating the landing of Christopher Columbus on the island of Guananí (in the Bahamas), which he called San Salvador, in 1492. In Latin America this day—the same date as Columbus Day—recognizes the fusion of the two races: European and Native American.

November 1–2: *Día de los Muertos* (Day of the Dead), a two-day fiesta including All Saints' Day (honoring saints and deceased children) and All Souls' Day (honoring deceased adults). During this major celebration for Mexicans and Mexican Americans, families visit the cemetery, first cleaning up their relatives' grave sites, later arriving with candles, flowers, and food for the honored souls, and frequently spending the night there in a communal vigil. In addition, many families decorate altars in their homes in honor of deceased relatives, including photos and other relics, offerings of food and flowers, and brightly colored paper skeletons and other symbols. Among the special foods baked for the deceased is *pan de muerto* (bread of the dead), a sweetened bread, usually with a skull or crossbones shape on top and colorfully decorated with sugar crystals. Candy makers also prepare elaborate *calaveras,* or sugar skulls, which may then be adorned with the name of a deceased friend or relative. For many Mexican Americans this is a time to honor not only the dead but also their heritage. Some dress in traditional costumes for a communal procession to the cemetery, others don colorful Mexican masks, and many participate in folk dancing after a ritual of prayers and songs for the dead.

November 19: *Discovery Day,* celebrating the landing of Columbus on the island of Puerto Rico in 1493, then called Borinquén by native Taínos.

December 4: Feast of *Santa Barbará* (Saint Barbara), associated with the Santería god Changó.

December 12: Feast of the *Virgen de Guadalupe,* the patron saint of Mexico. The champion of the Mexican people, the brown-skinned Virgin of Guadalupe is believed to have appeared to a small boy, Juan Diego, on this date in 1531 on a Mexico City hill. To convince the bishop of her appearance, the boy pointed to his cloak, where she had left her image. Today, many Mexicans and Mexican Americans make a pilgrimage to the shrine where this cloak hangs at the place where the Virgin appeared so many years ago. Both in Mexico and the United States the joyous celebrations on her feast day include church masses, religious processions, fairs, dances, and fireworks. In some places musicians begin serenading the Virgin at daybreak. For many, this holiday signals the beginning of the Christmas season.

Mid-December through January 6: *Las Navidades* (Christmas season). The entire Christmas season is a time of rejoicing for Latinos. Puerto Ricans sing carols *(villancicos)* and throw parties *(parrandas),* including *asaltos* (attacks), when groups of friends travel from house to house, paying surprise visits that become impromptu parties.

During the 12 nights leading up to Christmas, some Mexican

Americans reenact the Holy Family's search for an inn in celebrations called *posadas,* which means inns. Carrying candles, a group goes from house to house, knocking on doors and asking in song for a room. Refused again and again, they finally arrive at the chosen host's house, where the real party begins, including such traditional treats as *buñuelos* (sweet fritters) and tamales and the fun of breaking a piñata.

Some southwestern communities continue the tradition of the *pastorela,* or shepherds' play recounting the shepherds' journey as they followed the star of Bethlehem to find the baby Jesus. The informal play may be performed privately in someone's home or by a local theater group in a public spot. Afterward it's time for food and drink.

December 17: Feast of *San Lázaro* (Saint Lazarus), equivalent to the Santería god Babalú Ayé.

December 24: *Nochebuena* (Christmas Eve). For many Latinos this is the major Christmas celebration, when families come together for a huge meal. Puerto Ricans feast on roast pig, pigeon peas, sausages, and other native dishes. For Cuban families, a succulent roast pig takes the center place on the table, accompanied by such traditional dishes as white rice and black beans, yuca, and sweet plantains. At midnight Catholics flock to the church for the *misa del gallo* (rooster's mass) — for many, the most important church service of the year.

December 25: *La Navidad* (Christmas). Traditionally, this is a relatively quiet day, spent visiting with family and friends.

December 28: *Feast of the Holy Innocents.* Drawing on a Canary Islands tradition, this day is a time for fun, when children in Mexico play at being adults and anyone can promise the sky, much as on April Fool's Day. Just remember, if you lend something on this day, you may never get it back.

III

people

To UNDERSTAND who the Americans are one must know who the Latinos are, and were. Since 1493, millions of Latinos — including the original Spanish explorers and settlers — have lived in the United States (and the territories that would become the United States). Thousands of them have played crucial historical, civic, and social roles in American history, some in less than obvious ways. Clearly, not all of them could be included in even the most comprehensive listing. But the biographical sketches that are included here highlight the lives of some of the most important Latino men and women in U.S. history.

A couple of points do need to be made. One is that some names, such as those of the military man Alexander O'Reilly or the singer Linda Ronstadt, may not on first glance seem to belong in a list of Latinos. After all, don't Latinos all have Spanish names? The answer in part is that some of these figures are not technically Latinos but rather, as it were, "adoptive" Latinos. Notwithstanding, say, an entirely Irish heritage (such as O'Reilly's), the subject earns his or her place in this listing by virtue of having cleaved on to the Hispanic community for life. Indeed, even some of the figures with Latino-sounding names, such as the missionary Father Eusebio Francisco Kino, aren't Latino; the Italian-born Kino changed his name from Chino so it would be properly pronounced when he threw in his lot with the Spanish.

At the same time, many of these non-Latino-sounding names, like those of Ronstadt and the actor Anthony Quinn, belong to people who do indeed have significantly Hispanic heritages. Even a single non-Latino ancestor, so long as he is male, is enough to determine the family name—however ethnically inappropriate it might appear—for generations. Of course, some of these names are total fabrications anyway; like many entertainers in early Hollywood, Margarita Carmen Cansino reinvented herself as Rita Hayworth, and that's how she's listed.

Beyond the great explorers of the Spanish empire, almost all the figures listed here lived all or much of their lives on U.S., or future U.S., soil. Thus, prominent Cuban American, Mexican American, and Puerto Rican citizens are included. But so are quite a few folks from the Spanish-speaking Americas who settled here but never officially acquired citizenship, such as baseball great Martín Dihigo, a decidedly Cuban star of American baseball's Negro Leagues. Any attempt to draw a line between the former and the latter groups would be petty, pointless, and probably futile. As O'Reilly and Kino did with Spain, these resident Latinos have thrown in their lot with the United States, for better and for worse, and must be recognized.

That there are also a lot more men than women in these listings should not be seen as a simple case of chauvinism. It would be historically misleading merely to name as many women as men and thereby ignore the fact (revealing in itself) that in all the relevant cultures—Spanish, military, Catholic, American, Latin American, and Latino—women were not (and in many cases still are not) given the opportunities to be history-making leaders of society. The number of Latina movers and shakers is increasing, though. The likes of *conquistadores* such as Juan Ponce de León are making room for courtroom warriors such as Antonia Hernández as time marches on, and there's every reason to believe there will be more like her in the future.

EXPLORATION AND SETTLEMENT

Cristóbal Colón (Christopher Columbus) (1451–1506) is neither a Latino nor a Spaniard. But in Spain's service the Italian-born sailor, one of the most accomplished of his day, "discovered" the New World, including Puerto Rico and the Virgin Islands, both of which would one day be part of the United States.

Colón, born in Genoa, Italy, spent years sailing under the Portuguese flag along the African coast, as well as to England and the Madeiras Islands. Colón was intrigued by the theory that one could sail due west across the Atlantic to reach China, Japan, and the East Indies, and was anxious to try it. Portugal's rulers scoffed at his ideas, but their Spanish rivals, Fernando (Ferdinand) and Isabel (Isabella), were less skeptical. Colón set sail with the title of admiral in August 1492 in the *Niña, Pinta,* and *Santa María.* On October 12, his expedition arrived in the present-day Bahamas, which he dubbed San Salvador. Colón and his crew went on to explore Cuba and Hispaniola, on the latter of which he laid down fortifications. After the wreck of the *Santa María* off Haiti, he returned to Spain. In September 1493, the admiral set out again, as he would twice more, each time exploring the Caribbean region, "discovering" its islands and coasts, and parts of Latin America.

On his third journey, in 1498, Colón was installed as governor of Hispaniola. But reports of chaotic conditions there, Colón's mistreatment of both Spanish settlers and natives, and his failure to deliver promised gold and jewels to his royal patrons, led to his arrest and return to Spain in chains. Not long after, Colón was restored to royal service, and he made a fourth voyage in 1502. This final voyage proved disastrous as well; pressing still for a passage to the East Indies, he was marooned on Jamaica for a year. He returned to Spain in 1504 and died two years later.

Ironically, the man who changed the maps of the world went to his grave believing he had reached Asia, and was responsible for the European practice of calling Native Americans "Indians." More important, however, Colón's encounter with the Americas led to Spain's expansion overseas and the very genesis of the people today known as Latinos.

Juan Ponce de León (1460–1521) was the first Spaniard to set foot on what is now the continental United States. Ponce grew up in the royal household of King Fernando of Aragon, where as a young knight he fought the Muslims in Granada. He accompanied Columbus on his second voyage to the New World in 1493. After fighting the Taíno Indians of Hispaniola, Ponce conquered and established a settlement on Puerto Rico near present-day San Juan in 1508, and was appointed as the island's first governor. In 1513, not long after his removal from office due to a political dispute, Ponce set out to explore the region north of Puerto Rico (see pages 9–10) — partly in hopes of finding the legendary island of Bimini, believed to be the site of the Fountain of Youth.

After sighting the coast of Florida on Easter Sunday (known in Spain as *Pascua Florida*) and landing near present-day Melbourne Beach, Ponce turned south and explored the Florida Keys, then sailed up the west coast of Florida to the vicinity of Sanibel Island. There he battled Calusa Indian warriors. After seven months of exploration and a stop back in Puerto Rico, he sailed to Spain to report to the king, who in 1514 gave him permission to colonize and govern Florida (which at this point Ponce thought to be an island).

In 1521, he sailed with two ships and 200 colonists from Santo Domingo, landing again in the Charlotte Harbor area (near today's Fort Myers) on the western Florida coast and again battled the Calusas. This time, however, Ponce was fatally wounded by an Indian arrow. Withdrawing to Havana, Cuba, he soon succumbed and was buried in a church in San Juan, Puerto Rico. His epitaph reads: "This narrow place is the tomb of a man who was a lion ["León"] in name, but more in deed."

Juan Garrido (dates unknown) was the first free African to come to the New World and to the lands of the future United States, which he did as a soldier in the Spanish ranks. Known as *El Con-quistador Negro* (the Black Conquistador), he was born in Africa and later settled in Spain, where he converted to Christianity. Having enlisted in the military, Garrido came to Hispaniola and fought alongside Juan Ponce de Léon in the 1508 conquest of Puerto Rico. He also participated in Hernán Cortés's conquest of the Aztec empire in Mexico between 1519 and 1521. In 1538, he was granted a large estate in Mexico for his more than three decades of service to Spain.

Pánfilo de Narváez (1470–1528) was a Spanish conquistador who led an important expedition to the newly discovered La Florida (see pages 12–14). A lieutenant in Spain's 1511 invasion of Cuba, Narváez became a wealthy landowner on the island but was publicly criticized for his cruelty toward Cuba's Taíno Indians. His fierceness, however, recommended him to longtime associate Diego Velázquez, governor of Cuba. In 1520, Velázquez dispatched Narváez to displace the insubordinate Hernán Cortés, the great conquistador who seemed to be building a vast empire for himself in Mexico. But Cortés proved a worthy foe, and Narváez was defeated (losing an eye) and imprisoned. Allowed to return home after two years, he was given permission to colonize La Florida. He landed in Tampa Bay in 1528, but the expedition failed because of poor supplies and constant Indian harrassment. His ships, due to a miscue, having returned to Mexico, Narváez and his desperate party fashioned a fleet of crudely built barges and set sail. Virtually all, including Narváez, drowned at sea.

Lucas Vázquez de Ayllón (1475–1526) founded the first European settlement on the present-day U.S. mainland, near the mouth of the Savannah River in Georgia (see pages 11–12). Born in Toledo, Spain, Ayllón arrived in 1502 at Santo Domingo, Hispaniola, where he flourished, owning gold mines, sugar plantations, and a sugar mill, as well as 400 Indian slaves, and was appointed a judge to the Royal Council and later governor of the still unsettled La Florida. In 1520, at his own expense, he sent Francisco Gordillo on a North American expedition, which may have gone as far north as the Chesapeake Bay. In 1526, to secure Gordillo's discovery of the new land that natives called Chicora, Ayllón quickly received permission from Spain to settle and govern the area. He and six ships set sail from Hispaniola with more than 500 men (including three missionaries). Although the settlement he built on the Georgia coast, San Miguel de Gualdape, was the first European settlement—boasting the first Catholic mission—in the present-day United States, its location amid malaria-ridden swamps soon led to its failure. Ayllón and two-thirds of his party died of disease and hunger, and he was buried at sea on the survivors' return to Hispaniola.

Esteban Gómez (1474/78?–1530/4?) was a Portuguese sailor who explored America's Atlantic coast as far north as Canada on behalf of the Spanish (see page 11). Born Estevâo Gomes, he assumed a Spanish name when he joined Ferdinand Magellan's expedition around the world in 1519 as the captain of one of his ships. He deserted the expedition in Patagonia, Argentina, and a few years later won approval from Emperor Carlos V to search for a water route across North America to Asia—the dreamed-of Northwest Passage. In 1525, Gómez sailed north. He eventually visited the future New York Harbor, Hudson River, Cape Cod, and Penobscot River in Maine, among other New England sites. He never, however, found the elusive strait. A 1529 Spanish map calls New England the Land of Gómez.

Álvar Núñez Cabeza de Vaca (1490–1560) was a Spanish army veteran who wrote the first book about the exploration of the present-day United States. Cabeza de Vaca was one of the few survivors of the disastrous Narváez expedition of 1528 (see pages 12–14). When his barge went down, he washed ashore on present-day Galveston Island, Texas, and was promptly captured by natives. After six years of servitude, he and three other survivors escaped. They then proceeded to walk across the entire length of Texas, arriving in Culiacán on Mexico's west coast a full eight years after the original landing in Florida (see pages 14–15). The survivors' exaggerated tales gave rise to the fable of the Seven Cities of Cíbola, and formed the basis of Cabeza de Vaca's book, *La relación (The Story)*. Rewarded for his valor with an appointment as governor of Río de la Plata (Uruguay) and the assignment of settling Paraguay, he returned to Spain in chains, victim of a mutiny for his insistence on fair treatment of the Indians. (He wrote a second book about his Paraguay experience.) Perhaps to keep him out of trouble—i.e., out of the New World—the crown appointed Cabeza de Vaca a judge of the royal court in Seville, where he lived out the rest of his life.

Father Marcos de Niza (1495?–1558) was a missionary and explorer who, with the Moroccan-born Esteban, led the first expedition into the future U.S. Southwest. Father Marcos had joined in explorations of Peru and Guatemala before coming to Mexico. There, in 1539, he was tapped by the viceroy of New Spain to find the legendary Seven Cities of Cíbola about which the Indians had reportedly spoken so glowingly. He traveled with Esteban and a small party into today's New Mexico and Arizona, where Esteban was killed by natives (see page 50). On his return to Mexico City, however, Father Marcos reiterated tales of the mythical golden cities, which prompted Francisco Vázquez de Coronado to make a 1540 foray into the region, along with the padre. Coronado's failure to find any riches (see pages 50–53), however, led to Father Marcos's dismissal and disgrace.

Esteban or Estebanico (?–1539), a Moroccan-born slave, was the guide who joined with Father Marcos de Niza to lead the first expedition into the future U.S. Southwest. Esteban and his master comprised half the survivors of the failed Narváez expedition (see pages 12–14). On their eventual arrival in Mexico City, the survivors told of the Indian fable of the golden Seven Cities of Cíbola, thereby getting the attention of Antonio de Mendoza, the Spanish viceroy of New Spain. Mendoza acquired Esteban and in 1539 sent him with the Franciscan Father Marcos to find the cities of gold (see page 50). Esteban was sent ahead of the party with a number of Indians and told to send back crosses whose size would signal the importance of his discoveries. Increasingly large crosses arrived until a man-size cross appeared—followed by no more. Esteban, Father Marcos learned, had found not a golden city, but the Zuni Indians of New Mexico, and death at their hands.

Hernando de Soto (1500–1542) was the quintessential Spanish explorer, and the first European to cross the Mississippi River. At age 14 he joined an expedition to what is now Panama, and he later took part in conquistador Francisco Pizarro's conquest of Peru's Inca empire during the 1520s and 1530s. Returning to Spain a wealthy man, he was named governor of Cuba and La Florida and granted the right by the Emperor Carlos V to subdue the latter. De Soto and his 600 men landed at Tampa Bay in May 1539, and explored the region, searching for riches and clashing frequently with Indians. Over the next four years, the de Soto expedition traveled through ten present-day southern states and increased Spain's knowledge of the geography of North America. De Soto and his band were the first Europeans to see the inland Mississippi, in whose muddy waters de Soto was buried after succumbing to illness in June of 1542 (see pages 15–17).

Juan Rodríguez Cabrillo (?–1543) was the first European to explore the present-day California coast (see page 66). Historians debate whether his origins were Spanish or Portuguese. As a settler in Cuba he was recruited for Pánfilo Narváez's expedition, on behalf of Cuba's governor, to remove Hernán Cortés from power in Mexico; upon arrival, Cabrillo joined many of his comrades in promptly switching sides. As a member of Cortés's corps of crossbowmen, he assisted in the conquest of Guatemala. On his return to Mexico,

Viceroy Antonio de Mendoza asked Cabrillo to explore the Alta California coast and to find the fabled Straits of Anian, the North American passage that was believed to connect the Atlantic and Pacific Oceans.

In 1542 Cabrillo discovered San Diego Bay and dealt peacefully there with the native Yuman-speaking Indians. He continued north but sailed past the great San Francisco Bay. Returning for the winter to the Channel Islands off the Santa Barbara coast, he succumbed in early 1543 to an injury incurred earlier in the expedition.

Francisco Vásquez de Coronado (1510–1554) led a vain quest for the mythical Seven Cities of Cíbola and the similarly legendary Quivira, but extended the Spanish presence in the American South west. Arriving in the New World in 1535 as an aide to the viceroy of New Spain Antonio de Mendoza, he was appointed governor of the region of Nueva Galicia in 1538. When Father Marcos de Niza returned from Nuevo México to Mexico City with stories of the great Indian cities to the north, Coronado volunteered to lead an expedition to the area (see pages 50–53). Guided by Father Marcos, Coronado's party of more than a thousand arrived in present-day Arizona in the spring of 1540, then on to New Mexico in search of the Seven Cities of Cíbola and later the equally touted Quivira. To his disappointment, he found only the mud huts of the Zuni and Wichita Indians.

Coronado's exploration of the Southwest, however, was phenomenal. His men were the first Europeans to see the Grand Canyon and to encounter the Hopi Indians of northern Arizona, and they explored the Colorado River, the Gulf of California, Oklahoma, and Kansas.

In 1542, an injured Coronado—his party much shrunken by desertions and casualties from Indian clashes—returned to Nueva Galicia and took part in the fierce Mixtón War, an Indian uprising precipitated in part by the vacuum caused by Coronado's earlier recruitment of Spanish soldiers for his expedition. Coronado was dismissed from his governorship in 1544, after having spent his and the viceroy's fortunes in his vain search for gold. He died in obscurity in 1554.

Pedro Menéndez de Avilés (1519–1574) founded the first permanent European settlement in the future United States and governed Spain's claims along the eastern seaboard for almost ten years (see pages 19–20). A lifelong sailor, he was in 1554 appointed captain general of the Fleet of the Indies, and for almost 12 years he saw to the safe passage to and from Spain of treasure ships carrying the Americas' plundered riches. He also fought pirates in North Africa and supplied the Spanish army in the Netherlands. Impressed with Menéndez's naval skill, King Felipe II made him governor of La Florida, which brought with it the task of ousting the French from their Fort Caroline in what is now Jacksonville. In September 1565, Menéndez founded the city of Saint Augustine and—55 years before the Pilgrims landed on Plymouth Rock—celebrated a thanksgiving meal and mass with the local Indians. He and his men then killed virtually all the French in the area. Menéndez founded a string of settlements and forts, and the Jesuits he later welcomed founded several missions in present-day Florida, Georgia, the Carolinas, and Virginia. Menéndez was also given the responsibility by King Felipe of protecting the Spanish Caribbean settlements from Spain's European rivals. After 10 years of governing La Florida, and eventually Cuba as well, Menéndez was called to naval duty in Spain, where he died in 1574.

Juan de Oñate (1552–1626), explorer and first governor of Nuevo México (see pages 54–55), solidified Spain's hold on the American Southwest. One of only three Mexican-born leaders of explorations in the United States, Oñate was married to a woman who was both the granddaughter of Hernán Cortés, the conqueror of Mexico, and great-granddaughter of the legendary Aztec emperor Moctezuma. Oñate spent 20 years tending to the family mining business and participating in campaigns against the Chichimeca Indians. Viceroy Luis de Velasco selected Oñate to head the campaign to colonize

Nuevo México. After establishing a settlement near today's Santa Fe, Oñate and his soldiers fought the Pueblo Indians and leveled the Acoma Pueblo. He then led his army across Kansas, failing, like Coronado before him, to find the riches of Quivira. Three years later he led an expedition west in search of the Pacific Ocean but stopped at the Colorado River, which he rode to the Gulf of California. Accused of mistreating the Indians, he was forced to resign his governorship in 1607, and though he returned to the silver-mining business, he was convicted in 1614 of misconduct in office. Oñate was eventually pardoned, and by 1624, his rehabilitation complete, he was named mining inspector for all of Spain. He died there two years later at a mine site.

Sister María Jesús de Agreda (1602–1665) is fabled as the "Lady in Blue" who, without ever leaving Spain, claimed to have "journeyed" by trance to Tejas 500 times between 1620 and 1631 to preach the gospel to the Indians. Her claims surely would not have prompted a visit from Spain's King Felipe IV but for contemporaneous reports, supposedly made by west Tejas Indians to a local padre, of a lady in blue who had taught them Christianity.

Alonso de León (1637–1691) was a Mexican-born soldier and explorer who led several expeditions into Tejas and was involved in the founding of its first missions (see pages 36–38). As governor of Coahuila province in Mexico, he was sent in 1686 by the viceroy to search out a French fort supposedly built in Tejas. De León, on his fourth foray, found Fort Saint Louis—or what was left of it. Two French survivors told him that its commander, Sieur de La Salle, had been murdered by his own men, who were then themselves killed by the Indians. Nonetheless, perceiving a French threat, Spain ordered de León to occupy Tejas. In 1690, de León and Father Damián Mazanet, together with a small army, established two missions in east Texas. De León returned to Coahuila late in 1690, where he died soon thereafter.

Diego de Vargas Zapata y Luján Ponce de León (1643–1704) was a governor of Nuevo México who in the years after 1691 effectively recaptured the region for Spain (see pages 58–59) following a successful revolt of the Pueblo Indians in 1680 (see pages 57–59). The scion of a noble Madrid family, Vargas served in the Spanish court before his appointment in the New World. His show of military firmness led to substantial success with minimal casualties. In 1696, he suppressed another Pueblo revolt. He died after battle with the Apache Indians in 1704.

Father Eusebio Francisco Kino (1645–1711) was an Italian-born Jesuit who established numerous missions in northern Mexico and the American Southwest. Like most Jesuits, Kino was broadly educated, and he distinguished himself in mathematics, cartography, and astronomy in his studies in Europe. Turning down a professorship to become a missionary, he headed to New Spain (where his Italian family name, "Chino," was transliterated to effect proper pronunciation by Spaniards) in 1681. He was assigned to an expedition to the modern-day Mexican state of Baja (Lower) California.

When the Baja settlement was abandoned, Kino was reassigned to Pimería Alta—northern Sonora (in Mexico) and southern Arizona—where he spent the next 24 years. In that time he founded more than two dozen missions or satellites and made substantial strides in converting the Indians of Pimería Alta (see page 60). His cartographic work on the area remained the standard basis of mapmaking into the nineteenth century, and he wrote of his extensive experiences in a book, *Favores celestiales* (Heavenly Favors). Kino also introduced a variety of new plants and animals and made dozens of explorations, many in southern Arizona. He established cattle ranches among the Indians of the missions, as well as supplying them with seed grain.

Joseph Azlor Vitro de Vera (?–1723), as governor of Tejas, solidified Spanish military control over the province (see page 38). Holding the title of marqués of San Miguel de Aguayo by virtue of his

---

marriage to a noblewoman, he in 1719 volunteered to drive the French out of the Spanish mission of San Miguel de los Adaes in east Tejas. Aguayo raised an army of 500 men at his own expense—the largest that Spain had ever sent into Tejas—and as governor of Coahuila (in Mexico) and Tejas, secured a French retreat merely by the show of force. Aguayo followed up his success by constructing the presidio of Los Adaes only 12 miles from the French settlement at Natchitoches in Louisiana. The presidio, to which a 100-man detachment was assigned, became the temporary capital of Tejas. Aguayo left Tejas in 1722 firmly in Spanish control with four presidios, 250 soldiers, 10 missions, and a new settlement at San Antonio.

María Betancour (1703–1779) was a widowed mother of five who is regarded as one of the early pioneers of Tejas. She led 31 fellow Canary Islanders in the establishment of San Antonio; the city's main square, Plaza de las Islas, was named in honor of these founders.

Father Junípero Serra (1713–1784), founder of a string of missions along the Pacific coast, was a key figure in the Spanish settlement of Alta California (see pages 68–69). A Franciscan priest and accomplished academician, the Majorca-born Serra arrived in Mexico as a missionary in 1749. After nine years among the Pames Indians in Mexico's Sierra Gorda region and Mexico City, the mystical and energetic Serra developed a large and devoted following. For nine years Serra served as administrator of the Apostolic College of San Fernando. He was later stationed in Baja California when the region's governor, Gaspar de Portolá, asked him to lead a group of 17 missionaries as part of a settlement expedition northward. Serra agreed, despite a disabled leg, convinced of his mission to bring the Gospel to the natives. From 1769 on, he founded nine missions along a route still called *El Camino Real* (the Royal Road, or King's Highway)—missions that were later to grow into such cities as Monterey and Los Angeles. (He and his followers eventually constructed a total of 21 such missions.) Over his career he personally baptized more than 6,000 Indians, though some modern historians have responded to recent talk of Serra's canonization with charges that he mistreated the natives. Serra made the mission of San Carlos de Borromeo de Carmelo (Carmel) his home, and it was here that he died in 1784 and is still buried.

Gaspar de Portolá (1723–1784) was a Spanish army officer and explorer who became the first governor of Alta California. Born to a noble family in Catalonia, Spain, he joined the army at 17 and fought in campaigns in Italy and Portugal. When he arrived in Mexico in 1764, he was already a grizzled veteran. Three years later he was appointed governor of Baja California and charged with implementing a royal edict to expel the Jesuits from the region. (The Jesuit order had fallen into disfavor back in Europe for its supposed meddling in politics.) It was in the midst of this campaign that he met the Franciscan father Junípero Serra. In 1769, Spain ordered Portolá and Serra to settle Alta California (see pages 68–69). Two land parties and two ships were sent north; Portolá and Serra each headed one of the land expeditions, which between them included some 70 soldiers.

Soon after founding the San Diego mission in 1769, Portolá led a party in search of the Monterey Bay, which he passed but failed to recognize—though he did discover the San Francisco Bay. The next year, a second expedition sought, and this time found, Monterey Bay, where a presidio was established in June 1770. A month later, Portolá left Alta California for Spain, where he continued his military and government career until the end of his life.

Andrés Almonester y Rojas (1725–1798) was a rich Spanish merchant and philanthropist in New Orleans whose considerable contributions to the city during the era of Spanish rule helped make it the architectural gem it remains today. In 1779, he spent $100,000 of his own money to rebuild New Orleans Charity Hospital, which had been destroyed by a hurricane. Nine years later, following a calamitous fire that destroyed more than 800 buildings. Almonester replaced Saint Louis Cathedral (in which his tomb now lies) and the Cabildo (municipal building), and organized the reconstruction of the old French market. After a 1794 fire devastated 200 buildings, he again stepped forward, this time building a new customs house. His daughter, Michaela Almonester, baroness of Pontalba (1795–1874), continued his tradition of philanthropy by adding a row of elegant town houses to the city's main plaza.

Father Francisco de Garcés (?–1781) was a missionary and explorer in the Southwest. His horseback travels through the desert country of the lower Colorado River between 1768 and 1771 convinced Juan Bautista de Anza that an overland route from southern Arizona to California was indeed possible. Father Garcés joined in Anza's successful expedition to Monterey in 1774 (see page 69). Two years later, he set out on his own again, venturing north along the Colorado River and through the Mojave Desert, visiting Hopi Indian villages. He eventually met his death at the hands of the Yuma Indians.

Juan Bautista de Anza (1736–1788) was a Mexican-born army officer, governor, and explorer of today's Arizona, New Mexico, and California. He joined the army at 16 and eight years later was promoted to captain and commander of the presidio of Tubac in southern Arizona. In 1774, Anza led an expedition to Monterey, proving that an overland route was possible; the following spring he led a larger expedition that left Culiacán, Mexico, hit Tubac in October, and after taking on additional members and livestock, continued for 1,200 miles to San Francisco, arriving in March 1776 (see pages 69–71). On his return to Mexico City, Anza was appointed governor of Nuevo México, serving for 10 years. One of his chief accomplishments as governor was the establishment of a lasting peace with the Comanches. He died in Sonora, Mexico.

Alejandro Malaspina (1754–1809) was an Italian-born sailor who led a five-year Spanish scientific exploration of the Americas' Pacific coast, and ventured as far north as Alaska (see page 67). Having joined the Spanish navy at 20, Malaspina spent his early career sailing the Atlantic and Indian Oceans, and even visited China. In 1789, the seasoned sailor and his second-in-command, José Bustamente, left Spain with a royal mandate to study the coast, mountains, and jungles of Chile and Peru. They continued up the coast of Mexico and the U.S. west coast. Between 1791 and 1792, Malaspina led Spanish scientists and artists in examination of the native people, flora, fauna, and land of the Pacific Northwest, including Alaska. The last explorer to seek a strait between the Atlantic and Pacific Oceans, Malaspina mapped Alaska and its glaciers and claimed the land for Spain. Alaska's 1,500-square-mile Malaspina Glacier bears his name.

María Hinojosa de Ballí (1760–1801) was Texas's first cattle queen. De Ballí inherited her husband's land grant in 1790, which put her in control of a third of the present Rio Grande Valley.

Manuel Lisa (1772–1820) explored and traded in the Great Plains. At age 18 he left New Orleans for Saint Louis, Missouri, and prospered as a trader. In 1807, he led a party of 42 men up the Missouri River to central Montana and built the aptly named Manuel's Fort, which opened up the Upper Missouri region. Lisa traded with almost all the Indian tribes in the area. His explorations, and the development that followed in his wake, set the stage for the establishment of Saint Louis as the region's transportation and commercial hub.

Patricia de la Garza de León (1777–1849) was one of Texas's great pioneer women. Born in Mexico, she helped her wealthy husband Martín found the city of Victoria in 1824; after Martín's death nine years later, she became one of the richest women in Texas. Garza de

León supported Texas independence from Mexico and made significant financial contributions to the war effort. Nevertheless, she suffered the same discrimination as other Mexicans in independent
Texas and ultimately lost her fortune and lived out the rest of her
life in poverty.

Warfare

Alejandro (Alexander) O'Reilly (1722–1794) doesn't sound like
an Hispanic name, but this son of Dublin spent his life in the service of the Spanish army, part of it in Luisiana and Puerto Rico.
Marshal O'Reilly's first assignment in the New World came in
1762, when he was asked to organize a black militia in Cuba. Seven
years later he was sent as governor to Luisiana, of which Spain had
recently taken control, to put down a revolt of French settlers in
New Orleans antagonized by Spain's efforts to regulate commerce
(see pages 32–33). Appearing on the horizon with 2,000 soldiers in
21 ships, Marshal O'Reilly swiftly captured, tried, and executed the
ringleaders, then issued a general amnesty. In the ensuing year he
brought order to the colony, established Spanish law, and placed
the territory on the road to prosperity. In 1765, he was sent to
Puerto Rico with the charge of placing the island's economy on a
more solid footing. His overhaul of trade and land distribution policies ushered in a flourishing era for the colony. On his return to
Spain, he led 22,000 soldiers in an abortive invasion of North Africa. O'Reilly continued serving his adopted country in various
posts until his death.

Bernardo de Gálvez (1746–1786) led a Spanish army of more than
7,000 soldiers against the British in the American Revolution (see
pages 33–35). Son of the viceroy of New Spain and a military man
from the age of 16, Captain Gálvez came to New Spain, where he
fought the Apaches in Tejas and was twice wounded in action.

Gálvez returned to Spain in 1772 and spent the next three years with his regiment in France and Algeria. In 1776, now a colonel, he returned to the New World, where at age 29 he succeeded Luis de Unzaga as governor of Luisiana (see pages 32–34). In that position he assisted the American revolutionaries: opening the port of New Orleans to their ships, expelling all British subjects, and providing money and war matériel. When Spain declared war on Britain, Gálvez immediately attacked. He led a force that captured Baton Rouge, Natchez, Mobile, and Pensacola, effectively ousting the British from along the Mississippi Valley and the Gulf of Mexico. General Gálvez was richly rewarded by Spain. He was made a count and given a coat of arms, and later appointed governor of West Florida and Cuba. Upon the death of his father, who was viceroy of New Spain, Gálvez assumed the post himself. For all his precocity, Gálvez died an early death. Galveston, Texas, was named in his honor.

Jorge Farragut (1755–1814) fought in the American navy and army during the War of Independence. Born in Spain, he gained experience as a seaman in the Mediterranean, even serving in the Russian navy. In 1772, he became a merchant marine captain in the Gulf of Mexico, and in 1776, he joined the patriot navy of South Carolina. After being captured and released by the British, he was partially paralyzed by a musket ball, forcing him to retire from the navy. Nonetheless, he succeeded in joining the forces of General Francis Marion and commanded an artillery company in North Carolina. After the war, he became a frontiersman in Tennessee, and eventually found himself a major of the state militia. He later supervised the construction of gunboats in Louisiana for the defense of New Orleans. He saw his final military action in two minor naval missions in the War of 1812.

Farragut's assistance to the mortally ill father of naval officer David Porter earned him the young seaman's gratitude. Porter took Farragut's son George, who later called himself David Glasgow Farragut, under his care.

Andrea Castañón Ramírez Candelaria (1785–1899) nursed the wounded, including frontiersman Jim Bowie, at the battle of the Alamo (see page 46). Born in Mexico, she moved to Texas as a child and spent her life in nursing, also serving in San Antonio's smallpox epidemic of the 1840s. A mother of four and twenty-two adopted orphans, she was recognized for her service and awarded a pension by the Texas legislature in 1891. She lived to the age of 113.

David Glasgow Farragut (1801–1870) was the greatest naval leader of the Civil War and the U.S. Navy's first four-star admiral. Born near Knoxville, Tennessee, to the American revolutionary military figure Jorge Farragut, the younger Farragut entered the navy as a midshipman at age nine. Farragut was serving under his mentor, Commander David Porter, on the frigate *Essex* during the War of 1812, when it was sunk by two British ships off the coast of Chile. In the 1848–50 Mexican War (see pages 77–81), Farragut commanded a ship of his own with the duty of blockading Veracruz. When the Civil War broke out, the lifelong southerner moved to New York and remained loyal to the Union, though his Southern ties delayed his being granted an important assignment by the naval command.

In 1862, however, he was ordered to sail up the Mississippi and capture New Orleans, past the Southern positions at Forts Jackson and Saint Philip. He and his squadron reduced New Orleans in April of that year, enabling Union troops to enter the city. Farragut then proceeded up the river, ultimately stifling the Confederates' attempts to run a Union blockade of the Gulf of Mexico. He is best remembered for his August 1864 capture of heavily defended Mobile, Alabama, during which he uttered his famous cry of "Damn the torpedoes, full speed ahead!" (see page 115). After the war he was named four-star admiral and given command of the European Squadron.

Juan Seguín (1806–1890) was a second-generation *tejano* who fought for the independence of the Lone Star Republic. A rancher like his father, Captain Seguín joined the movement to oust Mexico from Texas (see pages 45–47), and only escaped death at the Alamo when he was sent out with a message seeking reinforcements just before Santa Anna's decisive assault. He subsequently fought at the Battle of San Antonio (1835) and the Battle of San Jacinto (1836), ending the war as a lieutenant colonel and military commander of San Antonio, his birthplace. Seguín served in the Texas Senate and was mayor of San Antonio for two terms. But like so many *tejanos*, he, too, was subject to intense discrimination by Anglos. Despite his attempts to protect *tejanos* from mistreatment at the hands of the Anglo majority in Texas, his later move to Mexico was not welcomed. He was jailed and then forced to serve in the Mexican army. In 1848 he made his way back to Texas, where he lived the rest of his life.

Manuel Chaves (1818–1889) was the scion of an "old" Nuevo Mexican family who originally fought against the United States in the Mexican War (see pages 77–81) but later was a Union hero in the Civil War (see pages 115–116). Nicknamed *El Leoncito* (the Little Lion) for his wartime exploits, Chaves remained in New Mexico after it became part of the United States. He became a loyal citizen rancher and later served as chief scout for the U.S. Army in a campaign against the Apaches. He was commander of Fort Fauntleroy in New Mexico when the Civil War began. At the battle at Glorieta Pass on the Santa Fe Trail in March 1862, Lieutenant Colonel Chaves led nearly 500 soldiers (many of them Hispanic) in a daring attack on Confederate troops—lowering themselves down a 200-foot mountain to surprise the rebels.

Ambrosio José Gonzales (1818–1893) was a Cuban-born Confederate colonel during the Civil War. Gonzales fled Cuba for South Carolina after participating in a failed expedition to free the island from Spanish rule in 1850. There, he married the daughter of a rich plantation owner whose family had lived in the region for generations. Gonzales was reputed to be South Carolina's first volunteer in the war against the Union. He served as an artillery officer under P. T. Beauregard and later became inspector of South Carolina's troops and coastal defenses. His children, Narciso (?–1903) and Ambrose (1857–1926) were later prominent progressive journalists, attacking the lynching of African Americans and child labor; Narciso was killed by a failed gubernatorial candidate whose misdeeds Narciso had exposed in print.

Santos Benavides (1823–1892) was the highest-ranking Hispanic officer in the Confederacy, among the first to take up arms on its behalf and among the last to surrender. Born in Laredo, Tejas, he was elected mayor of that city in 1857. When the Civil War began, he raised a regiment and was eventually appointed colonel. His 33rd Cavalry Unit was known as the Benavides Regiment. With his two brothers as captains of the regiment, Benavides repulsed several Union forays into the Laredo area (see page 116). He did not surrender until a month after the war ended at Appomattox. After the war, he served in the Texas legislature, and founded the *Alianza Hispano Americana* to promote acculturation and civil rights of Mexican Americans.

Loreta Janeta Velázquez (1842–?) served the Confederacy in at least two roles (depending on how they are counted)—once, disguised as a male soldier ("Lieutenant Harry Buford") in battles such as Bull Run and Shiloh, and later, after her detection and discharge, as a Confederate spy (see page 116). The Cuban-born Velázquez later wrote an account of her wartime experiences called *The Woman in Battle* (1876). She outlived two of her three husbands, her first a former Confederate army officer.

Federico Fernández Cavada (1832–1871) was perhaps the most remarkable Latino to fight in the Union army, distinguishing himself as a soldier, poet, painter, writer, diplomat, and cartographer. Born in Cuba, he and his brother Adolfo came with his widowed American mother to Philadelphia. When the Civil War began, he and Adolfo joined a volunteer regiment as captains, and, because he could draw, Federico was drafted into service as an engineer. His responsibilities included supervising the use of hot-air balloons for surveillance. Promoted to lieutenant colonel, Fernández Cavada fought at many of the major battles of the war, including Antietam, Fredericksburg, and Gettysburg. One of the few survivors of his unit in the last of those battles, he was captured and sent to the notorious Libby Prison in Richmond, Virginia. The notes he took and the pictures he drew during his six months at Libby were eventually published as *Libby Life* (see page 116).

After the war Fernández Cavada requested, and was granted, a diplomatic post in Cuba. In 1869, he resigned his post to join the incipient Cuban uprising against Spanish rule, which had begun a year earlier (see pages 116–119). He was quickly given major military responsibility and promoted to general (as was Adolfo) but was captured in 1871. The intercession of President Grant came too late to save him from a Spanish firing squad.

Maximiliano Luna (1860–1900?) was a captain in Theodore Roosevelt's Rough Riders during the Spanish-Cuban-American War. He was born in New Mexico to a family that had lived along the Rio Grande since the seventeenth century. A member of New Mexico's Territorial Legislature and a former sheriff, the 38-year-old Luna left Santa Fe to join the Rough Riders. He fought at the battles of Las Guásimas and El Caney and in the famous Battle of San Juan Hill in Cuba (see page 121). After the defeat of the Spanish forces in Cuba, Luna served as interpreter to Colonel Leonard Wood, later the U.S. military governor of Cuba.

Luis R. Esteves (1893–1958) was the first Puerto Rican graduate of West Point and the founder of Puerto Rico's National Guard. Born in Puerto Rico when it was still part of Spain, he graduated from West Point in 1915 and participated in a U.S. Army foray into Mexico in search of Pancho Villa (following Villa's deadly 1916 attack on U.S. citizens in New Mexico). During World War I he returned to his native island to train Puerto Rican officers, who would go on to lead some 20,000 Puerto Rican soldiers in the Great War. He organized the first Puerto Rican National Guard units in 1919, and was promoted to the rank of adjutant general in 1937, a position he held until his retirement in 1957.

Mercedes O. Cubría (1903–1980), a Cuban-born U.S. Army officer, had one of the most distinguished careers of any woman in the American military. Emigrating to the United States as a young girl, she enlisted in what came to be known as the WAC (Women's Army Corps) in 1943, and enrolled in officer training school. She was commissioned as a second lieutenant and served in various intelligence functions throughout Europe during World War II. Retiring as a major near the end of the Korean War, she was recalled in 1962 when the flood of Cuban refugees provided important strategic resources for U.S. intelligence. She retired in 1973 as a lieutenant colonel, having received the Bronze Star and the Legion of Merit, and having assisted hundreds of Cuban refugees in obtaining employment, housing, education, and social services in America. After her death, Cubría was inducted into the Army Intelligence Officers Hall of Fame.

Horacio Rivero (1910–) was the first Puerto Rican to achieve the rank of four-star admiral in the U.S. Navy. Born in Ponce, Puerto Rico, Rivero graduated from the U.S. Naval Academy at Annapolis. In World War II he served in the Pacific aboard the *San Juan*, participating in the marine landing at Guadalcanal and the attacks on the Gilbert, Salomon, and Marshall Islands. Later, aboard the *Pittsburgh*, he participated in the Iwo Jima and Okinawa campaigns. In 1962, as vice admiral in command of the Atlantic Fleet's amphibious force, he led the naval quarantine of Cuba during the Cuban Missile Crisis. He became a full admiral with the post of vice chief of Naval Operations in 1964. In 1972, after 41 years of distinguished service, he retired from the navy and served as U.S. ambassador to Spain.

Richard E. Cavazos (1929–) was the U.S. Army's first Hispanic four-star general. Born in Kingsville, Texas, he was commissioned as a second lieutenant through the ROTC program in 1951. In 1967, he commanded a battalion in Vietnam. He eventually served various posts, including U.S. Army attaché at the U.S. embassy in Mexico. Cavazos was commander of the U.S. Armed Forces Command at Fort McPherson, Georgia, and he commanded combat troops in the U.S. invasion of Grenada. He retired in 1984. Cavazos is the brother of former secretary of education Lauro F. Cavazos.

Erneido A. Oliva (1932–) was the first Cuban-born general in the U.S. Army. He graduated from the Cuban military academy in 1954 but resigned his commission in 1960 and emigrated to Miami. Joining other expatriate Cuban freedom fighters to form Brigade 2506, he was made second-in-command and participated in a disastrous 1961 invasion of Cuba at the Bay of Pigs (see page 172). He spent 20 months in a Cuban prison. On his release he joined the U.S. Army, and after a short training period was made second lieutenant in 1963. He fought as a company commander of the 82nd Airborne Division in the U.S. invasion of the Dominican Republic in 1965, and retired from active duty the following year. In 1971, he joined the National Guard, where he was eventually made brigadier general of the District of Columbia National Guard. He retired in 1987 with the rank of major general.

POLITICS AND GOVERNMENT

Manuel Armijo (1792–1853), Nuevo México's last Mexican governor, by his own admission built his career on corruption. Born in Albuquerque to a peasant family, he acknowledged that he got his start by stealing sheep and selling them back to a local *rico*, or rich landowner. (He claimed to have resold one ewe 14 times.) On this small fortune he himself became a landowner and merchant, and was then appointed customs collector, which he exploited for its tremendous graft potential. Appointed governor of Nuevo México in 1827, he served for little more than a year but was reappointed 10 years later when he put down a revolution against another governor. In his second term he turned back a 300-strong Texan army that in 1841 attempted to claim part of Nuevo México for the Republic of Texas (see page 49). Armijo was appointed to a third term as governor in 1845. This time the invading army was that of the United States, now at war with Mexico. U.S. forces occupied Santa Fe without firing a shot as Armijo—possibly encouraged by a U.S. bribe—fled to Mexico (see page 79).

Mariano Guadalupe Vallejo (1808–1890) was the main Californio military and political leader during the territory's transition to U.S. rule. Born in Monterey to wealthy parents, he graduated from that city's military academy in 1823, when Alta California belonged to the newly independent Mexico. Soon thereafter he was appointed commander of the San Francisco presidio, and by age 22 he was Alta California's military commander in chief. In 1830, Vallejo was elected to the *Diputación* (Legislature). Four years later he developed the fertile Sonoma valley, north of San Francisco, and soon he became the largest landowner in Alta California.

When the United States acquired Alta California in the Mexican War (see pages 77–81), Vallejo was one of seven Californios chosen for the constitutional convention and later was elected state senator. But, like the majority of the Californios, he lost most of his property to Anglo land grabbers and found his holdings reduced to a relatively meager 280 acres at the time of his death. His contribution to California's early development was nonetheless recognized by the United States in 1965, when a Polaris submarine was named in his honor.

Lorenzo de Zavala (1788–1836) was a signer of Texas's declaration of independence from Mexico, designer of the Texas flag, and vice president of the so-called Texas Republic-in-Arms (that is, after the declaration of independence but before its victory over Mexico).

Born in Mexico's Yucatán Peninsula, Zavala was jailed in his youth for his advocacy of Mexican independence from Spain. After that independence was achieved (see pages 41–42), he was elected to the National Congress and helped write Mexico's 1824 constitution. He served Mexico as governor of a state, minister of the treasury, and a diplomat in France. Zavala was granted land in Tejas in 1829 and moved his family there after he split with the policies of Mexico's president, Antonio López de Santa Anna. In 1836, he joined 58 other Texans—including two other *tejanos* (Hispanics from Texas)—in signing Texas's declaration of independence from Mexico (see page 45). He was elected vice president of the Republic-in-Arms, but ill health soon forced his resignation.

José Mariano Hernández (1793–1857) was the first Hispanic to serve as mayor of a U.S. city, as a delegate to Congress, and as a general in the U.S. Army. Hernández was born in Saint Augustine, Florida, of Spanish parents. He took an oath of allegiance to the United States after the Spanish cession of La Florida in 1821 (see page 31), and came to play an important role in Florida's early history. Elected to the Saint Augustine City Council, and later elected mayor of that city, he was in 1822 appointed Florida's non-voting delegate to the U.S. Congress. He served as president of the Florida Legislative Council while owning and managing a plantation. During a conflict with the local Seminole Indians, Hernández raised an army of volunteers and was appointed brigadier general. His troops captured several Seminole chiefs, including the famed Osceola. When in 1845 Florida was admitted to the Union as a state, Hernández ran as Whig candidate for U.S. Senate but lost. He then moved to Cuba, where he ran a sugar plantation near Mantanzas until his death.

José Antonio Navarro (?–1871), born in San Antonio, was a Mexican lawyer and legislator, and a leader in the Texan independence movement. In his youth, Navarro fought in Mexico's struggle for independence from Spain (see pages 41–42). Later a major Tejas landowner (when Tejas was still a region of Mexico), he joined in the Lone Star Republic's nascent independence movement (see pages 45–46). Navarro was a signatory to the republic's declaration of independence and helped draft the Texas constitution. After Texas's war with Mexico had been won, Navarro participated in the abortive 1841 military expedition into New Mexico (see page 49) and escaped from a Mexican prison after serving three years of a life sentence. He served in the Third Congress of the Texas Republic and in the Texas Senate when the republic was later annexed to the United States. A county in Texas is named in his honor.

Miguel A. Otero (1829–1882) was a politician in New Mexico who was part of the so-called Santa Fe Ring. Born in Nuevo México to a prominent family, he was trained as a lawyer and, in 1852, was elected to the New Mexico territorial legislature. Two years later he was chosen as the territory's attorney general. In 1855, he won election as territorial delegate to Congress, where he eventually served six terms. In the years after the Civil War, Otero prospered financially as well, founding a bank and setting himself up as president. His powerful status soon led Otero into an alliance with wealthy Anglos and *ricos*, the so-called Santa Fe Ring, who would control the political and economic life of the territory (see page 105). Otero himself grew even richer, acquiring considerable real estate and becoming a director of the Atchison, Topeka, and Santa Fe Railroad.

Romualdo Pacheco (1831–1899) was a wealthy Californio who served briefly as the state's first and only Hispanic governor. Born in Santa Barbara to an aide to the territory's Mexican governor, Pacheco was educated at a missionary school in Hawaii before returning to work in the family shipping business and manage the family estate. He was elected as a judge and then a state senator while still in his twenties. During the Civil War, he joined the Republican Party, was reelected to the state senate, and served as state treasurer. In 1871, he was elected lieutenant governor; when Governor Newton Booth was appointed to the U.S. Senate in 1875, Pacheco succeeded him in the post. As elections approached a year later, however, he failed to win his own party's support for nomination. Pacheco ran instead for Congress and served two terms, then returned to business. Later, Pacheco was the country's representative in Central America.

José Francisco Chaves (1833–1904) was an important public servant and politician in the New Mexico territory. He was born near Albuquerque to a wealthy rancher who had been prominent in Mexican politics. Chaves studied in Saint Louis and New York but returned to New Mexico on his father's death. He fought in various Indian campaigns and in the Civil War as a lieutenant colonel for the Union. After the war he served two terms as New Mexico's delegate to Congress but in his second reelection bid lost his continuing struggle with the Santa Fe Ring (see page 105). He then served in the Territorial Senate for 12 years and as a district attorney and as president of the state constitutional convention in 1889. In 1903, Chaves was appointed New Mexico's superintendent of public instruction, championing federal funding to secure equal access to education. His assassination in 1904, though never solved, was likely linked to his Santa Fe Ring campaign.

Fernando Figueredo Socarrás (1846–1929) was the first Cuban American elected to the Florida legislature and the state's first Cuban American mayor. Figueredo, who was born in Cuba, fought Spain during the Ten Years' War (see pages 117–118). After the war, he came to Key West, which he represented upon his election to the state legislature. Later he moved to West Tampa, where he became superintendent of schools and later mayor.

Luis Muñoz Rivera (1859–1916) was a Puerto Rican journalist and politician who served as the island's first delegate in the U.S. Congress. Muñoz Rivera fought for Puerto Rican independence from Spain in his youth, and when Spain conceded an autonomous

Puerto Rican cabinet, he became its premier in 1877. He continued to push for full independence, eloquently voicing his sentiments in *La Democracia,* a paper he founded in 1889. In 1897, Spain granted full self-government to Puerto Rico (see page 119). Muñoz Rivera had just taken his seat as head of that government when, eight days later, a U.S. force overran the island—a spoil of the Spanish-Cuban-American War (see pages 120–123). It was Muñoz Rivera who negotiated with the invaders on behalf of Puerto Rico. In 1910, Muñoz Rivera began serving as the island's delegate to Congress, in which capacity he pressed for the extension of U.S. citizenship and the right to an elected legislature for Puerto Ricans (see pages 126–128). *La Democracia* and his New York paper, the *Puerto Rico Herald,* spread the gospel among his constituents. Ironically, the Jones Bill, which did just what Muñoz Rivera had demanded, did not pass until the year after he died in office. His son was Luis Muñoz Marín.

Ezequiel Cabeza de Baca (1864–1916) was an educator and newspaper editor who became the state of New Mexico's second governor—and the country's first-ever elected Hispanic governor. Born in New Mexico, Cabeza de Baca taught in one-room schoolhouses before he began working in 1890 at *La Voz del Pueblo* (the *People's Voice*), the most important Spanish-language newspaper in the territory. He eventually rose to become editor and part owner of the paper. In New Mexico's first state elections in 1911, Cabeza de Baca was elected lieutenant governor on the Democratic ticket. Five years later, he was elected governor, only to die less than two months after taking office.

Octaviano A. Larrazolo (1859–1930) was a governor of New Mexico who became the first Hispanic to serve in the U.S. Senate. Born in Mexico, Larrazolo came to the United States at age 11. He became a teacher, high school principal, and activist lawyer. He succeeded Ezequiel Cabeza de Baca as governor of New Mexico from 1919 to 1921. In 1928, he was appointed to the U.S. Senate to fill out the term of a deceased senator, and held the seat until his own death. During his brief tenure in the Senate, Larrazolo was a major supporter of bilingual education, and the rights and welfare of Hispanics were always at the top of his agenda.

Dennis Chávez (1888–1962) was the first U.S.-born Hispanic elected to the U.S. Senate. A native of Albuquerque, he was a lawyer and politically active Democrat who served in the New Mexico legislature and was elected to the House of Representatives in 1930. Appointed to the U.S. Senate in 1935 on the death of Bronson Cutting, he retained the seat by popular election in 1936. An ardent New Dealer, he spent the rest of his life in the Senate.

Luis Muñoz Marín (1898–1980) was the founder of the Commonwealth of Puerto Rico and remains a popular hero years after his death. Muñoz Marín spent most of his youth in the United States, where his father, Luis Muñoz Rivera, worked on behalf of Puerto Rico. In 1926, Muñoz Marín abandoned his career as a poet and journalist in New York and returned to Puerto Rico to take over the family newspaper, *La Democracia*. He was elected to the Puerto Rican senate in 1932, and six years later founded the Popular Democratic Party, whose slogan was "Bread, land, and liberty." Muñoz Marín became the first popularly elected governor of Puerto Rico in 1949, and was reelected three times before choosing to step aside in 1964. In 1952, he secured, with popular support, commonwealth status for Puerto Rico and was a lifelong advocate of economic expansion in close cooperation with the United States (see pages 127, 130).

Joseph M. Montoya (1915–1978) was the third Hispanic to serve in the U.S. Senate. Born in New Mexico to a family that had settled there almost two centuries earlier, he was, during his second year of law school, elected as a Democrat to the New Mexico House of Representatives—at 21, the youngest representative in state history. In 1940, four years later, Montoya was elected to the state senate, making him (at age 25) the youngest senator in state history. Montoya went on to serve as lieutenant governor and again as a state senator. In 1956, Congressman Antonio Fernández died in office; Montoya won a special election and in 1957 began the first of four terms in the U.S. House of Representatives. Montoya won the U.S. Senate seat of the deceased Dennis Chávez in 1964, and was subsequently elected to a second term. A powerful and influential supporter of Latino civil rights, Montoya was defeated in his 1976 reelection bid.

Edward R. Roybal (1916–) was a California congressman and Los Angeles City Council member, whose first electoral victory was a lightning rod for Mexican-American political action (see page 146). Born in Albuquerque, he attended college and became a teacher, then served in the military during World War II. After the war he settled in Los Angeles, where he was picked by a group of Mexican Americans eager to place one of their own on the Los Angeles City Council. Though Roybal was defeated in 1947, the group, known as the Community Service Organization (CSO), built on the groundwork it had laid and continued campaigning for the 1949 race. When Roybal won in that year, he became the first Hispanic on the council since 1881. After 13 years there, and unsuccessful runs for lieutenant governor and the Los Angeles County Board of Supervisors, Roybal was elected to Congress. He spent more than three decades in office, pushing consistently for the concerns of Hispanics. The CSO also continued its work as an advocate for the rights of Mexican Americans. Today Roybal's daughter, Lucille Roybal-Allard, is a Democratic representative from California.

Henry González (1916–) is a congressman from Texas who wielded considerable power during the Democratic Party's ascendancy over the House of Representatives. A son of San Antonio, González failed in his first attempt at election to his hometown's City Council in 1950 but won three years later. In 1956, he was elected to the state senate—the first Mexican American member of that body in 110 years. In 1962, after a special election the previous year, González entered Congress, where he became the first Texan of Mexican descent in that body. There, he became chairman of the Banking Committee and later of the Banking, Finance, and Urban Affairs Committee. A maverick liberal Democrat, González is an outspoken critic of discrimination and other forms of injustice.

Herman Badillo (1929–) was the first mainland Puerto Rican ever elected to Congress. Born on the island, Badillo was raised in New York City and Burbank, California. After an unsuccessful try for the New York State Assembly, he was elected Bronx borough president in 1965. He lost a run for mayor in 1969 but was elected to Congress the following year. Badillo resigned from Congress in 1978, and has since held a range of top city posts in both Democratic and Republican administrations. Badillo remains one of New York's most popular Latino politicians.

SOCIAL PROTEST AND CIVIL RIGHTS

Juan "Cheno" Nepomuceno Cortina (1824–1892), the "Red Robber of the Rio Grande," was a Mexican *bandido*-revolutionary. Cortina was born into privileged circumstances, the son of a prominent rancher who was also a small-town mayor in Mexico. The red-bearded Cortina, or "Cheno," as he became known, became a *vaquero* (cowboy), and along with other vaqueros fought in the Mexican cavalry in the war with the United States (see page 101). With the postwar shift of the Texas-Mexico border from the Nueces River to the Rio Grande, Cortina found himself a resident of the United States. He had settled down to life as a family man and rancher near Brownsville, Texas, when in 1859 he shot and wounded a U.S. marshal in Brownsville who was mercilessly beating a *tejano* hand.

The gentleman-turned-outlaw fled the country to save his life, then returned to the scene of the crime to publicize his people's grievances with their rulers. Cortina and several followers captured Brownsville, but, hunted by the U.S. Army and the Texas Rangers, the group turned back to Mexico. He later became governor of his native state of Tamaulipas and was named a general by Mexican president Benito Juárez. However, he was accused of stealing cattle and was imprisoned by President Porfirio Díaz, who had overthrown Juárez, and spent his last years under local arrest.

Ramón Emeterio Betances (1827–1898), a medical doctor and writer, was one the most impassioned voices pressing for independence from Spain of both his native Puerto Rico and Cuba. Betances studied medicine in France, but upon returning to Puerto Rico, he threw himself into the campaign for independence (and against the ongoing practice of slavery). Repeatedly deported for his activities, he eventually fled to New York City in 1867, where he founded the Puerto Rico Revolutionary Committee and plotted an insurgency with rebels on the island to oust Spain. After the failure of the *Grito de Lares* in 1868 (see page 117), Betances continued to press his cause in a long string of articles, arguing as well for Cuba's independence. He proposed the idea, never realized, of a confederation of all the islands of the Antilles to bring independence to the two Spanish colonies and protection to the rest. In 1896, the Cuban government-in-arms named him diplomatic agent to France, and he worked on Cuba's behalf there until his death.

Joaquín Murieta (1832–1853) was a Mexican social bandit whose fame spread throughout Latin America. Born in Sonora, Mexico, to wealthy parents, he and his girlfriend went to California in search of gold when he was 18. Like many Mexicans who were killed or driven off their claims by force, however, they found themselves less than warmly received by the Anglos and were rousted from wherever they settled. By age 19, Murieta had taken to robbing and killing miners, eventually heading a gang that rampaged throughout California. With a $5,000 dead-or-alive price on his head, he became a hunted man, and was eventually caught and killed by the California Rangers (see page 101).

Tiburcio Vázquez (1835–1875) was a famous Mexican social bandit in California (see pages 101–102). He was born on his parents' ranch in Monterey. A teenage brawl at a Mexican dance led to the death of an Anglo policeman and the lynching of one of Vázquez's friends. Vázquez escaped and turned to a life of crime, heading a gang of horse thieves by 1856. A year later he was captured and spent a year at San Quentin prison; on his release he went back to rustling and spent another stretch in jail that ended in 1870. This time he turned to robbing stagecoaches. After a holdup led to the deaths of a number of store employees, California put a reward on his head. Apprehended in 1874, he became a celebrity in jail, where he was visited by thousands and, in a thoroughly modern gesture, sold cards with his picture. Convicted for murder in a highly publicized trial, he was finally hanged.

Eugenio María de Hostos (1839–1903) was an educator and writer who, like Betances, campaigned for the independence of Spain's two Caribbean island colonies. Born in Puerto Rico with both Cuban and Dominican ancestry, Hostos decamped to New York during Cuba's Ten Years' War (see pages 117–118). There he worked with the revolutionaries' government in New York and served as its delegate to South America. After the war, Hostos traveled across the South American continent, teaching law and writing articles attacking the Spanish colonial system. Later, when war flared up again in Cuba, José Martí (see pages 119–120) named Hostos the South American delegate of his own Cuban Revolutionary Party. The achievement of independence for Cuba in 1898 only enhanced Hostos's desire to see Puerto Rico free as well, and in his writings he pressed that aim with new vehemence. In 1938, the Organization of American States conferred upon Hostos the status of "Citizen of the Americas." Today, many schools and colleges on the U.S. mainland and in Puerto Rico are named in his honor.

Juan José Herrera (dates unknown), a native of New Mexico, founded the *Gorras Blancas* (White Caps) around 1887 to fight the land encroachments by railroads in his state. Herrera lived in Santa Fe and San Miguel counties until 1866, when he moved to Colorado and became familiar with the ideas of Joseph P. Buchanan, the founder of the Red International, an anarchist organization. This led to his involvement with the Knights of Labor, an early union. Returning to Las Vegas, New Mexico, in San Miguel County, he organized the *Gorras Blancas*, which claimed a membership of 1,500, to fight Anglo land grabbers who had taken public lands belonging to the town. Night riders cut fences and destroyed property; Herrera and his brother Pablo and 24 others were indicted for these illegal actions in 1890. The *Gorras Blancas* continued cutting fences and destroying property and spread their raids to Santa Fe County. But the *Gorras Blancas* were ultimately unable to stop the influx of Anglos and the loss of public lands.

Elfeco Baca (1865–1945) was not an actual criminal—just an accused one—but his aggressive advocacy of the rights of Mexicans in New Mexico made him a legend in his own time. Born in New Mexico, Baca grew up in Topeka, Kansas. His family later returned to New Mexico, where his father became marshal of a small town but later had to escape from jail, with Baca's aid, after a fight over a horse race. Baca himself became famous when, as a young U.S. marshal himself, he arrested an Anglo Texan in the town of Frisco for disturbing the peace. A mob of at least 80 Texans descended on Baca's building and fired on it for 36 hours. Baca killed two Texans and wounded several others. Arrested by an Anglo deputy sheriff who betrayed Baca's trust, Baca stood trial at Albuquerque for his actions at the "Battle of Frisco" and was acquitted.

In 1894, Baca became a lawyer and champion of the rights of New Mexico Hispanics. He also served in many local offices, including mayor, district attorney, and sheriff of Socorro. He became well acquainted with Mexican revolutionary leaders at the turn of the century, acting as the Mexican government's U.S. representative in 1913–14. He also made powerful enemies; at one time Pancho Villa offered $30,000 for Baca's life.

Gregorio Cortez (1875–1916) became an outlaw as a result of a cross-cultural mistake, and was immortalized in the ballad *"Corrido de Gregorio Cortez"* (see page 101). Born in Mexico, Cortez and his family moved to the Austin area when he was 12. In 1901, a sheriff, searching for a horse thief, mistranslated a Mexican's statement that he had acquired a horse from Cortez as an accusation that Cortez was a thief. The sheriff arrived at the young rancher's house and, after a brief discussion, shot Cortez's brother and fired at Cortez, who fired back and mortally wounded the sheriff. This led to a 10-day chase involving hundreds of people; Cortez himself walked more than 120 miles, and rode more than 400, until he was arrested. (His entire family was also put in jail, where his brother, mortally wounded, died.)

Sentenced to death, Cortez appealed. Fund-raising campaigns on both sides of the border, involving both the Mexican and Mexican American press, brought in substantial support. The verdict was reversed, and in a subsequent trial he was acquitted on the grounds that the arrest was illegal and that Cortez had acted in self-defense. In the interim, however, Cortez had been convicted of the death of one of his pursuers. After 12 years of imprisonment, he was pardoned by the governor of Texas in 1913. Upon his release he returned to Mexico, fought in the Mexican Revolution, and died shortly thereafter.

Luisa Moreno (1906?–1992) was a union organizer and activist during the 1930s and 1940s. Born in Guatemala, she moved to Mexico and worked as a newspaper reporter before coming to the United States in 1928, where she found work as a seamstress in a sweatshop. The injustice and deplorable conditions she encountered there led her into union organizing, and she went on to organize tobacco-rolling workers in cigar factories in Florida, New York, and Pennsylvania. She worked for (and eventually became vice president of) the leftist United Cannery, Agricultural, Packing, and Allied Workers of America (UCAPAWA), and followed Emma Tenayuca as leader of the great 1938 San Antonio pecan-shellers strike (see page 139). Moreno also took it upon herself to travel throughout the United States in an attempt to create a confederation of Latino organizations to fight for immigrants' rights. The result was *El Congreso de los Pueblos de Habla Español* (The Congress of Spanish-Speaking Peoples), which met for the first time in Los Angeles in 1938 (see pages 145–146) and lasted for four years. Moreno herself, labeled a communist or communist sympathizer, was deported in the early 1950s.

Emma Tenayuca (1916–) organized and fought on behalf of Mexicans working at pecan shelling and in the garment, cement, and laundry industries. In the face of the meager wages and terrible working conditions of San Antonio pecan shellers, she organized 10,000 shellers and in 1938 led them in the largest (if ultimately futile) strike in Texas history (see page 139). The United Cannery, Agricultural, Packing, and Allied Workers of America (UCAPAWA)—sensitive to accusations that Tenayuca was a communist—replaced her as strike leader with Luisa Moreno. Tenayuca later organized workers in other industries, and then attended college and became a schoolteacher. She retired in 1982.

Héctor Pérez García (1914–1996) alerted Americans to the ugly treatment received by non-Anglo veterans. A physician, García earned the rank of major, and the Bronze Star, in World War II. Returning to private practice in Corpus Christi, Texas, García was horrified to learn that he could not place wounded and sick American veterans at the Corpus Christi Naval Air Station Hospital—if they were Mexican Americans. Later García learned that a Mexican American casualty of the Battle of the Philippines was denied burial in a Texas cemetery (President Truman arranged for his burial at Arlington National Cemetery). In response García founded the American GI Forum (see page 145), which initially addressed discrimination against Mexican American veterans but broadened its mission as the years went on. In 1968, García was appointed U.S. civil rights commissioner by Lyndon Johnson. Ronald Reagan awarded him the Presidential Medal of Freedom in 1984.

Reies López Tijerina (1926–) was a Chicano leader who fought in the 1960s to regain land lost decades earlier by Mexican Americans in New Mexico (see pages 154–156). "El Tigre" ("The Tiger"), as he was nicknamed, was born on a farm near Fall City, Texas, and worked in the fields. He became an itinerant fundamentalist preacher among the Southwest's poor farmworkers and briefly tried to establish a utopian community in Arizona. Tijerina traced the sorry lot of Mexican Americans to their ancestors' displacement from their land following the 1846–48 Mexican War, in violation of the Treaty of Guadalupe Hidalgo (see pages 80–83). His advocacy of that cause, through *La Alianza Federal de Mercedes* (later to be called the *Alianza Federal de Pueblos Libres*), led to marches and civil disobedience, culminating in the occupation by *aliancistas* of the Kit Carson National Forest in New Mexico and Tijerina's subsequent arrest. While awaiting trial, he and several followers attempted to make a citizen's arrest of the district attorney in Tierra Amarilla; a gunfight broke out, and several people were wounded. Tijerina eventually served one year in jail on assault charges.

César Chávez (1927–1994) was one of the greatest union organizers in American history and a symbol of Latino empowerment. He was born in Yuma, Arizona, to a family of poor migrant workers—migrating so much that, when he wasn't working in the fields, he attended about 30 schools until he left after seventh grade. Chávez served in the navy in World War II, after which he settled in San Jose, California. There he worked for and eventually came to lead the Community Service Organization (CSO), a Mexican rights group.

Chávez started working solely at organizing farmworkers in

1962, when he formed the National Farm Workers Association (NFWA), later to be called the United Farm Workers (UFW). He was a pioneer in the effective use of nationwide boycotts of non-union agricultural products such as grapes, wine, and lettuce, along with strikes, pickets, fasts, and marches. His most celebrated accomplishment was a five-year strike by migrant grape pickers, coupled with a nationwide boycott of table grapes, that forced California grape growers to recognize the UFW in 1970 (see pages 149–151). The UFW eventually became a member union of the powerful national labor union, the AFL-CIO, in 1972. Chávez, as president of the union, extended his efforts to migrant workers in Florida. He is seen as the driving force behind California's passage of the Labor Relations Act in 1975. Chávez's achievements in California were, over time, undermined by the encroachment of the rival Teamsters Union and internecine disputes in his own organization. But even beyond the UFW's 100,000 members, Chávez was a hero to struggling Latinos, whose world he changed.

Rodolfo "Corky" Gonzáles (1928–) is a poet, playwright, and activist who was one of the most inspiring leaders of the Latino civil rights movement (see pages 151–152). Born in Denver to migrant sugar-beet workers, Gonzáles competed for the featherweight boxing title for eight years and ran an auto insurance agency before becoming increasingly involved in community affairs. In 1965, he was appointed director of a federal youth program in Denver, and the following year he founded the Crusade for Justice, a political activism program for Mexican Americans. Gonzáles, whose emphasis was on self-empowerment and pride, wrote plays about "bronze people with a bronze culture," hearkening back to the great Aztec civilization. He pressed for Latino autonomy, even an independent Hispanic entity in the Southwest. His epic poem *Yo Soy Joaquín/I Am Joaquín*—with its final words proudly insisting, "I will endure"—is a standard of the Chicano canon. In 1970, Gonzáles started the Colorado branch of La Raza Unida Party (LRUP), an independent Chicano political party created by José Ángel Gutiérrez a few months earlier in Texas. But at the party's first convention in 1972, the membership rejected Gonzáles's radical politics and instead embraced a considerably more mainstream Gutiérrez (see pages 158–159). Gonzáles's views and the increasingly conservative temper of the nation largely ended his career as an active nationwide Chicano leader.

Dolores Fernández Huerta (1930–) was one of the civil rights movement's top Chicana activists. Huerta was born Dolores Fernández in New Mexico and raised in rural California; her coal miner–migrant worker father was himself a labor activist and worked for a time for the Congress of Industrial Organizations (CIO). She graduated from college and soon became involved with the Community Service Organization (CSO), pushing for voter registration and better treatment for migrant farmers. In 1958 she became an aide to César Chávez, head of the statewide CSO, and when he left to form the National Farm Workers Association (NFWA)—later, the United Farm Workers (UFW)—she joined him. Throughout *el movimiento* she was a central figure, organizing strikes, boycotts, and demonstrations and serving as a principal negotiator on behalf of migrant farmworkers (see pages 149–151). She later served as vice president of the UFW from 1970 to 1973, and continues to work for the organization.

Vilma Martínez (1943–) is a lawyer and civil rights activist who was president of the Mexican American Legal Defense and Education Fund (MALDEF). Born in San Antonio, she became a lawyer and served as consultant to the U.S. Commission on Civil Rights from 1969 to 1973. As general counsel for MALDEF from 1973 to 1982, Martínez fought for greater access for and increased participation of Hispanics in politics (see pages 160–161). She was instrumental in persuading Congress to pass the Voting Rights Act amendments of 1975, extending the law to cover many predominantly Hispanic districts. Since 1982, she has continued to practice law privately in Los Angeles and has served on the California Board of Regents, which oversees the state university system.

José Ángel Gutiérrez (1947–) was a student leader who founded the Mexican American Youth Organization (MAYO) and cofounded the short-lived La Raza Unida Party (LRUP). While a student at Texas A&I University, the physician's son joined with several other students to protest discrimination in admissions, dormitory segregation, the lack of Latino employees, and an exclusionary curriculum; the organization would take the name MAYO in 1967. Gutiérrez won national attention in 1969, when he organized a march to protest the cancellation of a government social program in San Felipe Del Rio (west of San Antonio). With fierce rhetoric, Gutiérrez condemned Anglo oppression and won a commitment from the participants, in the form of the so-called Del Rio Manifesto, to embrace cultural identity and fight racism (see pages 152–153). The Texas LRUP was formed in 1970 and in that same year Gutiérrez and two other Chicanos were elected to the Crystal City (Texas) School Board. (Others won seats on the city council and on both bodies in nearby cities as well.) By the time of the party's first convention in 1972, however, Gutiérrez had grown considerably more moderate and pushed for working in cooperation with the two-party system (see pages 158–159). In 1974, Gutiérrez was elected judge in Zavala County; he resigned seven years later to become a college professor.

Linda Chávez (1947–) is a leading conservative Latino activist. A descendant of Spanish settlers in New Mexico, Chávez was born in Albuquerque and studied and taught at UCLA before getting involved in Republican politics. She worked in a variety of political jobs in Washington and eventually won the attention of the Reagan administration with her writing, as editor of *American Educator*, in support of traditional values in the schools. As staff director of the U.S. Commission on Civil Rights, she drew fire from the civil rights establishment for her challenges to affirmative action and other racial preferences. After an unsuccessful campaign for the U.S. Senate as a Republican in 1986, Chávez became president of U.S. English, an organization that aimed to make English the nation's official language; she resigned soon after, when one of its founders was revealed to have expressed racist views toward Hispanics. Chávez has continued to arouse considerable controversy within the Latino community for her outspoken opposition to special treatment for Latinos, which she believes to be an obstacle to real progress, a position detailed in her 1991 book *Out of the Barrio: Toward a New Politics of Hispanic Assimilation.*

Antonia Hernández (1948–) is president of the Mexican American Legal Defense and Education Fund (MALDEF), one of the most effective advocates of Hispanic rights in the United States. Born to a poor family in Coahuila, Mexico, Hernández moved to East Los Angeles at age eight and picked crops during the summer. After studying at UCLA Law School, she worked for the East Los Angeles Center for Law and Justice and the Legal Aid Foundation. In 1978, she became the first Latina to join the staff of the U.S. Senate Judiciary Committee, where she worked on immigration and civil rights legislation. She joined MALDEF's staff in Los Angeles in 1980 and became its president in 1985.

SCIENCE AND TECHNOLOGY

Carlos Juan Finlay (1833–1915) discovered the link between yellow fever and mosquitoes. Born in Cuba of a Scottish physician father and Trinidad-born French mother, Finlay attended Philadelphia's Jefferson Medical College in 1855 and, after additional study in France, began his medical practice in Havana 10 years later. In 1879, he was assigned by Cuba's Spanish government to work with a U.S. medical team studying yellow fever in Cuba. In 1881, Finlay, now working alone, announced his finding that yellow fever was transmitted from infected humans to susceptible humans through the agency of mosquitoes.

Yet subsequent U.S. medical teams studying yellow fever in Cuba rejected Finlay's theory until the U.S. governor ordered the fourth such team to reconsider Finlay's approach. U.S. soldiers and doctors were bitten with Finlay's infected mosquitos, and they contracted the disease, confirming Finlay's conclusions. Ironically, Dr. Walter Reed, the leader of that medical team—which, like its predecessors, would not consider Finlay's findings—was wrongly credited with Finlay's discovery. (Finlay was later credited with the discovery by various international medical congresses.) Finlay's work led to the virtual eradication of yellow fever.

Severo Ochoa (1905–1993) was the United States' first Hispanic winner of the Nobel Prize in 1959, which he earned in medicine for his synthesis of RNA (ribonucleic acid, an organic compound central to transmission of hereditary traits). Ochoa was born in Luarca, Spain, and received his medical degree in Madrid in 1929. He emigrated to the United States in 1941 and became a citizen in 1956. Shortly thereafter, he began a 40-year tenure at New York University, where he eventually headed the pharmacy and biochemistry departments.

Luis Walter Álvarez (1911–1988), a member of the Manhattan Project, which developed the atomic bomb, he received the Nobel Prize in physics for his discovery of certain subatomic particles. A native of San Francisco, Álvarez was the first U.S.-born Hispanic to receive a Nobel Prize. He studied physics at the University of Chicago and after graduation did cyclotron research at the University of California at Berkeley. During World War II he helped develop a radar system called Ground-Controlled Approach (GCA), still in use today. After the war Álvarez returned to Berkeley and continued the physics research that led to his Nobel Prize in 1968.

After retirement, Álvarez worked with his son, a geologist, in analyzing fossils in layered rocks. Their discovery of iridium—an element found in asteroids—in these rocks led to their theory that the dinosaurs were destroyed when a huge asteroid struck the earth, sending dust and smoke into the air and killing the vegetation on which the dinosaurs fed.

Mario Molina (1943–) is a scientist and winner of the Nobel Prize in chemistry—making him the United States' third Hispanic Nobel laureate. Born in Mexico, Dr. Molina studied at the University of California at Berkeley, and teaches at the Massachusetts Institute of Technology. His work as part of an international team studying the damaging effects of chlorofluorocarbon gases (found in spray cans and refrigerators) on the ozone layer won him a share of the Nobel Prize in 1995.

Franklin R. Chang-Díaz (1950–) is an astronaut who in 1986 was the first Hispanic in space. Chang-Díaz was born in Costa Rica; his paternal grandfather was from China. He came to the United States to attend college, eventually receiving a Ph.D. in applied plasma physics from the Massachusetts Institute of Technology. He became an astronaut in 1981 and has participated in four space flights, beginning with his journey on the space shuttle *Columbia* in 1986. He was the first to speak in Spanish from outer space, transmitting a message to millions of Spanish-speaking television viewers throughout the world.

Ellen Ochoa (1958–) was the first Latina in space. She was born in Los Angeles and received a doctorate in electrical engineering from Stanford in 1985. After graduation she did research at the Sandia National Laboratories in Livermore, California, winning patents for some of her work. In 1988, she joined NASA's Ames Research Center and helped develop high-performance computational systems for aerospace missions. She became an astronaut in 1991 and flew her first mission two years later on the space shuttle *Discovery*. In 1994, she was a member of the space shuttle *Atlantis* crew.

Sidney M. Gutiérrez (1951–) is an experimental test pilot and two-time space traveler. Born in Albuquerque, New Mexico, he attended the U.S. Air Force Academy and the Air Force Test Pilot School. Following a string of assignments, including the testing of the F-16 aircraft, Gutiérrez became an astronaut in 1985. He served as pilot of the space shuttle *Columbia* on his first space mission in 1991. On his second mission, aboard the shuttle *Endeavour*, Gutiérrez, now promoted to colonel, served as commander of the Space Radar Laboratory. In total, Gutiérrez has logged more than 4,500 hours flying time in approximately 30 different types of airplanes, sailplanes, balloons, and rockets.

ENTERTAINMENT

Pablo Casals (1876–1973) was one of the world's greatest cello players. Born in Spain, he was considered a master cellist by the age of 21. He began conducting in his thirties and founded the Orquesta Pau (Pablo) Casals in Barcelona in 1919. Fleeing Franco's fascist regime in Spain, he settled in Puerto Rico, his mother's birthplace, in 1956. In 1957, he founded the annual Festival Casals in Puerto Rico and was later instrumental, so to speak, in establishing the Puerto Rico Symphony Orchestra. He died in San Juan, having achieved worldwide fame.

Ernesto Lecuona (1896–1963) was probably the most famous Cuban-born composer. A musical prodigy who performed in New York City as a teenager, he studied with Maurice Ravel in France while in his twenties. Lecuona composed more than 400 songs, some of which were used in Hollywood movies. Besides "Siboney," which was published in the United States in 1929, other popular Lecuona compositions were "María la O" (1931) and *"Para Vigo me voy"* (1933). He also composed classical pieces such as *"Malagueña"* (1927) and *"Andalucía"* (1930). Lecuona organized a band called The Lecuona Rumba Boys, which performed in the United States and Europe. His music is still enjoyed today, especially among the Cuban Americans of South Florida.

Ramón Novarro (1899–1968) was one of first "Latin lovers" of Hollywood and was considered a rival to Rudolph Valentino in the 1920s. Born in Durango, Mexico, with the name José Ramón Samaniegos, he began his career as a singing waiter and vaudeville performer. Novarro's breakthrough performance was in *The Prisoner of Zenda* (1922). His later film roles include the title role in the 1925 epic *Ben-Hur*, and *Mata Hari* with Greta Garbo (1931). Like those of many of his colleagues, Novarro's career waned after the coming of sound to cinema.

Xavier Cugat (1900–1990) was a bandleader known as the "Rumba King" in the 1930s and 1940s. Born in Barcelona, Spain, he moved with his family to Cuba as a young child and later emigrated to the United States, where he drew cartoons for the *Los Angeles Times*. He quit scribbling and started swinging in 1928, forming a band that played at Hollywood's Coconut Grove nightclub. Cugat's band caught on in Hollywood, becoming not only a staple of the airwaves but a frequent feature in movies.

Walt Disney (1901–1966), the creator of Mickey Mouse and all his friends, and founder of the Walt Disney Studios, was born José Luis Guirao in Mojácar, Spain, to a philandering Spanish doctor and his mistress, and was subsequently adopted by Elias and Flora Disney in Chicago. . . . At least, that's what one credible but unconfirmed account holds.

After studying at Chicago's Academy of Fine Arts, Disney turned to cartoons. His own Kansas City animation studio failed in 1923. He tried again in Hollywood and in 1928 created Mickey Mouse in the groundbreaking *Steamboat Willy*. With Mickey's success, Disney began a thriving career as creator of animated films and movie producer. He later went on to produce such classics as *Snow White and the Seven Dwarfs* and *Bambi*. Disney studios later had great success with classic live-action films as well. His Disney studio was and remains one of the most significant forces in Hollywood. Disney won 32 Academy Awards for the movies his studios produced during his lifetime plus his other contributions to film, and of course inspired countless vacations with the mother of all theme parks, Disneyland (and its younger sister, Disney World).

It is said that Disney sought his birth certificate in the Cook County clerk's office when he wanted to enlist in the army and then learned of his secret past. Given the morals of the time concerning illegitimacy, and the prejudice against Hispanics, it's no surprise that he kept his story to himself. He was posthumously "outed" when *Hispanic* magazine gave him the Hispanic in the Closet Award for 1993. (Food for thought: A common theme in Disney movies is parentless or adopted children and animals.)

Jesús María Sanromá (1902–1984) was one of the top concert pianists of his age. Born in Carolina, Puerto Rico, he studied in Boston, Paris, and Berlin. From 1926 to 1943, Sanromá was the pianist for the Boston Symphony, and he later served as musical adviser to the University of Puerto Rico.

Gilbert Roland (1905–1983) played dashing leading men on-screen in the 1920s. Born in Juárez, Mexico, as Luis Antonio Dámaso de Alonso, he originally considered becoming a bullfighter like his father before finding his way to Hollywood at the age of 13 with dreams of becoming a star. His first major role was as Armand in the silent film version of *Camille* in 1927. (Ramón Novarro, for whom Roland had been a double on an earlier film, lobbied for Roland to get the part.) Roland became an instant star after *Camille*. Though his stature diminished with the coming of talkies, Roland continued to get swashbuckling roles into the 1950s.

Dolores Del Río (1905–1983), whose original name was Lolita Dolores Martínez Asunsolo y López Negrete, was a popular movie actress during Hollywood's golden age. She was born in Durango,

Mexico; her wealthy family had trained her as a dancer. A Hollywood talent scout discovered her in Mexico City, where she was living as a newlywed. She made her film debut in *Joanna* in 1925; she also appeared in other silent films such as *What Price Glory?* (1926) and *Ramona* (1928). Unlike many silent-era stars, she survived the coming of sound. She appeared in 1933's *Flying Down to Rio* (1934), which also featured the first appearance of the Fred Astaire and Ginger Rogers dance team; *Journey into Fear* (1943) with Orson Welles; and John Ford's *The Fugitive* (1947). Frustrated with being typecast as a "Latin spitfire," she turned to Mexican films before returning to Hollywood in smaller roles in the 1960s.

César Romero (1907–1994) was best known to modern audiences as the Joker in the 1960s *Batman* television series or perhaps for his role in the more recent *Falcon Crest*. In fact he had a distinguished Hollywood career—as was only appropriate for a grandson of Cuba's greatest hero, José Martí (see pages 119–120). The New York–born Romero began as a dancer in the New York theater. In Hollywood he debuted in 1934's *The Thin Man* and later played the Latin lover opposite film legends such as Alice Faye and Betty Grable.

José Limón (1908–1972) was one of the greatest dancers and choreographers of the century. Born in Culiacán in Mexico and raised in Los Angeles, he abandoned an early interest in fine arts and turned instead to modern dance, first as a performer, then as a choreographer. Exploring Mexican and Spanish dance themes, Limón began to win great acclaim for his work. The José Limón Dance Company debuted in 1945 and continues to tour nationally and around the world. Over three decades Limón choreographed dozens of works, mostly for his company and often starring himself.

Mario Bauza (1911–1993) introduced Afro-Cuban music to the United States. An arranger and trumpet player, Bauza came to the United States from Cuba in 1926 as a clarinetist in Antonio María

Romeu's Charanga Orchestra and later switched to trumpet in Chick Webb's orchestra. He joined the renowned Cab Calloway's band in 1939 and soon discovered and brought in trumpeter Dizzy Gillespie. With his brother-in-law Machito he formed the Afro-Cubans in 1940 (see page 228). The band, arguably the most important Latin orchestra in the United States, played frequently in New York's Palladium. Among Bauza's orchestral works are *"Lona"* (1928) and *"Tanga"* (1949); the latter was important for its synthesis of Afro-Cuban rhythms with jazz (see page 236).

José Ferrer (1912–1992) had a distinguished career on stage and screen. Born in Santurce, Puerto Rico, he graduated in 1933 from Princeton University. He appeared onstage in such plays as *Stalag 17* (1951), *Man of La Mancha* (1966), and *Cyrano de Bergerac* (1975) and on-screen in *Joan of Arc* (1948), *Moulin Rouge* (1952), *The Caine Mutiny* (1954), *Lawrence of Arabia* (1962), and *A Midsummer Night's Sex Comedy* (1982). He won an Oscar in 1950 for his performance in the film version of *Cyrano de Bergerac.*

Frank Grillo (aka Machito) (1912–1984) was a singer, bandleader, and percussionist who, along with his brother-in-law Mario Bauza, revolutionized Latin music in the United States by integrating it with jazz. A founder of the popular Afro-Cubans in 1940 (see page 228), he and Mario Bauza also helped introduce the cha-cha, the mambo, and the rumba to U.S. audiences.

Anthony Quinn (1915–), whose full name is Anthony Rudolph Oaxaca Quinn, possesses one of Hollywood's great, distinctive screen personas. He has appeared in more than 120 pictures and received two Academy Awards. Born in Chihuahua, Mexico, he and his family came to the United States when he was a child. He was a migrant worker, studied architecture with Frank Lloyd Wright, and considered becoming a preacher before his Hollywood debut in *Parole!* (1936). He won an Oscar for best supporting actor in *Viva Zapata!* in 1952 and a second one four years later for *Lust for*

Life. His many other films include *Blood and Sand* (1941), *Sinbad the Sailor* (1947), *Zorba the Greek* (1964), and *The Last Action Hero* (1993).

Desi Arnaz (1917–1986) will always be "Ricky Ricardo" to millions around the world. Together with his wife of 20 years, Lucille Ball, he produced the most successful television series of all time, *I Love Lucy,* from 1951 to 1956; reruns of the show are still aired regularly. Their company, Desilu Productions, pioneered both the production and distribution of television series. He was born Desiderio Alberto Arnaz y de Acha III and came to the United States as an exile from Cuba with his family when he was 16. Arnaz became famous as a singer and drummer and helped popularize the Cuban conga dance (see page 229). In 1940 he married Lucille Ball, his costar in the movie *Too Many Girls* (1940). Among his other films are *Cuban Pete* (1946), *Holiday in Havana* (1949), *The Long Trailer* (1954), and *Forever Darling* (1956). One of his last performances was hosting television's *Saturday Night Live.*

Israel "Cachao" López (1918–) is one of several figures credited with the invention of the mambo (see page 230). A bassist, bandleader, arranger, and composer, López is also known for his *descargas* (improvisations). Born to a musical family in Havana, he played with many Cuban orchestras including José Fajardo's Orquestra América. He left Cuba for good for New York in 1963 and played in various bands, including those of Tito Rodríguez, Johnny Pacheco, Pupi Campo, and Julio Gutiérrez. Cachao's records remain popular among Cuban expatriates in the United States, and he continues to perform at nightclubs in South Florida.

Rita Hayworth (1918–1987) was one of the dominant Hollywood sex symbols of the 1940s. Born Margarita Carmen Cansino in New York, both her parents were dancers: Her Spanish father danced flamenco and her mother performed in the Ziegfeld Follies. Her Hollywood debut was in 1935, when she appeared in *Under the*

Pampas. Two years later she married Edward Judson, who advised her to drop her Spanish name and "look." Her subsequent films, under her screen name, include *Blood and Sand* (1941), *Gilda* (1946), and *Pal Joey* (1957). Her later husbands included cinematic auteur Orson Welles and the playboy Prince Aly Khan.

Dámaso Pérez Prado (1922–1989) was the "King of the Mambo" (a title he shares with Tito Puente), a bandleader, arranger, and composer who sold millions of mambo records around the world (see page 230). A native of Cuba, he played piano and worked as an arranger in the Orquesta Casino de la Playa in Havana. In 1948, he started his own band, achieving renown throughout Latin America and the United States. Pérez Prado moved to Mexico in 1950 and began writing a series of mambos in popular and classic styles.

His first international hit was *"Qué rico el mambo."* Through the 1950s he toured the United States and continued releasing mambo hits, earning a gold record with "Cherry Pink and Apple Blossom White," which eventually sold 4 million copies. By 1955, he led the most popular orchestra in the United States, regularly playing New York's Palladium and the Waldorf Astoria. Eventually Hollywood called, and Pérez Prado himself danced a screen mambo with Jane Russell. Prado died in Mexico City.

Tito Puente (1923–) is one of the biggest stars in Latin music. Puente was born in New York and began his career at 13, as a drummer for the orchestra of Noro Morales. In 1941, he joined Machito's Afro-Cubans (see page 228), the most influential Latin band of the era. After naval service in World War II, he played with the orchestras of Tito Rodríguez and Pupi Campo, and then organized his own group, Tito Puente and His Orchestra. He shares the "Mambo King" crown with Dámaso Pérez Prado, an honor underscored by his appearance in the 1992 movie *Mambo Kings.* Puente has recorded more than 100 albums and remains a popular headliner in the Latin music world.

Celia Cruz (1929?–) is the "Queen of Salsa." She refuses to give her age but she has reigned over the world of salsa music (see pages 231–232) for more than four decades. Born in Havana, she was for 15 years the lead vocalist of the Sonora Matancera orchestra, mainstays of the famous Tropicana nightclub and stars of Cuban television. Cruz and much of the band left Cuba in 1960 and came to the United States after a year and a half in Mexico (where they appeared in five Mexican movies). Cruz has recorded numerous albums, including records with Tito Puente, Johnny Pacheco, and Willie Colón.

Rita Moreno (1931–) holds the distinction of having won the grand slam of entertainment awards: an Oscar, a Tony, an Emmy, and a Grammy. Born Rosa Dolores Alverio in Puerto Rico, she came as a baby to New York City with her seamstress mother. Moreno started earning money singing and dancing as a child, winning her first Broadway role at age 13 and her first film role six years later. In 1962, she won an Oscar as best supporting actress for her performance in the film version of *West Side Story*. She also appeared in *Singin' in the Rain* (1952), *The King and I* (1956), and *Carnal Knowledge* (1971). Her stage credits include *Elmer Gantry* (1969–70), *The Last of the Red Hot Lovers* (1970–71), and the play for which she won a Tony as best supporting actress, *The Ritz* (1975).

In 1972, she shared a Grammy with fellow cast members for their record album of the children's educational television program *The Electric Company*, which she joined in 1971. She won her two Emmy awards for guest appearances on television's *The Muppet Show* (1977) and *The Rockford Files* (1978).

Trinidad "Trini" López (1937–), whose albums stayed on the charts throughout the 1960s, formed his first band when he was just 15. Born in Dallas, he performed in Texas nightclubs and was "discovered" by Frank Sinatra at a club called PJ's. López signed with Sinatra's own Reprise Records, and the album *Trini López at PJ's* was the number-two-selling album of 1963. By the end of the decade he had recorded 14 albums and 13 singles that made it onto the charts, including "Lemon Tree," his take on a Latin folk number; López's *Greatest Hits* album was released in 1966. He also appeared in a number of films, most notably *The Dirty Dozen.* López continues to sing in clubs.

Raúl Julia (1940–1994) was among the most accomplished Hispanic actors in the United States. Born in San Juan, Puerto Rico, he began his stage career in Spanish-language plays such as *La carreta (The Oxcart)*, and moved on to Shakesperean and classical roles in such plays as *Titus Andronicus* (1967) and *Hamlet* (1972). He also starred in a revival of the musical *Man of La Mancha* (1992). He achieved national fame for his role in *Kiss of the Spider Woman* (1985). Younger audiences may know him for his role as Gomez Addams in the film *The Addams Family* (1991). Julia died in 1994 after a brief illness and was given a state funeral in Puerto Rico.

Vikki Carr (1941–) is a singer best known for her English-language song hits of the 1960s. She was born in El Paso, Texas, with the name Florencia Bicenta de Casillas Martínez Cardona to a family with a Mexican background, and grew up in the San Gabriel Valley near Los Angeles. Among her hits, "It Must Be Him" reached number three on the pop charts; she also had success with "Can't Take My Eyes Off of You" and "With Pen in Hand." She recorded a Spanish album, *Vikki Carr en español*, in 1972, and eventually won two Grammy awards: for *Simplemente mujer* (Simply Woman) in 1985, and *Cosas de Amor* (*Things of Love*) in 1992. By 1994, she had released 50 best-selling singles.

Joan Baez (1941–) is one of the most famous American woman folksingers and is known also for her civil rights and antiwar activism in the 1960s. Born in Staten Island, New York, to a Mexican father and a mother of Scottish ancestry, she began singing in coffeehouses in Cambridge, Massachusetts, at age 18. Her talent was quickly recognized, and she performed before 13,000 people at the

1959 Newport Folk Festival; her first album was released the following year, with great success. She soon paired up with Bob Dylan and began recording many of his songs. In 1974, she recorded a Spanish-language album, *Gracias a la vida (Gratitude to Life)*. Baez's voice is one of the most resonant of the Vietnam protest era.

Ritchie Valens (1941–1958) was one of the three prodigious young musicians to die in a 1958 plane crash, along with Buddy Holly and the Big Bopper. His career spanned only two years. Born Richard Valenzuela, he was a sensation when he was barely 16 with his debut single, "Come on Let's Go," followed by "Donna." But his place in the archives of popular music is secured by his version of the Mexican folk song "La Bamba" (see page 236). Ironically, Valens did not speak Spanish. He is the first Latino rock singer to have a star on Hollywood's Walk of Fame and to be featured on a U.S. postage stamp. A movie about Valens's life, *La Bamba*, was released in 1988.

Geraldo Rivera (1943–) is one of the masters of "tabloid television." His father was born in Puerto Rico and came to America in 1940. Rivera established a reputation as an aggressive investigative reporter, and later as an "ambush" journalist, on New York's *Eyewitness News* and on *Good Morning, America* and *20/20*, for which he won a number of Emmy awards. Rivera went on to become a dominant force in the daytime talk show category, first as host of *Geraldo* and then of *Rivera Live*.

José Feliciano (1945–) is one of the most popular singers to record in both Spanish and English. Born in Lares, Puerto Rico, his family moved to Spanish Harlem. Feliciano was born blind but learned to play the guitar and the accordion. As a teenager he began performing in coffeehouses in New York's Greenwich Village and had a hit with his 1964 version of "Light My Fire," for which he won best new artist and best male pop vocalist Grammy Awards. Feliciano has also recorded albums in Argentina, Venezuela, and Mexico. A Grammy winner in 1983 for his album *Me enamoré (I Fell in Love)*, Feliciano has had a performing arts school in Harlem named in his honor.

Linda Ronstadt (1946–) was a top female pop vocalist beginning in the late 1960s and into the 1980s, who later achieved critical success in a Broadway revival of Gilbert and Sullivan's operetta *The Pirates of Penzance* and, later still, as a singer of lush big-band standards. She was born in Tucson, Arizona. Her grandfather, Federico Ronstadt, was born in Sonora, Mexico. He became a successful businessman in Tucson. His avocation was Mexican music, however, and he was the founder of the Club Filarmónico, which became Tucson's leading orchestra. Singing in a country mode, Linda Ronstadt's first hit was "Different Drum" in 1967. She dominated the pop charts in the 1970s with her versions of songs such as "Blue Bayou," "Poor, Poor Pitiful Me," "When Will I Be Loved?," and "Heat Wave." Her 1988 album, *Canciones de mi padre (Songs of My Father)*, featured the *ranchera* songs (see page 234) she heard as a child and alluded to a like-named 1946 collection of Mexican folk songs published by her aunt, Luisa Ronstadt.

Edward James Olmos (1947–) is one of today's top Latino actors. Born in East Los Angeles, the descendant of a radical Mexico City newspaperman, Olmos set aside an early interest in rock and roll to try his hand in the world of acting. After years of bit parts, his big break came in the 1978 play *Zoot Suit*, Luis Valdez's musical about the 1942 Sleepy Lagoon case. Olmos won a Tony nomination and an L.A. Drama Critics award for his performance. He appeared later in the hit movie *Blade Runner* (1982) and in PBS's *The Ballad of Gregorio Cortez* (1983). But Olmos is still probably best known as Lieutenant Castillo from the 1980s hit show *Miami Vice*, for which he won the 1985 best supporting actor Emmy. He later garnered an

Oscar nomination for *Stand and Deliver* (1988). He directed, produced, and starred in 1992's *American Me*. Olmos is also known for his humanitarian interests and his encouragement of Latino culture, priorities reflected not only in his choice of roles and the work he does promoting them but in his dedication to community service.

Carlos Santana (1947–) is an outstanding guitarist and bandleader. Born in Mexico, he played the violin and the clarinet as a child and picked up the guitar at age 14. In 1962, he and his family moved to San Francisco, and in 1967, he organized the Santana Blues Band, which played at Woodstock the following year. Santana is considered if not the creator then certainly the master of the hybrid sound known as Latin Rock. His best-known album, *Abraxas* (see page 237), included the songs *"Samba pa ti"* and his cover of Tito Puente's *"Oye como va"*; one of his best-known singles is "Evil Ways," from his debut album.

Rubén Blades (1948–) has made his mark as a musician, actor, lawyer, and politician. He was born in Panama City, Panama, to a Cuban mother who was a pianist-singer and a Panamanian father who was a police detective and musician. His early love was U.S.-style pop music, but he gave it up after U.S. troops killed 21 rioting Panamanians in 1964. He switched to salsa and took his act to the United States, where he released his own album and joined Willie Colón's orchestra as a singer and composer. His songs' leftist politics offended many in the anti-Castro Miami community, resulting in his music being banned from some Cuban radio stations there.

Forming his own group, he shortly released the album *Buscando América (Searching for America)*, which sold 300,000 copies. With his music career in full swing, he moved on to Hollywood, where in 1985 he starred in a movie about Latino musicians yearning for mainstream acceptance, *Crossover Dreams* (see pages 223–224). Having earlier earned a law degree in Panama, he later returned with his second law degree, a master's in international law from Harvard. In Panama, he ran unsuccessfully for president.

Fernando Bujones (1955–) is considered one of the top ballet dancers of his generation. Born in Miami, he went to Cuba and took classes at the famous ballet school of Alicia Alonso, returning home at age 10. He later received a full scholarship to the prestigious School of American Ballet. After graduation at 17 he joined American Ballet Theater. When he was 19, he became the first American to win a gold medal at the Varna, Bulgaria, international ballet contest. In 1985, Bujones left ABT after a falling out with its director, Mikhail Baryshnikov, and went on to dance as a guest artist with virtually every top ballet company in the world. In 1994, he became artistic director of Ballet Mississippi.

Gloria Estefan (1957–) is one of the most successful Hispanic entertainers in American history. Born in Cuba as Gloria Fajardo, she came to the United States as a child and joined Emilio Estefan's Miami Sound Machine. She married Estefan in 1978. Together they pioneered a lively pop-Latin hybrid music dubbed the Miami sound (see page 231). Starting in 1984, the group had a string of big hits, including "Conga" (see pages 237–238), "Words Get in the Way," "Rhythm Is Gonna Get You," and "Anything for You." In 1989, Estefan released her first solo album, *Cuts Both Ways*. Since then her albums have sold in the tens of millions. Estefan inspired legions of fans around the world with her phenomenal comeback after suffering a broken vertebra in a traffic accident.

Selena Quintanilla Pérez (1972–1995) was a rising *tejano* music (see pages 233–235) star whose tragic murder sparked such an interest in her work that she posthumously became one of the most successful Latino recording artists. The Texas-born singer, who went simply by the name Selena, had already won a Grammy Award in 1993 and earned a gold record when she cut *Dreaming of You* (see page 238) her first English-language album, which was to be her crossover debut. It was released shortly after she had been murdered by a disgruntled former employee, immediately became the fastest-selling album ever by a woman, and soon became the first album by a Latin artist to reach number one on *Billboard*'s Top 200. Selena soon had five albums on the *Billboard* Top 200 chart — the first such accomplishment by a single artist.

LITERATURE, DRAMA, AND SOCIAL THOUGHT

Gaspar Pérez de Villagrá (1555–1620) was one of New Mexico pioneer Juan de Oñate's lieutenants and the author of the United States' first epic poem. Born in Spain, Villagrá graduated from the University of Salamanca in 1580 and worked in the royal court. He later journeyed to New Spain and joined Oñate's expedition. His epic poem about the experience, *Historia de la Nuevo México (History of New Mexico)*, conveyed both the bravery of the Spanish explorer-colonists and the travails of the Indians who got in the way (see pages 56–57).

Father Félix Varela (1787–1853) was the outstanding Cuban intellectual of his time and lived more than 30 years of his life in exile in the United States. He was born in Havana but attended school in Saint Augustine, Florida, where his grandfather was stationed at Fort Castillo de San Marcos. He returned to Cuba to join the priesthood and the faculty of the Seminario de San Carlos. There he helped revolutionize Cuba's education system. He left for Spain on his election to the Cortes (Parliament), but was forced into a New York exile because of his public stance against slavery and monarchy.

In New York, Father Varela continued both his priestly vocation and his revolutionary avocation, working and writing for Cuban independence and finding time to found three religious schools, two churches, and a hospital. With an optimistic eye to emerging Latin American democracy, he translated Jefferson's *Manual of Parliamentary Procedure* into Spanish. As he had done since his Cuban teaching days, he published philosophy textbooks in Spanish, which were used throughout Latin America. Named vicar general of the church in New York, he dissipated his considerable fortune on charity and died in poverty in Saint Augustine.

Miguel Ángel Otero (1859–1944) was one of the first Hispanic writers to publish his work in English. A native of New Mexico, he served as governor of the territory from 1897 to 1906. It was after this that he made his name in the world of letters. His two-volume English-language autobiography, *My Life on the Frontier*, published in 1935, was a stirring account of New Mexico in the days of the Wild West. He later wrote a biography of bandit Billy the Kid, whom he had known personally.

Jesús Colón (1901–1974) was one of the first Puerto Rican English-language writers in the United States. He came to New York from the island at 16 and worked as a laborer. His class consciousness raised by the experience—and by the discrimination he faced due to his Afro–Puerto Rican heritage—he joined the Communist Party and ran unsuccessfully for office. He wrote for the party's *Daily Worker* and published a collection of essays and columns, *A Puerto Rican in New York and Other Sketches* (see page 216), in 1961.

Father Angelico Chávez (1910–1996) was one of the United States' most important contemporary religious poets. Born Manuel Ezequiel Chávez in Wagon Mound, New Mexico, he was the first son of that state to be ordained as a Franciscan priest. A twelfth-generation *nuevomexicano*, Father Chávez wrote 23 books and innumerable articles and stories, many about or set in old New Mexico. Among his books of poetry are *Clothed with Sun* (1939) and *Selected Poems, with an Apologia* (1969).

René Marqués (1919–1979) was Puerto Rico's foremost playwright and short-fiction writer with a reputation that extended far beyond the island. A student of agronomy, Marqués worked briefly in the field before decamping to Spain to study the classics. Upon his return to Puerto Rico, Marqués founded a theater group and soon became a prolific writer of plays, stories, and essays. His most important play is *La carreta (The Oxcart)* (see page 216), first performed in 1953, which described the travails of Puerto Rican peasants trying to find their way in New York City. Among his other plays are *Un niño azul para esa sombra (A Blue Child for That Shadow)* and *La muerte no entrará en palacio (Death Will Not Enter the Palace).* He also published several books of poetry.

Celedonio González (1923–) is a prominent Cuban exile writer whose work focuses on the travails of Castro's refugees. As a young man, González managed his family's farm in central Cuba. When his initial support for Castro turned sour, however, he was imprisoned briefly as a counterrevolutionary. He fled with his family to the United States in 1960 but did not write his first book, *Los primos (The Cousins)* (1971) (see page 219), until the age of 41. His later books include *La soledad es una amiga que vendrá (Solitude Is a Friend Who Will Come)* (1971), *Los cuatro embajadores (The Four Ambassadors)* (1973), and *El espesor del pellejo de un gato ya cadáver (The Thickness of a Dead Cat's Skin)* (1978), the last of which encourages Cubans to accommodate themselves to living in the United States.

Carlos Castañeda (1925–) is the author of a string of best-selling books based on his mystical search for a separate reality. Born in Peru, he moved to the United States in the 1920s and studied anthropology at the University of California at Los Angeles. It was in the course of his study-related visits to the Southwest that Castañeda claims to have come across, and become apprenticed to, a Yaqui Indian sorcerer named Don Juan—who, he says, led him to challenge conventional views of reality and to suggest there was more to the universe than science could understand. Castañeda's first book was the *The Teachings of Don Juan: A Yaqui Way of Knowledge* (1968) (see page 221), one of whose major effects was to popularize mind-altering natural substances such as peyote. He later wrote the best-seller *Journey to Ixtlán: The Lessons of Don Juan* (1972).

Piri Thomas (1928–) is the author of 1967's *Down These Mean Streets* (see page 217), a pioneering autobiographical account of an Afro-Cuban–Puerto Rican youth in New York's ghettos. Thomas was born in New York City to a Cuban father and a Puerto Rican mother. He grew up poor and victimized by discrimination. His youth followed a now familiar pattern: gangs, drugs, and crime. He was eventually arrested, convicted, and sentenced to prison, where he began to write. Thomas's account of his experiences of hopelessness and despair helped create a genre of "mean streets" literature by Latinos and others. He also wrote *Savior, Savior Hold My Hand* (1972) and *Seven Long Times* (1972), the latter about his years in Sing Sing prison.

José Antonio Villareal (1929–) wrote what is generally considered to be the first Chicano novel, *Pocho* (1959) (see page 212). The son of Mexican migrant workers, he was raised in Los Angeles and served in the navy before getting his education at the University of California at Berkeley. While working as an editor, Villareal wrote *Pocho*, an autobiographical novel about being caught between two worlds, a reflection of Villareal's own youthful experiences of racism and cultural conflict. The book's extraordinary reception won Villareal a string of university teaching jobs. He later published *The Fifth Horseman* (1974), a saga of the Mexican Revolution, and *Clemente Chacón* (1984), about the rise to fame of an impoverished Mexican boy. Ironically, Villareal has refused to identify himself as a Chicano writer per se or even to accept the notion of a Chicano literature, a stand for which he has drawn much fire within the Latino community.

Oscar "Zeta" Acosta (1936–1974) was a civil rights activist and controversial author. Born in El Paso, Acosta studied to become a lawyer but did not find his activist vocation until inspired by the nascent civil rights movement. He wrote two semiautobiographical novels: *The Autobiography of a Brown Buffalo* (1972) (see page 213), in which he portrayed himself as Robin Hood, and *The Revolt of the Cockroach People* (1973), in which he appears as a lawyer defending Chicanos accused of rioting in Los Angeles. In 1974, he disappeared under mysterious circumstances while on vacation in Mexico.

Luis Valdez (1940–) is an actor, director, playwright, and filmmaker who is considered the father of Chicano theater. That distinction was earned when he created the *Teatro Campesino,* a theater of farmworkers in California, by which he inspired young Mexican Americans to use theater as a means of organizing. Born into a family of migrant farmers in Delano, California (seat of César Chávez's United Farm Workers union), Valdez worked in various theater troops after college, then joined Chávez in 1965, and began Teatro Campesino to dramatize the plight of Chicano workers. In the late 1960s, even as many of his plays continued to be produced by the Teatro Campesino, Valdez expanded his range. In 1969, he wrote the film version of Corky Gonzales's *Yo Soy Joaquín/I Am Joaquín.* Valdez eventually broke into the mainstream in 1979 with the Broadway hit *Zoot Suit* (see page 214), later made into a movie (see page 223). His 1986 *I Don't Have to Show You No Stinking Badges* was also adapted by Hollywood. Valdez later wrote and directed the successful film *La Bamba* (see page 224).

Richard Rodriguez (1944–) is a journalist and author whose unconventional views have made him a lightning rod for establishment Latino criticism. A child of Mexican immigrants, he was raised in Sacramento. Rodriguez thrived academically and turned to writing. His first book, *Hunger of Memory: The Education of Richard Rodriguez* (1982) (see page 214), challenged bilingual education and affirmative action as harmful to Hispanics, preventing them from entering mainstream society. His critics regard Rodriguez as "self-hating."

He has since written another autobiographical narrative, *Days of Obligation: An Argument with My Mexican Father* (1993).

Isabel Allende (1942–) is one of the best-regarded and most successful Latino writers of her generation. Born to a Chilean family in Peru, where her father was a diplomat, she eventually went to Chile and began to write while still a teenager. After the coup that overthrew the government of her uncle, Salvador Allende, she fled with her husband and child to Venezuela. There she achieved her first fame with *La casa de los espíritus (The House of the Spirits)* (1982) (see page 222). This success was followed by *De amor y de sombra (Of Love and Shadow)* (1987) and *Cuentos de Eva Luna (The Stories of Eva Luna)* (1991). Allende has since settled in California, where she wrote her latest book, the nonfiction *Paula* (1995).

Oscar Hijuelos (1951–) is the first Hispanic to have won the Pulitzer Prize in literature, for his work *The Mambo Kings Play Songs of Love* (1989) (see pages 220–221). Born in New York City to Cuban American parents, he published his first novel, the autobiographical *Our House in the Last World*, in 1983, at a small press. Its reception led to a number of prizes, and after several years of travel, he wrote *The Mambo Kings*, about two Cuban musician brothers who come to New York in 1949 with hopes of making the big time. Published in 1989, the book not only won the Pulitzer but made the best-seller lists and was later turned into a movie (see page 224). His novel *Mr. Ives' Christmas* was published in 1995.

Gary Soto (1952–) is America's most celebrated Latino poet. A native of Fresno, California, he studied under the poet Philip Levine before becoming a university professor himself. Drawing frequently on social themes in his work and on his own life experiences, Soto has won a string of prestigious awards and fellowships. His books of poetry include *The Tale of Sunlight* (1978) and *Who Will Know Us?* (1990). He has also written works of prose, including the autobiographical *A Summer Life* (1990) (see page 215).

ART, ARCHITECTURE, AND DESIGN

José Rafael Aragón (1796?–1862) was one of the earliest major *santeros* (see pages 239–241)—religious folk artists—in New Mexico. Born in the town of Cordova, he was active from the mid-1820s to 1860, creating *bultos* (carved and painted religious sculptures) as well as panel paintings and altar screens. Typical of his *bultos* is *Santo Tomás de Aquino* (in the Museum of New Mexico), an expressive elongated figure accented by strong lines and pure colors.

José Benito Ortega (1858–1941) produced some of the most cherished santos in the history of the craft (see page 240). Born in New Mexico, Ortega spent most of his life traveling from one village in the region to the next, carving holy figures for different patrons. His brightly painted wooden sculptures are simply designed with distinctively Spanish faces. Many sport the black-pegged boots introduced by Anglo traders.

César Pelli (1922–) is one of contemporary architecture's leading lights. A native of Argentina, he apprenticed with the celebrated Eero Saarinen and in 1977 cofounded a firm of his own and later became dean of the Yale School of Architecture. In the early 1980s, Pelli rose to prominence with such works as Manhattan's World Financial Center—with its arching, 125-foot-high, glass-enclosed public hall—and the renovated Museum of Modern Art. Among his other projects are the Pacific Design Center in Los Angeles, Herring Hall at Rice University, the Norwest Center in Minneapolis, and Indiana Tower in Indianapolis.

Marisol Escobar (1930–) is an internationally celebrated sculptor known simply as Marisol. She was born in Paris to Venezuelan parents and came to New York City at age 19. Influenced by pre-Columbian art and folk sculptures, as well as Dada and other European movements, she began to create witty assemblages out of wood, paint, and found materials. In the 1960s, she was acclaimed as a member of Andy Warhol's pop art circle and was chosen to represent Venezuela in the 1968 Venice Biennale. Her satirical social commentary is evident in *The Party* (1965–66), an installation piece with two servants catering to thirteen wooden guests, all bearing plaster casts of Marisol's face. Other works, combining sculpted forms and painted wooden blocks, portray such political and cultural celebrities as Lyndon Johnson, the British royal family, John Wayne, and Georgia O'Keeffe. Today, Marisol's work is displayed at such premier institutions as the Metropolitan Museum of Art, the Museum of Modern Art, and the Whitney Museum of American Art (see page 245).

Oscar de la Renta (1932–) is one of the age's top fashion designers. Born in the Dominican Republic, he studied art in Madrid before landing a job with the famed Spanish fashion designer Cristóbal Balenciaga. He soon moved on to Paris and then to New York, where after a few years of working at Elizabeth Arden, he started his own design company in 1965. Over the following decades, de la Renta became one of the premier designers of haute couture, winning widespread kudos, numerous awards, and an international reputation.

Rafael Ferrer (1933–) is a major contemporary experimental artist. Born in Puerto Rico and initially influenced by the European surrealist movement, he moved to Philadelphia in the late 1960s and became a central figure in the process art movement, which emphasized materials and procedures rather than finished art objects. His ephemeral works included a huge block of melting ice and piles of pungent dead leaves, strategically placed so that viewers had to walk through them. During the 1970s, Ferrer shifted to evocations of explorations and imaginary journeys with his colorful displays of maps, boats, and tents. More recently, since the 1980s, he has created brightly colored figurative paintings of Puerto Rican life.

Adolfo (1933–) is a celebrated fashion designer. Born Adolfo Sardiña to a wealthy Havana family, he began his career as a hat designer, working in a succession of jobs in Paris and New York before establishing his reputation with the Emme fashion house in the 1950s. In 1962, he started his own company and soon moved beyond millinery into dress design. His already considerable popularity among the fashion set grew throughout the decade and has continued to this day.

Rupert García (1934–) is a leading contemporary Chicano artist. Born and educated in California, where he has taught at the university level for decades, García is known for politically charged silkscreen posters and prints that often feature graphic portraits of such recognizable figures as Frida Kahlo or Nelson Mandela, delineated by bold areas of black and one or two strong colors. In his paintings and large pastels, García also uses simplified forms and bright colors to make an activist statement. For example, in *Nose to Nose* (1985), a silhouetted black bomber flies (nose to nose) into the huge abstracted face of a Mexican mask.

Judy Baca (1946–) has been a key figure in the California Chicano mural movement since the 1970s. Born in Los Angeles, she studied art and later initiated and headed the Citywide Mural Project, which has created some 250 murals since 1974. Baca's best-known project is *The Great Wall of Los Angeles*, a 13-foot-high mural extending for half a mile along a drainage canal in the San Fernando Valley (see pages 242–243). Painted over five summers by hundreds of youngsters from different ethnic communities, the mural traces the social history of California's diverse population from pre-Columbian times to the present. Baca sees two major benefits from her projects: the finished mural and the interracial harmony among the people working on it.

Arnaldo Roche Rabell (1955–) creates evocative, dreamlike, textured figurative paintings. Born in Puerto Rico, he studied art in

Chicago where he lives on-and-off today. Roche Rabell is noted for his technique of rubbing paint on canvas pressed over his models' bodies or various objects. Other works include large, close-up self-portraits, in which his face emerges almost ghostlike from the densely painted surface. Roche Rabell's work has been included in such major group shows as *Hispanic Art in the United States* (1987) and *The Decade Show* (1990).

SPORTS

Adolfo "Dolph" Luque (1890–1957) was one of the National League's dominant pitchers between 1914 and 1935, mostly with the Cincinnati Reds. The Cuban-born Luque won the fifth and deciding game in the 1933 World Series while on the mound for the New York Giants.

Martín Dihigo (1905–1971), the "Black Babe Ruth," is one of the Negro League's few Hall of Famers. Born in Matanzas, Cuba, he played every position and in just about every league except the majors: the American Negro League, the Mexican League, and the professional leagues of the Dominican Republic and Cuba. Although there are no reliable records of his statistics, he was nonetheless recognized by teammates and opponents to have been one of the best ever, especially on the mound and at the plate. Dihigo was too old to play in the majors by the time baseball was desegregated, but he won election to the Hall of Fame all the same—an honor to put beside his membership in the baseball halls of fame of a number of Latin American countries. After the Cuban revolution, Castro named Dihigo minister of sports.

Vernon L. "Lefty" Gómez (1908–1989) was one of baseball's most successful pitchers, third all-time in regular season wins. The California-born Gómez, son of a Spanish father and an Anglo mother, had four 20-game-winning seasons during his career, which spanned 1930 to 1943. He had a 6–0 record in World Series play and was a two-time triple-crown pitcher (league leader in ERA, strikeouts, and wins). The repeat all-star and Hall of Famer was a classic pitcher, with a great fastball and curve, which he was able to put to good use as a member of the dominant New York Yankees teams of the era. Gómez coined the phrase, "I'd rather be lucky than good."

Alfonso R. "Al" López (1908–) was a Hall of Fame player and manager with the Cleveland Indians and Chicago White Sox. The Tampa-born López was a strong-hitting and stronger-fielding catcher with a number of teams in the 1920s through the 1940s. After managing in the minors, he was taken on as skipper of the Cleveland Indians and led them to the World Series in 1954. Though they lost to the New York Giants, their 110 wins in one season have still never been equaled. In 1953, López moved to the White Sox and two years later led them to the World Series (only to lose again, to the Brooklyn Dodgers). López's winning percentage as a manager is the third-best ever.

Richard Alonzo "Pancho" González (1928–1995) was one of tennis's all-time stars. He was born in Los Angeles to Mexican parents and learned to play tennis on public courts. The strong-serving, hot-tempered González became a champion in a sport that did not welcome the poor or the non-Anglo. He won the U.S. singles championship at Forest Hills in 1948 (the second-youngest winner ever) and 1949 and reigned as the world champion singles professional from 1954 to 1962. The 1969 Wimbledon tournament was his last moment in the spotlight, when, at the age of 41, he beat 25-year-old Charles Pasarell in the longest match in Wimbledon history—5 hours and 12 minutes. González is a member of the International Tennis Hall of Fame.

Roberto Clemente (1934–1972) was one of baseball's all-time greats and the first Latino ever named to the Hall of Fame. Born in

Puerto Rico, he played for the Pittsburgh Pirates from 1955 to 1972, won four National League batting championship titles, and was the National League most valuable player in 1966. Clemente also won multiple Gold Gloves for his defensive play, and was a 14-time all-star. His greatest moment came in the 1971 World Series, in which he hit .414 with two home runs. Overall, Clemente had a lifetime average of .317, with exactly 3,000 hits, 240 home runs, and 1,305 RBIs. Clemente's career was marked by his willingness to speak out against discrimination against Latinos and blacks in sports. It was cut short by a plane crash while Clemente was on an earthquake-relief mission to Nicaragua. He was elevated to the Hall of Fame immediately thereafter in recognition of his heroic life and tragic death.

Luis Aparicio (1934–) was one of the game's best shortstops. The son of Venezuela's greatest shortstop, Aparicio combined sterling defensive skills with superb speed on the base paths, which made him a top base stealer. His career spanned from 1956 to 1973, mostly with the Chicago White Sox. Aparicio was named Rookie of the Year in his debut season, was repeatedly elected to the all-star team, won numerous Gold Gloves, and was ultimately inducted into the Hall of Fame.

Juan "Chi Chi" Rodríguez (1935–) is a member of the World Golf Hall of Fame. Born in Puerto Rico, he started as a caddy and rose to become a top player, noted for his long drives. Though long one of the best players in the game, Rodríguez never won a major championship. He is also well known for his charitable work for Puerto Rico. Rodríguez continues to golf professionally on the PGA Senior Tour, where he is still a dominant player.

Thomas Raymond "Tom" Flores (1937–) is the only Hispanic to have been a pro football coach and general manager, and is the top Latino executive in the National Football League. The Fresno-born Flores was a solid quarterback for the Oakland Raiders, Buffalo

Bills, and Kansas City Chiefs between 1960 and 1970. After his retirement from the field, he became an assistant coach for the Raiders, and in 1979 was named head coach. He led the power-house team to Super Bowl victories in 1981 and 1984. After eight seasons as Raiders coach, where he compiled a 78–43 regular sea-son and 8–3 postseason record, and a year in the Raider front office, he was named president and general manager of the Seattle Seahawks. He named himself coach of the team in 1992 but gave up the post a few years later.

Lee Trevino (1939–) is one of golf's finest players. Born in Dallas to a poor Mexican American family, he learned golf by watching duffers at the course where he was a groundskeeper and caddy, and started competing in the Far East while stationed in Okinawa as a marine. After several years as a golf hustler in Dallas, he joined the PGA tour in 1967 and was named Rookie of the Year. He won the U.S. Open in 1968 and 1971, the British Open in 1971 and 1972, and the PGA championship in 1974 and 1984. Trevino, who was named PGA player of the year in 1971 and 1974, continues to play on the Senior Tour, and has won senior PGA Player of the Year honors three times.

Angel Cordero (1942–) is one of horse racing's most successful jockeys. He was born in San Juan, Puerto Rico. Cordero won six Triple Crown races: He rode the Kentucky Derby winners in 1974, 1976, and 1985; the Belmont Stakes winners in 1980 and 1984; and the Preakness winner in 1976. Cordero was named Jockey of the Year in 1982 and 1983, and is one of the all-time winningest jockeys and top money earners in the field. He is a member of the National Horse Racing Hall of Fame.

Rod Carew (1945–) was one of modern baseball's greatest hitters, winning seven American League batting titles and posting a career average of .328. Born in the Panama Canal Zone, the 1967 Rookie of the Year and frequent all-star was named the American League's most valuable player in 1977, when his .388 batting average tied with Ted Williams's 1957 average as the best since 1941 (when Williams hit .406). Carew played with the Minnesota Twins and the California Angels. He retired in 1985 and is now a member of the Hall of Fame.

James "Jim" Plunkett (1947–) was a two-time Super Bowl–winning quarterback. Born in Santa Clara, California, of Mexican descent, Plunkett excelled at football at Stanford University. The young quarterback won the 1970 Heisman Trophy as the best college player in the country. His professional career started well; he won Rookie of the Year honors in 1971 with the Boston (later New England) Patriots. His career then sputtered. He had several sub-par years with the Patriots, then two more with the San Francisco 49ers before being picked up as a backup passer for the Oakland Raiders. But when he was brought in to replace the hurt starter in the middle of the 1980 season, he led the team to a Super Bowl victory (and won most valuable player honors), a feat he repeated in 1984.

Nancy López (1957–) is one of the greatest stars of women's golf. She was born in Torrance, California, to Mexican American parents, who initiated her into the game. López was women's champion of New Mexico at age 12, finished second (while still an 18-year-old amateur) in the 1975 U.S. Open, and won five consecutive tournaments in 1978—including the LPGA Championship Tournament—earning her the titles of LPGA Rookie of the Year and Player of the Year. She has since won two more LPGA championships and three more Player of the Year awards. A member of the LPGA Hall of Fame and the World Golf Hall of Fame, she is among the sport's top all-time winners and earners.

Alberto Baudy Salazar (1958–) is one of the world's premier distance runners. The Cuban-born Salazar won the NCAA individual championship and helped his University of Oregon team win the

NCAA title in 1977. He made the U.S. Olympic team in 1980 but could not compete due to the U.S. boycott of the Moscow games; instead, he ran in and won that year's New York Marathon with the fastest first marathon in history and the second-fastest ever run by an American. He won it again, along with the Boston Marathon, in 1982. In all, he has set one world record and six U.S. records.

latinos today and *mañana*

♦

Contrasting snapshots of the Latino worlds of half a century ago and today reveal profound changes flecked with stubborn problems. As a result of the civil rights revolution and the social trend toward tolerance and away from gross discrimination, the lives of Latinos in this country are better than they have been at any other time in U.S. history.

More Latinos have more education than ever before. They have moved into a whole range of jobs previously unavailable to them. An affluent Hispanic middle class is growing rapidly, and Latinos across the board are seeing a gradual but significant rise in their standard of living. Restaurants, clubs, and other facilities that once formally or informally kept Latinos out now welcome them. Overall, the barriers to entry into—and advancement within—the spectrum of political, professional, and social realms have been if not eradicated completely then at least substantially lowered. Today, few are surprised to see Latinos in high elected and appointed offices, prestigious academic posts, and positions of cultural leadership.

Similarly, as the historic "melting pot" model of assimilation into the greater Anglo culture has given way to the "mosaic" model of cultural pluralism, more that is Latino is American, and more that is American is Latino. Not even the most Middle American Anglo family thinks of a night at a Mexican restaurant or an hour spent listening to a Gloria Estefan CD as a foray into a culture any different from its own.

And yet, all is not well in the Hispanic community. Despite recent progress, Hispanics still suffer disproportionately from economic deprivation, with all its attendant social ills. Latino household incomes hover some 20 percent below those of the overall population; their unemployment rate is 60 percent higher; their college graduation rate 60 percent lower. One in six Latinos lives below the poverty line, twice as many as in the overall population. There is, to be sure, much differentiation between (and within) the various national groups that make up the Latino community, but even Cuban Americans, by far the most well-off group, have sharply lower incomes and education levels than the population as a whole. Along with this economic distress comes a similarly disproportionate incidence of crime, drug use, teenage pregnancy, and the like. At the same time, notwithstanding the changed laws and (somewhat) changed hearts, residual bias still lingers. It takes the form not only of social slights but of more concrete phenomena, such as professional glass ceilings and police harassment. And, as much as anything, it stands in the way of further economic advancement.

Meanwhile, public policies that Hispanics have looked to over the past two decades to address their community's problems are under fire. In the name of traditional values and freedom from government interference—and often with a wink to antiminority prejudice—social services (such as public housing, welfare, and health care), antidiscrimination legislation, affirmative action, multicultural education, and political empowerment face dismantling or watering down at the hands of local, state, and federal legislators and judges. The widespread unease engendered by corporate downsizing and other recent economic dislocations have only fed this trend. Bilingual education and Latin American immigration, two issues uniquely dear to Hispanics, have also come under severe challenge. The increasing political strength of the Latino community can still only accomplish so much.

These, then, are among the most critical issues that will occupy Latinos in the coming years:

Political Empowerment: The 1982 amendments to the Voting Rights Act of 1965 had acted as a de facto guarantee that Latino and other minority communities would be assured representation in Congress, even if radical redistricting was necessary to assure such a result (see page 161). In the early 1990s, however, legal challenges to this procedure began to make significant headway in the federal courts. One notable decision was the Supreme Court's 1993 ruling that North Carolina's 12th Congressional District, meant to guarantee an African American seat or at least an African American district in that state's congressional delegation, was unconstitutional. In June 1996, the Court reaffirmed that decision and also invalidated three districts in Texas, including the majority-Hispanic 29th district in Houston. With these rulings, racially redistricted seats everywhere are now threatened—and indeed, a recently created Latino district in New York City that in 1992 made Nydia Velázquez the first Puerto Rican woman representative is now being challenged in a federal lawsuit.

Opponents of the redistricting system have generally concurred with the court's 1993 opinion, written by Justice Sandra Day O'Connor, which stated that it "may Balkanize us into competing racial factions [and] bears an uncomfortable resemblance to political apartheid." They argue that it is inherently racist to assume that blacks or Latinos can only effectively be represented by people of their own ethnic background. But the system's supporters note that minorities are underrepresented at all levels of government. Hispanic leaders point out that even though Hispanics comprise 10 percent of the population, they make up barely 2 percent of elected officials. And the very election results in these districts themselves suggest that the voters do believe they are best represented by "one of their own," who understands their problems and aspirations first-hand. (Interestingly, the 29th district in Texas is represented by a non-Hispanic.)

The ultimate effect of the Supreme Court's ruling is still unclear. In the meantime, Latinos continue to fight off other attempts to water down their political representation at lower levels of government through such devices as at-large and multidistrict elections, which effectively disenfranchise minority voting by dispersing the minority vote in as large a pool as possible.

The largest single obstacle to Latino political empowerment, however, remains the noncitizen status of millions of Latinos—perhaps as many as 8 million adults alone. For this reason, numerous activist organizations are conducting citizenship campaigns among documented immigrants and pushing for documentation of others. The next step, of course, is voter registration. The formerly arcane process of voter registration has been made easier in recent years through various federal initiatives that have been supported by Latinos, including the National Voter Registration Act of 1993, familiarly known as the motor voter law. This law requires that eligible citizens be allowed to register to vote when they apply for or renew their driver's licenses. The law also requires states to permit registration by mail and to make registration forms available at designated social-service agencies.

Affirmative Action and Set-Asides: The debate over affirmative action—the granting of preferential treatment to minorities in hiring, promotion, and admission to higher education—and set-asides—the practice of limiting the bidding on certain government projects to minority businesses only—is one of the hottest topics in American politics today. Supporters contend that American society is obligated to remedy the past injustices of Latinos and other minorities, injustices perpetrated by the whole society.

They argue that, rather than guaranteeing a color-blind society, the legal system can at best stop only overt discrimination. But this leaves unaffected the "old-boys network" through which the vast majority of professional and educational opportunities are made available—and not to Latinos. Since the many decades of discrimination (including exclusion from government contracts) prevented Hispanics from gaining a foothold in better-paying, middle-class fields, there has been no network through which subsequent generations of Latinos could be brought in. For example, discrimination kept even qualified Latinos out of elite universities for so long that today they are unable to take advantage of the favorable consideration given the children of alumni. This legacy of discrimination still hobbles the Latino population.

Supporters of affirmative action and set-asides argue that only by guaranteeing what appears to be special treatment in many categories of employment and education can Latinos (and other minorities) receive what is really simply fair treatment. At the same time, these policies will permit Hispanics to establish their own networks to build on in the future.

Opponents of affirmative action and set-asides maintain that they foster a victim mentality among minorities, who are constantly reminded of their past victimization and come to define themselves by it each time they check off the appropriate boxes on job and college applications and contract bids. They note that preference programs cause resentment on the part of majorities who doubt that two wrongs make a right—and who don't appreciate being the recipients of the second "wrong." Some observers doubt that the vast majority of those who benefit from these programs are the barrio residents and new immigrants who need the help most. Rather, they say, they are a gift to the already assimilated members of the minority middle class.

On these issues, the main body of Latino opinion remains in favor of affirmative action and set-asides. Even those who admit that these policies, applied at the top levels, may largely benefit second- or third-generation Latinos who sometimes don't speak a word of Spanish, disagree that this is fatal to the programs. They believe that just as it was critical to get Latinos into the middle class, it is necessary to propel them into the elite so that they can be role models and trailblazers for others. At the same time, there is a significant minority of Latinos, among them Linda Chávez (see pages 315–316) and Richard Rodriguez (see pages 336–337) who are tired of being regarded as recipients of special treatment and having their own accomplishments discounted. They have joined in opposition to affirmative action.

Some sort of affirmative action has been standard policy in a range of public and private institutions since the early 1970s. And for almost 20 years, the federal government has used set-asides in the awarding of contracts. But from the beginning, under pressure from the policies' opponents, the courts and state governments have been chipping away at affirmative action and set-asides, especially in the public realm. In 1995 and 1996 alone, the Supreme Court strictly limited the instances in which the federal government could use racial preferences, the University of California eliminated race-based admissions policies altogether, and one federal court all but completely outlawed the use of racial considerations in public university admissions. The explicit recognition by all sides in the debate that these decisions will mean a severe reduction in Latino (and other minority) hiring and admissions has not slowed the trend to dismantle affirmative action and set-asides.

Immigration: Perhaps no single issue is as critical to Latinos, and the rest of the country, as immigration, and all that comes with it. It is estimated that a third of all Hispanics in the United States are immigrants and half of all Hispanic adults are foreign born. In 1994, legal immigration to the United States totaled just over 800,000, with an additional 200,000 undocumented individuals estimated to enter each year. The 8.7 million immigrants that came here in the 1980s reflect the fact that the United States accepts more immigration than the rest of the world combined. And since the 1960s, the vast majority of these immigrants have been from Latin America.

The current political climate has not been friendly to immigration, future or past. As in many periods of tight economic conditions, the "host" population is reluctant to slice another piece of a pie that it does not believe is growing and share it with the newcomers. Regions with the most Latino immigrants tend to feature the greatest anti-immigrant sentiment. Thus a hotbed of anti-immigrant sentiment has been California, where, for example, state education officials estimate that more than 400,000 undocumented immigrants attend the public schools.

Opponents of liberal immigration policies essentially argue the following: U.S. cities, where many immigrants locate, are already overpopulated and underserviced. Because the immigrant pool tends to be unskilled and uneducated, new immigrants provide competition to the least-skilled and neediest population, such as African Americans and Latinos. Since today's cultural atmosphere no longer encourages the ultimate goal of assimilation, further immigration therefore leads only to the development of self-contained subcultures. The money spent on social services for needy immigrants would be better spent on providing services and training to Americans.

One of the big battles of the 1996 federal budget surrounded the denial of many social services to even legal immigrants, though Republicans seem to have backed down from a measure that would have denied education aid to noncitizens—a move that arguably would have guaranteed that the doors of opportunity be closed to countless immigrants. Later, welfare reform legislation made all noncitizens ineligible for benefits. And legislation tightening immigration law enforcement, border control, and even the number of legal immigrants has been moving through Congress. Steps have even been taken to bring in the military to assist in patrolling the Mexican border. In California, Proposition 187, the so-called Save Our State initiative, which would deny all nonemergency social services and education to nondocumented immigrants, passed with 59 percent of the vote in late 1994. The law will be tied up in the courts for years before its effect can be calculated; indeed, one federal judge has already determined that crucial sections overreach state authority and are therefore unconstitutional. But the fact of its passage, and by a solid margin, reflects the depth of anti-immigrant sentiment.

The end of the cold war has had a devastating effect on immigrants who were once tolerated for their political usefulness. Thus thousands of Nicaraguans who entered the country during the Sandinista-Contra conflict of the Reagan years (see pages 180–181) now face deportation. Similarly, the Clinton administration tightened Cuban immigration in a way unimaginable in the days of the U.S.-Soviet rivalry (see pages 173–174). Even undocumented Mexican workers are being rounded up by the thousands in an unprecedented enforcement effort.

Many free-market advocates insist that immigration is the engine of American productivity and economic growth. Most economists believe that immigration tends to improve income and spur economic growth, not the opposite. Native-born Americans are not prepared to do the menial work immigrants will accept, at a price that could realistically be paid for such work. In any case, some immigrants do, in fact, come with skills and educational backgrounds that are in short supply in this country. Immigrants, who tend to be young, healthy, and well-motivated, invigorate the society and can balance the "graying" of the U.S. population. Nonetheless, the anti-immigration political pressure from an increasingly insecure Anglo population continues.

Bilingual Education: Bilingual education is school instruction in English along with another language, such as Spanish. Its purpose is to teach the student whose English proficiency is limited so that his substantive education can continue while he learns English. Its opponents, however, argue that in the years since the Bilingual Education Act of 1968 (see page 158), the primary accomplishment of bilingual education has been to reduce or eliminate the incentive for non-English-speakers to learn English at all. The result is a population of ever unassimilated Latinos and a culturally and linguistically divided nation. Among those opponents are Latino cultural figures such as Richard Rodriguez and Linda Chávez.

Latinos (supported by many non-Latinos as well), however, tend to favor bilingual education for their children. While recognizing the need for English skills for anyone who expects to compete in the national economy, they believe that the alternative to bilingual education inevitably results in the withering of students' native language skills—skills that themselves are valuable in a globalized economy. Educators argue that standardized test scores do not support the argument that overall educational achievement is harmed by bilingual teaching. Furthermore, the overwhelming majority of Latinos that attend public schools do end up learning English.

Here, too, the political trends do not bode well for the position held by most Latinos. Although the Clinton administration has supported bilingual education, opponents of federal funding of bilingual education, which has totaled more than $2 billion since 1968, are closer than ever to achieving their goals.

English Only: In the early 1980s, Hispanic demands for bilingual and multicultural education, bilingual ballots and license examinations, and their growing numbers in certain parts of the country, resulted in a backlash that coalesced in the organization U.S. English. Inspired by former U.S. Senator S. I. Hayakawa, a one-term Republican who sponsored a constitutional amendment making English the official language of the U.S. government, the organization—along with another like-minded group, English First—has succeeded in making English the official language of 23 states. Among these states are California, Florida, Colorado, and Arizona, all of which have large Latino populations and in all of which the vote resulted in serious polarization of the Anglo and Latino communities. And a bill was also passed by the House of Representatives that would require that most federal government business be conducted in English.

Latino leaders have denounced these initiatives as anti-Hispanic and racist, despite the involvement of figures such as Linda Chávez in U.S. English. Indeed, a leaked memorandum by the Michigan ophthalmologist who founded U.S. English described Hispanics as fast-breeding carriers of corruption who were incapable of being educated, and asked, "Can *homo contraceptivus* compete with *homo pregentiva* if borders are not controlled? . . . [P]erhaps this is the first instance in which those with their pants up are going to get caught by those with their pants down!" (This led to the resignation of Chávez, as well as journalist Walter Cronkite, from the organization.)

The rancor and divisiveness raised by the English initiatives has made life for Latinos especially unpleasant. It became commonplace for total strangers to admonish Latinos to cease "abusing" their children by speaking to them in their native tongue—practices that none of the measures ever sought to forbid. One Texas judge in a 1995 custody case awarded a child to her father on the grounds that the Spanish-speaking mother was "damaging" the child by teaching her the "language of maids." (The ruling was subsequently reversed.)

Despite these atmospheric changes, however, the effect of these laws is unclear. Ironically, Chávez, who by her own account has been demonized as an Uncle Tom for her stands on bilingual education and official English, notes in her book, *Out of the Barrio,* that "official English laws have had virtually no impact on public policy." At any rate, in the long run attempts to enforce them may not stand up to constitutional tests (unless the Constitution itself is altered): An Arizona state law limiting governmental discourse to English was found by two federal courts to be in violation of the First Amendment right to freedom of speech.

Multicultural Education: Multicultural education was developed with the intention of serving as an interdisciplinary, cross-cultural educational process that seeks to prepare students to live, learn, and work together in a culturally diverse world. Its explicit goals are to foster appreciation, respect, and understanding among people who differ in sex, race, ethnic background, religion, language, or other fundamental perspective. Its proponents believe that multicultural curricula provide students with a positive self-image because they learn about the cultural and historical forces that make them what they are. And, it is argued, this teaching approach also helps students appreciate that other forces, just as undeniable, have shaped others differently.

A major undertaking of educators who focus on multiethnic education is the reduction of bias in textbooks and other instructional materials. Studies have shown that students who see themselves portrayed in biased or stereotyped ways internalize these ideas and fall short of their potential. Bias of this kind is identified in all kinds of classroom materials, from nursery rhymes and fairy tales to literature and history texts, from audiovisual aids to computer software.

Except for the most radical proponents of the idea, proponents of multiculturalism believe fundamental "American" values, such as due process of law, civic responsibility, and democracy, should be conveyed to all students. But many multiculturalists reject assimilation—the "melting pot"—and believe that different groups should affirmatively maintain their distinctive ways of life.

Critics of multiculturalism include the historian Arthur Schlesinger, Jr., who has written that "we should be alert to the danger of a society divided into distinct and immutable ethnic and racial groups, each taught to cherish its apartness from the rest." Others have condemned the search for bias in instructional materials as a search for "political correctness" and asserted that this political correctness has not only distorted the representation of history (in order to enhance the self-esteem of minorities) but had a chilling effect on those who would express different views.

There are, of course, other political matters in which Latinos take a special interest. Foreign policy toward Latin America, which has been instrumental in creating or supporting situations that have resulted in substantial immigration, is one. Cuban Americans, in particular, generally support continued pressure on Castro's Cuba in hopes of one day seeing a democratic government again in place (see pages 172–173). Another matter, of particular concern to Mexican Americans, is the effect of the North American Free Trade Agreement (NAFTA), both in terms of U.S.-Mexican relations and economic exchange and in terms of the effect on immigration and the livelihoods of Hispanics who have made their home "north of the border." Latinos also anxiously await the first appointment of a leading jurist of Hispanic extraction, such as Judge José Cabranés, to the United States Supreme Court. The future of the civil rights movement in general, besides affirmative action, is of keen concern to Latinos as well.

That is not to say that all Latinos agree on these matters, or any other. Just as with the rest of the world, those who share the same goals may disagree about how to meet them. One of the most notable political divergences within the Latino community is actually between, on the one hand, conservative Cuban Americans, 64 percent of whom tend to vote Republican, and, on the other hand, more liberal Puerto Ricans (64 percent Democratic) and Mexican Americans (60 percent Democratic). But, even within political blocs, there are splits, as demonstrated by the divergence of opinions among Latino leaders on the NAFTA treaty: While many Hispanic Democratic members of Congress ultimately joined the majority of Republicans in voting in the treaty's favor, other Hispanic legislators—both Democrats and Republicans—voted in opposition.

In any event, the Latinos are here to stay, and then some. Their numbers are now too large to ignore, and between immigration— officially sanctioned and otherwise—and a relatively high birthrate, this will be even more true in the coming century. They have moved, and will continue to move, decisively from the fringes to the mainstream of American life. So where next for Latino America? It is, of course, impossible to predict. But one thing is certain: More than ever before, Latinos will be the ones who do the deciding.

SELECTED BIBLIOGRAPHY

◆

Acuña, Rodolfo. *Occupied America: A History of Chicano,* third edition. New York: Harper & Row, 1988.

Arana, Luis Rafael, and Albert Manucy. *The Building of Castillo San Marcos.* Saint Augustine: Eastern National Park & Monument Association, 1977.

Arias, David. *Spanish Roots of America.* Huntington: Our Sunday Visitor Publishing Division, 1992.

Armstrong, Ruth W. *New Mexico: From Arrowhead to Atom,* second edition, revised. New York: A. S. Barnes and Company, 1976.

Bannon, John Francis. *The Spanish Borderlands Frontier, 1513–1821.* Albuquerque: University of New Mexico Press, 1974.

Beardsley, John, and Jane Livingston. *Hispanic Art in the United States: 30 Contemporary Painters and Sculptors.* Houston/New York: Museum of Fine Arts/Abbeville, 1987.

Belous, Richard S., and Jonathan Lemco, editors. *NAFTA as a Model of Development.* Washington, D.C.: National Planning Association, 1993.

Bronx Museum of the Arts, *The Latin American Spirit: Art and Artists in the United States, 1920–70.* New York: Harry N. Abrams, 1988.

Carner-Ribalta, J. *Gaspar de Portolá, Explorer of California*. San Diego: Tecolote Publications, 1990.

Chávez, Linda. *Out of the Barrio: Toward a New Politics of Hispanic Assimilation*. New York: Basic Books, 1991.

Cocina al Minuto. Miami: Ediciones Cubamerica, 1968.

Cummings, W. D.; R. A. Skelton; and D. B. Quinn, editors. *The Discovery of North America*. New York: American Heritage Press, 1972.

De Reparaz, Carmen. *Yo solo: Bernardo de Gálvez y la toma de Panzacola en 1781*. Barcelona: Ediciones del Serbal S.A., 1986.

De Varona, Frank, editor. *Hispanic Presence in the United States*. Miami: Mnemosyne Publishing Company, 1993.

De Varona, Frank, and Eden Force Eskin. *Hispanics in the U.S. Through 1865*, volume 1. Englewood Cliffs, N.J.: Globe Book Company, 1989.

De Varona, Frank, and Steven Otfinoski. *Hispanics in U.S. History: 1865 to the Present*, volume 2. Englewood Cliffs, N.J.: Globe Book Company, 1989.

Dudley, William, editor. *Immigration: Opposing Viewpoints*. San Diego: Greenhaven Press, 1990.

Fernández-Shaw, Carlos M. *The Hispanic Presence in North America from 1492 to Today*. New York: Facts On File, 1991.

———. *Presencia española en los Estados Unidos*. Madrid: Ediciones Cultura Hispánica, 1987.

Flexner, Stuart Berg. *I Hear America Talking: An Illustrated History of American Words and Phrases*. New York: Simon & Schuster, 1976.

Fuentes-Pérez, Ileana; Graciella Cruz-Taura; and Ricardo Pau-Llosa, editors. *Outside Cuba/Fuera de Cuba*. Office of Hispanic Arts, Mason Gross School of the Arts, Rutgers, the State University of New Jersey, and the Research Institute for Cuban Studies, University of Miami, Florida, 1988.

Gannon, Michael V. *The Cross in the Sand: The Early Catholic Church in Florida, 1513–1870*. Gainesville: University Press of Florida, 1983.

———. *Florida: A Short History*. Gainesville: University Press of Florida, 1993.

García, Mario T. *Mexican Americans: Leadership, Ideology, and Identity*. New Haven and London: Yale University Press, 1989.

Gómez, Rudolph, editor. *The Changing Mexican-American*. Boulder, Colo.: Pruett, 1972.

Gómez Sicre, José. *Art of Cuba in Exile.* Miami: Editora Munder, 1987.

Gonzáles, Rodolfo. *I Am Joaquín/Yo soy Joaquín.* New York: Bantam Books, 1972.

Griswold del Castillo, Richard, et al. *Chicano Art: Resistance and Affirmation, 1965–1985.* Los Angeles: Wight Art Gallery, 1991.

Hadley-García, George. *Hispanic Hollywood: The Latins in Motion Pictures.* Secaucus, N.J.: Carol Publishing Group, 1990.

Hafen, Leroy R., and Ann W. Hafen. *Old Spanish Trail, Santa Fe to Los Angeles.* Lincoln, Neb.: University of Nebraska, 1993.

Hauberg, Clifford A. *Puerto Rico and the Puerto Ricans: A Study of Puerto Rican History and Immigration to the United States.* New York: Hippocrene Books, 1974.

Hobbler, Dorothy, and Thomas Hobbler. *The Mexican American Family Album.* Oxford: Oxford University Press, 1994.

Jones, Oscar, and Joy Jones. *Hippocrene U.S.A. Guide to Historic Hispanic America.* New York: Hippocrene Books, 1993.

Kane, Robert S. *Spain at Its Best.* Lincolnwood, Ill.: Passport Books, 1985.

Kanellos, Nicolás. *The Hispanic Almanac: From Columbus to Corporate America.* Detroit: Visible Ink Press, 1994.

Kennedy, Diana. *The Cuisine of Mexico.* New York: Harper & Row, 1986.

Krell, Dorothy, editor. *The California Missions, A Pictorial History.* Menlo Park, N.J.: Lane Publishing Company, 1979.

Larsen, Ronald J. *The Puerto Ricans in America.* Minneapolis: Lerner Publications Company, 1989.

Levadi, Barbara, senior editor. *Latino Biographies.* Paramus, N.J.: Globe Fearon, 1995.

Lewin, Stephen, executive editor. *The Latino Experience in U.S. History.* Paramus, N.J.: Globe Fearon, 1994.

Lluriá de O'Higgins, María Josefa. *A Taste of Old Cuba.* New York: HarperCollins, 1994.

Lomelí, Francisco, editor, *Handbook of Hispanic Cultures in the United States: Literature and Art.* Houston: Arte Público Press, 1993.

Maltby, William S. *The Black Legend in England: The Development of Anti-Spanish Sentiment, 1559–1660.* Durham, N.C.: Duke Historical Publications, 1971.

Manucy, Albert. *Florida's Menéndez, Captain General of the Ocean Sea.* Saint Augustine Historical Society, 1965.

McDermott, John Francis, editor. *The Spanish in the Mississippi Valley 1762–1804*. Champaign, Ill.: University of Illinois Press, 1974.

Meier, Matt S., and Feliciano Rivera. *Dictionary of Mexican American History*. Westport, Conn.: Greenwood Press, 1981.

———. *Mexican Americans/American Mexicans from Conquistadors to Chicanos*. New York: Hill and Wang, 1972.

Mexican Cooking Made Easy. New York: Galahad Books, 1979.

Milanich, Jerald T., and Charles Hudson. *Hernando de Soto and the Indians of Florida*. Gainesville: University Press of Florida, 1993.

Montero de Pedro, José. *Españoles en Nueva Orleans y Luisiana*. Madrid: Ediciones Cultura Hispánica, 1979.

Moore, Joan, and Harry Pachon. *Hispanics in the United States*. Englewood Cliffs, N.J.: Prentice-Hall, 1985.

Moquin, Wayne, editor, with Charles Van Doren. *A Documentary History of the Mexican Americans*. New York: Praeger, 1971.

Novas, Himilce. *Everything You Need to Know About Latino History*. New York: Plume/Penguin Books, 1994.

———. *The Hispanic 100*. New York: Citadel Press/Carol Publishing, 1995.

Officer, James E. *Hispanic Arizona, 1536–1856*. Tucson: University of Arizona Press, 1989.

Ortiz, Yvonne. *A Taste of Puerto Rico: Traditional and New Dishes from the Puerto Rican Community*. New York: Penguin Books, 1994.

Pérez San Jurio, Elena. *Historia de la música cubana*. Miami: La Moderna Poesia, 1986.

Pichot, Jane. *The Mexicans in America*. Minneapolis: Lerner Publications Company, 1989.

Quirarte, Jacinto. *Mexican American Artists*. Austin: University of Texas Press, 1973.

Reyes, Luis, and Peter Rubie. *Hispanics in Hollywood: An Encyclopedia of Film and Television*. New York: Garland, 1994.

Rivera, Oswald. *Puerto Rican Cuisine in America, Nuyorican and Bodega Recipes*. New York: Four Walls Eight Windows, 1993.

Roberts, John Storm. *The Latin Tinge: The Impact of Latin American Music in the United States*. Tivoli, N.Y.: Original Music, 1985 (originally published by Oxford University Press, 1979).

Sale, Kirkpatrick. *The Conquest of Paradise: Christopher Columbus and the Columbian Legacy*. New York: Alfred A. Knopf, 1990.

Sauer, Carl Ortwin. *Sixteenth Century North America: The Land and the People as Seen by the Europeans*. Berkeley and Los Angeles: University of California Press, 1971.

Selby, John. *The Eagle and the Serpent: The Invasions of Mexico, 1519 and 1846*. New York: Hippocrene Books, n.d.

Shorris, Earl. *Latinos: A Biography of the People*. New York: Avon Books, 1992.

Sinnott, Susan. *Extraordinary Hispanic Americans*. Chicago: Children's Press, 1991.

Weber, David J. *The Spanish Frontier in North America*. New Haven: Yale University Press, 1992.

Wallace, Katherine. *California Through Five Centuries*. New York: Amsco School Publications, 1974.

Waterbury, Jean Parker, editor. *The Oldest City: St. Augustine's Saga of Survival*. Saint Augustine Historical Society, 1983.

INDEX

♦